Voices of the Civil War

Voices of the Civil War · Antietam

By the Editors of Time-Life Books, Alexandria, Virginia

Contents

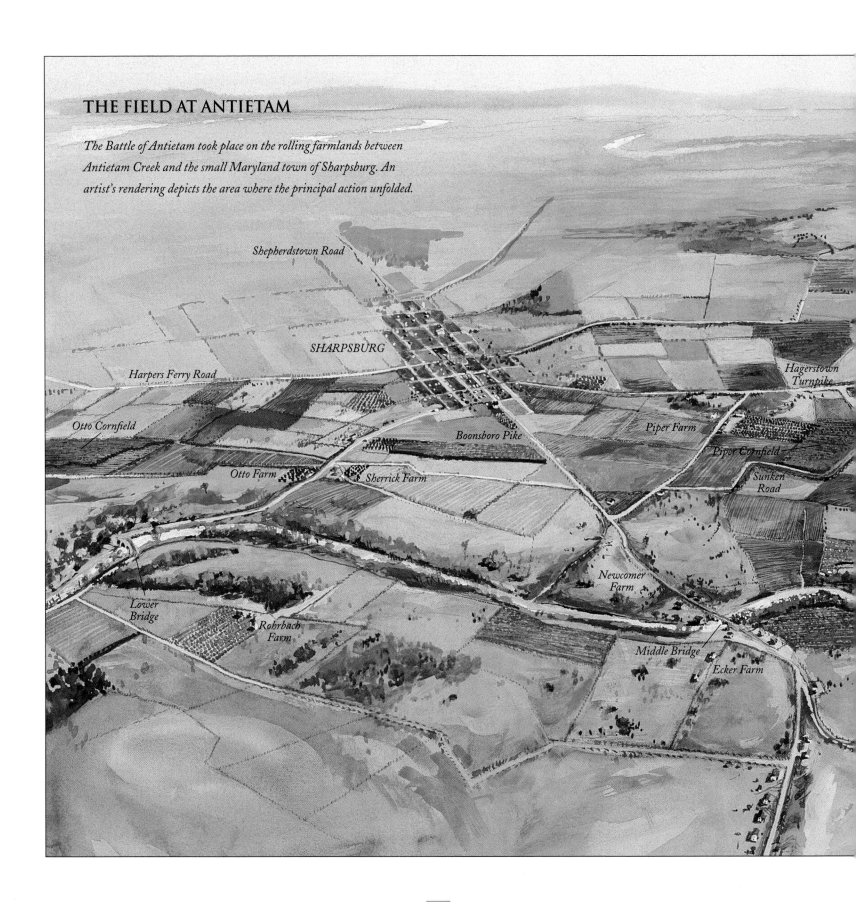

THE FIELD AT ANTIETAM

The Battle of Antietam took place on the rolling farmlands between Antietam Creek and the small Maryland town of Sharpsburg. An artist's rendering depicts the area where the principal action unfolded.

Shepherdstown Road

SHARPSBURG

Harpers Ferry Road

Hagerstown Turnpike

Otto Cornfield

Boonsboro Pike

Piper Farm

Piper Cornfield

Otto Farm

Sherrick Farm

Sunken Road

Lower Bridge

Newcomer Farm

Rohrbach Farm

Middle Bridge

Ecker Farm

Hauser's Ridge

West Woods

Nicodemus
Hill

Nicodemus Farm

North Woods

D. Miller Farm

Miller
Cornfield

J. Poffenberger
Farm

Middlekauf Farm

Dunker
Church

Mumma
Farm

Smoketown Road

East
Woods

S. Poffenberger Farm

M. Miller Farm

Roulette Farm

Kennedy
Farm

Neikirk Farm

Antietam Creek

Smith Farm

S. Pry
Farm

P. Pry Farm

Upper Bridge

Little Antietam Creek

Potomac River

N

Previous to Antietam

Across the Potomac

On Wednesday, September 3, 1862, some 40,000 Confederate troops were bivouacked in the fields surrounding the tiny hamlet of Dranesville, Virginia. They were lean and sun-browned, their uniforms soiled and tattered; some were barefoot, and many wore shoes that were in the last stages of dilapidation. But despite their motley appearance, and the exhaustion that followed weeks of strenuous marching, the Rebel soldiers were flushed with confidence. Four days earlier they had achieved the crowning glory of an epic campaign by inflicting a crushing defeat on Major General John Pope's Yankee forces —a victory to be savored all the more because it had occurred at Bull Run, the same battlefield where another Federal army had been put to flight in July 1861.

From the Maryland shore of the Potomac a Federal scout takes aim at Robert E. Lee's Rebels as they wade across the river from Virginia at White's Ford on September 4, 1862. One of James Ewell Brown "Jeb" Stuart's staff officers commented about the crossing that "there were few moments . . . of excitement more intense, of exhilaration more delightful."

Then, as now, the vanquished Union troops had pulled back into the defenses of Washington, D.C., leaving a Confederate army poised at the doorstep of the Federal capital. The Southern leaders had failed to follow up their success the preceding year, but now the troops were veterans and their commander a man whose genius for waging war was unexcelled—General Robert E. Lee.

In less than three months the revered commander, known to his admiring soldiers as Marse Robert, had managed to shift the field of operations from the very outskirts of the Confederate capital of Richmond to the environs of Washington. "His army had acquired that magnificent morale which made them equal to twice their numbers," recalled Lieutenant Colonel E. Porter Alexander, "and his confidence in them, & theirs in him, were so equal that no man can yet say which was greatest." Like their leader, the fighting men of the Army of Northern Virginia sensed that the scales of war had begun to tip in favor of the Confederacy.

Never one to rest on his laurels, Lee was determined to exploit the signal victory of Second Manassas—not by assaulting the formidable earthworks ringing Washington but by crossing the Potomac River—and for the first time carrying the war onto Northern soil.

As he outlined his plans in a communication to Confederate president Jefferson Davis, Lee was nursing a painful injury he had sustained the day following the engagement at Manassas. The general had dismounted from his favorite horse, Traveller, and was about to examine a map held by one of his staff officers when a gust of wind sent the parchment flapping in the animal's face. The horse shied, and when Lee grabbed for its bridle, he stumbled and fell heavily on his hands. He severely sprained both arms; for the next several weeks they would be splinted and bandaged, with the right arm confined to a sling. Though compelled to ride in an ambulance for several days, Lee shrugged off the inconvenience as he embarked on his daring new strategy.

Although he realized that his troops were undersupplied and numerically inferior to his Federal opponents, Lee felt that his army could "not afford to be idle." With the enemy seemingly in "a very demoralized and chaotic condition," Lee judged the time right to cross the Potomac into Maryland and, if all went well, to continue on across the Mason-Dixon line into Pennsylvania. Lee hoped the invasion would provide a temporary respite to war-ravaged Virginia, allow him to replenish his army's supplies in the verdant farmland of central Maryland and rally pro-Southern Marylanders to the Confederate cause. If and when the Federals sallied out of the Washington defenses, a Southern victory on Northern soil might well force President Abraham Lincoln to the negotiating table.

President Davis acceded to the general's proposal, and Lee's offensive quickly got under way. " 'On to Maryland!' is now the cry," wrote Confederate artillerist William M. Owen, "and the heads of columns are directed toward the Potomac." On September 4 the lead elements of the Southern force began crossing the river at White's Ford near Leesburg. "Just now it does appear as if God were truly with us," exulted Major Walter Taylor of Lee's staff. "All along our lines the movement is onward." As the regimental bands played "Maryland! My Maryland," the jubilant gray-clad columns emerged on the northern bank of the Potomac and continued toward the prosperous town of Frederick, 11 miles away. "A dirtier, more ragged, exhausted set would be hard to find the world over," Lieutenant John H. Chamberlayne confessed in a letter to his sister; but, he noted, "it is an army of which General Lee may well be proud, a better never shouted under a Roman Eagle." Chamberlayne added: "Whatever Lee's plans are, they will be good, and his army can carry them out."

As his proud fighters pushed on through a pristine countryside as yet untouched by war, Lee learned that the enemy forces at Washington had been placed under the command of Major General George B. McClellan. Having thwarted McClellan's efforts to take Richmond two months earlier, Lee assessed his opponent as "an able general but a very cautious one." If McClellan was true to form, Lee had every reason to expect that several weeks would pass before the reorganized enemy army marched forth to give battle.

The 35-year-old George McClellan possessed a sharp mind and charismatic presence; no officer was more proficient at organizing, training, and inspiring his soldiers. It was McClellan who had raised a magnificent fighting machine from the shambles of the defeat at First Manassas. And yet a year and a half of war had shown McClellan to be so deliberate in his strategy that time and again he had yielded the initiative to his Southern foes. Moreover, his disdain for civilian authority had made him a most contentious subordinate. McClellan seemed to view the Army of the Potomac as his personal property and to have taken a perverse delight in General Pope's misfortunes. Secretary of the Navy Gideon Welles noted that President Lincoln, in tendering command to McClellan, "was greatly distressed," but confessed that McClellan "had beyond any officer the confidence of the army."

The soldiers' adoration of McClellan was made strikingly evident when "Little Mac" rode forth to greet the disheartened survivors of Pope's debacle at Manassas. "Up went caps in the air and a cheer broke out which, as the news travelled, was taken up and carried to the rear of the column," Brigadier General John Gibbon recalled. "Such cheers I never heard before," noted Lieutenant Stephen Minot Weld Jr.; "Every one felt happy and jolly." Edmund R. Brown of the 27th Indiana thought "every one who was the least discouraged or doubtful before, was now buoyant and full of confidence." Within hours of McClellan's assumption of command, a measure of order began to return to the army as the war-weary troops pitched camp and stragglers made their way back to their units. Major Thomas Hyde of the 7th Maine expressed the prevailing opinion when he wrote to his mother, "McClellan is the only man who can save the country."

In a remarkable display of alacrity for the habitually deliberate commander, McClellan by September 7 had established his headquarters at Rockville, Maryland, 15 miles northwest of Washington. Rather than wait to complete his reorganization in the capital's defenses, McClellan was determined to confront Lee's invasion. Leaving two corps to safeguard the capital, he began shifting his force of some 70,000 men—a tenth of whom were new recruits—in three parallel columns across a 25-mile front. It was far from a lightning advance but much swifter than Lee had expected from the cautious leader of the Army of the Potomac.

As McClellan got his pursuit under way, Lee's forces were converging on the prosperous central Maryland town of Frederick. On September 8, the Confederate commander issued an appeal to the citizens of Maryland, stating: "The people of the South have long wished to aid you in throwing off this foreign yoke, to again enjoy the inalienable rights of freedom, and restore freedom and sovereignty to your state." Unfortunately for Southern hopes, the response to Lee's proclamation was lukewarm at best. Central Maryland proved to be predominantly Union in sentiment, and no groundswell of support was forthcoming.

A subordinate once wrote of Lee that the general was "audacity personified"; and at Frederick the Southern commander devised a plan fully in keeping with his reputation as a military gambler. He would divide his army into four columns, three of which—led by his ablest corps commander, Thomas J. "Stonewall" Jackson—would advance on the town of Harpers Ferry, the strategic Federal stronghold located at the convergence of the Shenandoah and Potomac Rivers. By capturing Harpers Ferry, Lee would free the vital corridor of Virginia's Shenandoah Valley from a potential enemy movement to his rear. Jackson would then march to Boonsboro, Maryland, 20 miles north of Harpers Ferry,

and reunite with the remainder of Lee's forces, under the command of General James Longstreet. If all went according to plan, the rendezvous of Jackson and Longstreet would occur on September 12, leaving Lee time to confront McClellan on ground of the Confederate commander's choosing.

With McClellan on the move, haste was vital. And with the issuing of Special Orders No. 191, the Army of Northern Virginia resumed its march, trudging through Frederick on September 10. The Rebels received a decidedly cool reception. "I have never seen a mass of such filthy, strong-smelling men," one local youth recalled. "They are the roughest set of creatures I ever saw: their features, hair, and clothing matted with dirt and filth, and the scratching they kept up gave warrant of vermin in abundance." Some citizens flaunted the Stars and Stripes at the passing columns; John E. Crow of the 12th Virginia remembered a local woman sporting the U.S. flag on her apron. "You *are* a nice specimen," she snapped, "you miserable ragamuffin rebel!"

McClellan reached the outskirts of Frederick on September 12 and prepared for the next phase of his move against Lee. General in Chief Henry W. Halleck had rejected McClellan's request that the vulnerable garrison of Harpers Ferry be evacuated, and the army commander feared that Lee was indeed moving against the isolated outpost. As so often in the past, Little Mac believed his force to be at a significant numerical disadvantage; he reported to Washington that Lee had "not less than 120,000 men"—far more than the Southern commander actually possessed north of the Potomac.

But McClellan's concerns gave way to jubilation on September 13 when soldiers of

the 27th Indiana stumbled on a copy of Lee's Special Orders No. 191, wrapped around three cigars and lying in a field formerly occupied by Southern troops. Apparently a Confederate courier or staff officer had accidentally dropped the document. The discovery provided the Federal commander with a detailed timetable and routes of march for the dispersed Southern columns. If the garrison of Harpers Ferry could continue to hold out, thus frustrating Lee's effort to reunite his forces, the Army of the Potomac would be able to divide and defeat the Rebels in detail. In possession of Lee's plans, McClellan felt that he now held a potentially decisive advantage over his foe, even if the enemy reunited at Boonsboro or Hagerstown. "I think Lee has made a gross mistake," McClellan wired President Lincoln, "and that he will be severely punished for it."

Portions of the Army of the Potomac got under way later that same day, although not with the "forced marches" that McClellan had promised General in Chief Halleck. It would be September 14 before the vast blue columns began wending their way over the Catoctin Mountain range, across the Middletown Valley, and on toward the ridge of South Mountain. McClellan directed his forces in the direction of the two principal gaps in South Mountain. The corps of Major Generals Joseph Hooker and Jesse L. Reno were to secure Turner's Gap and push on to Boonsboro. Major General William B. Franklin's VI Corps was given the crucial assignment of advancing through Crampton's Gap—seven miles farther south—and marching to relieve the beleaguered garrison at Harpers Ferry.

As the Federals passed through Frederick, they received a much warmer reception than the Confederates had experienced three days earlier. "The stars and stripes floated from every building and hung from every window," wrote Major Rufus Dawes of the 6th Wisconsin Infantry. "Little children stood at nearly every door, freely offering cool water, cakes, pies and dainties." When McClellan rode past, General Gibbon noted, "he was overwhelmed by the ladies, they kissed his clothes, threw their arms about his horse's neck, and committed all sorts of extravagances."

As McClellan made his triumphant passage through Frederick, Stonewall Jackson was tightening the noose on the Yankee defenders of Harpers Ferry—some 14,000 troops commanded by Colonel Dixon S. Miles. On the afternoon of September 13, two Confederate divisions led by Major General Lafayette McLaws seized the commanding elevation of Maryland Heights, overlooking the town. Meanwhile, Brigadier General John G. Walker's 2,000-man division had occupied Loudoun Heights, which commanded the Shenandoah River flank of Harpers Ferry. Having pushed his hard-marching "foot cavalry" on a wide-ranging arc across the Potomac and south through Martinsburg, Virginia, Stonewall Jackson and the remainder of his force were closing in on the western approaches to Harpers Ferry. On the afternoon of September 14, Jackson's artillery opened a heavy bombardment on Colonel Miles' garrison, now entirely surrounded and unable to offer effective resistance.

Frustrated that his risky plan was two days behind schedule, Robert E. Lee had left the division of Major General D. H. Hill to hold the gaps of South Mountain while he continued on to Hagerstown with Longstreet's corps. Early on September 14, when Lee received word that McClellan was approaching South Mountain in great strength, the

Confederate commander ordered Longstreet back to Hill's support. If the Southern troops were unable to delay the Federal columns at South Mountain, Lee risked disaster.

There had been nothing in the lost orders about a Confederate defense of South Mountain; and when the vanguard of McClellan's army encountered stiff resistance there, the Federal commander was caught off guard. For much of September 14, the fighting raged along the National Road as Hooker's troops slowly battled their way up the approaches to Turner's Gap. A mile farther south at Fox's Gap, General Reno's IX Corps reinforced Brigadier General Jacob D. Cox's Kanawha Division in an effort to flank Hill's position. The vanguard of Longstreet's column arrived to shore up Hill's embattled defenders, and as night fell the combat raged on. Eventually Federal numbers told, and both Turner's Gap and Fox's Gap were secured. McClellan judged his success "a glorious victory," but in fact the stubborn Rebel defense had purchased crucial time for Lee's scattered forces.

To Lee, however, time seemed to be running out, and the general reluctantly prepared to call off his invasion of Maryland. Fearing that McLaws' 8,000 men would be ensnared by the southernmost Federal column, Lee ordered that general to evacuate his position on Maryland Heights. "The day has gone against us," Lee wrote, "this army will go by Sharpsburg and cross the river."

Entrusted with the crucial mission of relieving the garrison at Harpers Ferry, General Franklin's VI Corps managed to disperse the outnumbered Confederate defenders of Crampton's Gap, the southernmost pass in the South Mountain range. Had Franklin pressed on across Pleasant Valley, he might well have broken the siege and surrounded

McLaws' force in the process. But believing he faced a superior and well-entrenched foe, the cautious Franklin decided to halt for the night, only six miles from Harpers Ferry.

Fate again smiled on the Southern cause. On the morning of September 15, Lee received a dispatch from Stonewall Jackson, stating: "Through God's blessing, Harpers Ferry and its garrison are to be surrendered." Nearly 12,500 troops and 73 Yankee artillery pieces fell into Rebel hands. Granted yet another reprieve, Lee reconsidered his decision to abandon Maryland without a fight. Shifting Longstreet's and D. H. Hill's columns toward the little town of Sharpsburg, Lee ordered Jackson to march north immediately and rejoin the rest of the Confederate force. Major General A. P. Hill's division would finish the task of paroling the Federal prisoners at Harpers Ferry, then likewise veer north for Sharpsburg. It was a remarkable turn of events for the Southern leader, whose daring strategy had now paid off. "That Lee was the man for the hour cannot be gainsaid," one Federal soldier admitted, "for, like the successful gambler, he was ever ready to take great chances at desperate odds."

Jackson's three divisions crossed the Potomac near Shepherdstown on the afternoon of September 16 and pushed on to Sharpsburg. His men straggled badly; many had not slept for 48 hours or more. Even with their arrival Lee was still greatly outnumbered by McClellan's forces, who were beginning to concentrate opposite him. McLaws' troops would not arrive at Sharpsburg until the morning of September 17, and A. P. Hill's division even later. Many of Lee's most trusted subordinates doubted the wisdom of giving battle against such odds. But with the future of the Confederacy at stake, the

Southern commander was determined to fight before retreating from Northern soil.

Throughout September 16 the opposing forces exchanged intermittent shellfire, as McClellan methodically positioned his forces for an assault. The valley of Antietam Creek provided a natural barrier between the two armies, and the Union commander wanted to establish a bridgehead on the western bank of the stream before committing his troops to the offensive. By nightfall of the 16th, Hooker had crossed the stream at a ford north of Lee's position and stood poised with three divisions facing the Confederate left flank. Following a brief but savage skirmish, both sides waited for the dawn and the great bloodletting all knew would come with the rising sun.

CHRONOLOGY

1862

August	28-30	*Battle of Second Manassas*
		Pope's defeated Federals fall back to Washington defenses
September	1	*Battle of Chantilly*
	3	*Confederates begin northward movement*
	4-7	*Lee crosses Potomac River*
	5	*Federal Army of Virginia and Army of the Potomac consolidate under McClellan's command; Federals begin march into Maryland*
	6	*Confederates enter Frederick*
	10	*Lee divides his army and moves west*
	12	*McClellan reaches Frederick*
	12-15	*Confederates besiege and capture Harpers Ferry*
	14	*Battles at South Mountain (Turner's Gap, Fox's Gap, Crampton's Gap)*
	15-16	*Lee falls back on Sharpsburg; Federals follow up*
	17	*Battle of Antietam*
	18-19	*Lee recrosses the Potomac*
	20	*Battle of Shepherdstown*
	22	*Emancipation Proclamation issued*
October	1-4	*Lincoln visits Antietam battlefield*
	26	*Federals begin crossing the Potomac into Virginia*
November	7	*McClellan relieved of command*

ORDER OF BATTLE

ARMY OF NORTHERN VIRGINIA (Confederate)

Lee   40,000 men

Left Wing (2d Corps) Jackson

Lawton's Division	J. R. Jones' Division	A. P. Hill's Division
Douglass' Brigade	*Grigsby's Brigade*	*Branch's Brigade*
Early's Brigade	*Warren's Brigade*	*Gregg's Brigade*
J. A. Walker's Brigade	*Johnson's Brigade*	*Brockenbrough's Brigade*
Hays' Brigade	*Starke's Brigade*	*Archer's Brigade*
		Pender's Brigade
D. H. Hill's Division		*Thomas' Brigade*
Ripley's Brigade		
Rodes' Brigade		
Garland's Brigade		
G. B. Anderson's Brigade		
Colquitt's Brigade		

Right Wing (1st Corps) Longstreet

McLaws' Division	J. G. Walker's Division	Hood's Division
Kershaw's Brigade	*Manning's Brigade*	*Wofford's Brigade*
Cobb's Brigade	*Ransom's Brigade*	*Law's Brigade*
Semmes' Brigade		*Evans' Brigade*
Barksdale's Brigade		
D. R. Jones' Division	R. H. Anderson's Division	
Toombs' Brigade	*Cumming's Brigade*	
Drayton's Brigade	*Posey's Brigade*	
Garnett's Brigade	*Armistead's Brigade*	
Kemper's Brigade	*Pryor's Brigade*	
J. Walker's Brigade	*Parham's Brigade*	
G. T. Anderson's Brigade	*Wright's Brigade*	

Cavalry Stuart

Hampton's Brigade
Munford's Brigade
F. Lee's Brigade

ARMY OF THE POTOMAC (Federal)

McClellan   90,000 men

Left Wing Franklin

VI Corps Franklin

1st Division Slocum	2d Division Smith
Torbert's Brigade	*Hancock's Brigade*
Bartlett's Brigade	*Brooks' Brigade*
Newton's Brigade	*Irwin's Brigade*

IV Corps

1st Division Couch
Devens' Brigade
Howe's Brigade
Cochrane's Brigade

V Corps Porter

1st Division Morell	2d Division Sykes	3d Division Humphreys
Barnes' Brigade	*Buchanan's Brigade*	*Tyler's Brigade*
Griffin's Brigade	*Lovell's Brigade*	*Allabach's Brigade*
Stockton's Brigade	*Warren's Brigade*	

Center Sumner

II Corps Sumner

1st Division Richardson	2d Division Sedgwick	3d Division French
Caldwell's Brigade	*Gorman's Brigade*	*Kimball's Brigade*
Meagher's Brigade	*Howard's Brigade*	*Morris' Brigade*
Brooke's Brigade	*Dana's Brigade*	*Weber's Brigade*

XII Corps Mansfield

1st Division Williams	2d Division Greene
Crawford's Brigade	*Tyndale's Brigade*
Gordon's Brigade	*Stainrook's Brigade*
	Goodrich's Brigade

Right Wing Burnside

I Corps Hooker

1st Division Doubleday	2d Division Ricketts	3d Division Meade
Phelps' Brigade	*Duryée's Brigade*	*Seymour's Brigade*
Hofmann's Brigade	*Christian's Brigade*	*Magilton's Brigade*
Patrick's Brigade	*Hartsuff's Brigade*	*Gallagher's Brigade*
Gibbon's Brigade		

IX Corps Reno

1st Division Willcox	2d Division Sturgis	3d Division Rodman
Christ's Brigade	*Nagle's Brigade*	*Fairchild's Brigade*
Welsh's Brigade	*Ferrero's Brigade*	*Harland's Brigade*

Kanawha Division Cox
Scammon's Brigade
Crook's Brigade

Cavalry Division Pleasonton

Whiting's Brigade
Farnsworth's Brigade
Rush's Brigade
McReynolds' Brigade
Davis' Brigade

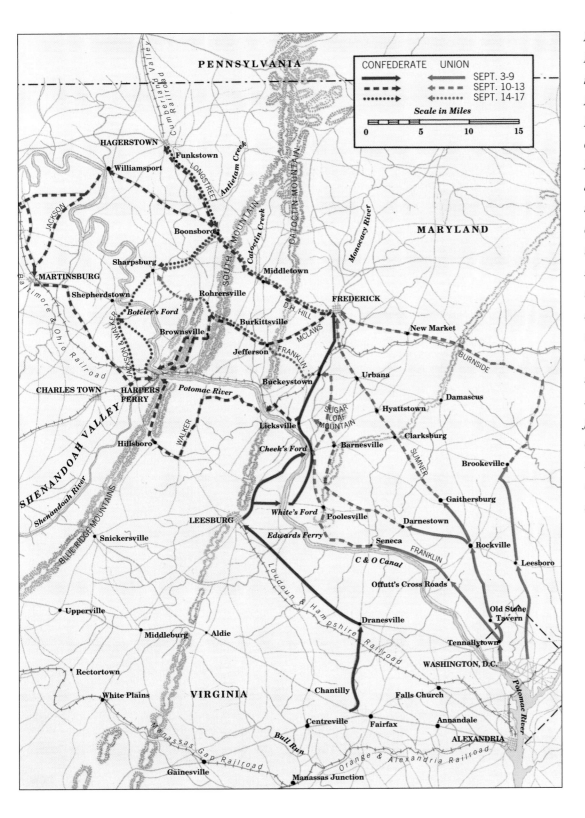

CONFEDERATE UNION
SEPT. 3–9
SEPT. 10–13
SEPT. 14–17
Scale in Miles
0   5   10   15

PENNSYLVANIA

HAGERSTOWN
Funkstown
Williamsport
Boonsboro
Sharpsburg
MARTINSBURG
Shepherdstown
Boteler's Ford
Rohrersville
Brownsville
Burkittsville
CHARLES TOWN
HARPERS FERRY
Jefferson
Buckeystown
Hillsboro
Licksville
Cheek's Ford
Snickersville
LEESBURG
White's Ford
Edwards Ferry
Upperville
Middleburg
Aldie
Rectortown
White Plains
VIRGINIA
Gainesville
Manassas Junction

MARYLAND
Middletown
FREDERICK
New Market
Urbana
Damascus
Hyattstown
Clarksburg
Barnesville
Brookeville
Gaithersburg
Poolesville
Darnestown
Seneca
Rockville
Leesboro
Offutt's Cross Roads
Old Stone Tavern
Tennallytown
Dranesville
WASHINGTON, D.C.
Chantilly
Falls Church
Annandale
Centreville
Fairfax
ALEXANDRIA
Bull Run

SHENANDOAH VALLEY
BLUE RIDGE MOUNTAINS
Potomac River
Shenandoah River
Baltimore & Ohio Railroad
Cumberland Valley Railroad
Antietam Creek
Catoctin Creek
Monocacy River
SOUTH MOUNTAIN
CATOCTIN MOUNTAIN
LONGSTREET
JACKSON
JACKSON & WALKER
WALKER
D.H. HILL
MCLAWS
FRANKLIN
BURNSIDE
SUMNER
FRANKLIN
SUGAR LOAF MOUNTAIN
C & O Canal
Loudoun & Hampshire Railroad
Manassas Gap Railroad
Orange & Alexandria Railroad
Potomac River

Fired by his stunning victory over John Pope's Federals at Second Manassas, Lee wasted little time carrying the war north. After shifting to Leesburg, the Rebel army swiftly crossed the Potomac and reached Frederick, Maryland, on September 6. Pausing there for a few days, Lee then ordered a bold four-way split of his army. Longstreet and D. H. Hill headed north toward Boonsboro and Hagerstown; the rest of the army, divided into three columns under Stonewall Jackson's command, converged on Harpers Ferry. The Federals, now reunited under McClellan, took up the pursuit on September 5. A week later they clashed with the Confederate rear guard at Frederick. All day on September 14 the Federals hammered at the screen of Rebel defenders holding the South Mountain passes, eventually forcing them to fall back that night. The next day, as the Federals ponderously resumed the chase, the garrison at Harpers Ferry surrendered, and Lee ordered his scattered army to recombine with all haste in the vicinity of Sharpsburg.

PRIVATE OTIS D. SMITH
6TH ALABAMA INFANTRY, RODES' BRIGADE

Mustered in as a private in 1861, Smith, who would become a college professor after the war, was among the first troops to cross the Potomac River in September 1862 during Robert E. Lee's advance into Maryland. Writing of the invasion, Smith recalled the high spirits and confidence that marked the Confederates' first foray into Union territory.

In due time our [regiment], [Col.] John B. Gordon in command, reached the Potomac, and were drawn up in line on a high bluff overlooking the river, and the country beyond. It was just before sundown, and the rays of the setting sun shimmering on the placid water, glimmering through the woods just tinged with autumn foliage, gilding with golden hues the distant rolling hills, the whole landscape thickly studded with substantial farmhouses, elegant mansions, lowing herds, and waving grain, presented a picture of placid beauty seldom seen.

There was nothing [Col.] Gordon loved better than speech-making, unless it was fighting. Inspired by the scene and the occasion, he made one of his most thrilling and eloquent speeches. "We were especially honored in being the first troops to cross the Potomac. Our names would go resounding down the corridors of time, our deeds be perpetuated in song and story. Our crossing the Potomac, rivaled only in the past by Washington and his heroes crossing the Delaware, should furnish subjects for the painter's canvas, inspiration to the sculptor's chisel. Future generations should rise up and call us blessed, to the end of time, &c, &c."

The woods and hills re-echoed with rebel yells. The brigade marched to the river singing "Maryland, My Maryland" with an enthusiasm, and abandon only equalled by Frenchmen shouting the Marseillaise.

On reaching the river our enthusiasm was decidedly dampened by the cold fact that we had to wade several hundred yards through water three or four feet deep.

Presto change. Two thousand men were struggling with the swift current, divested of their lower integuments, with gun, ammunition, and other impediments on head and shoulder. Every now and then "One more unfortunate" would disappear, and nothing remain visible but a bayonet with cartridge box attached. For they must "keep the powder dry" whether they trusted in God or not. I fear many trusted in "Massa Bob Lee."

When an anti-Union riot broke out in his hometown in April 1861, Baltimore native James Ryder Randall, an English professor teaching at a Louisiana college, was moved to write the secessionist poem "Maryland, My Maryland." Set to the music of "Tannenbaum, O Tannenbaum," the song became a favorite among Southerners, who were outraged by the Federal dominance of the state.

PRIVATE JOHN W. STEVENS
5TH TEXAS INFANTRY, WOFFORD'S BRIGADE

Serenaded by regimental bands playing their favorite tunes, soldiers of the Army of Northern Virginia waded into the shallow waters of the Potomac River filled with the enthusiasm and jubilation of a conquering force. While awaiting his regiment's turn to cross, Stevens, a native of Liberty County in east Texas and a future judge, turned his thoughts to matters of a more sobering nature.

Imagine a river (as I remember it) about 500 yards wide, from two to three feet deep, the water very swift. Now it is just as full of men as it can be for 600 or 700 yards, up and down, yelling and singing all sorts of war and jolly songs, and in this connection you must find room for eight or twelve regimental bands in the river all the time, the drums beating, the horns a tootin' and the fifes a screaming, possibly every one of them on a different air, some "Dixie," some "My Maryland, My Maryland," some "The Girl I Left Behind Me," some

"I could not for the life of me suppress a feeling of sadness as I beheld this vast concourse of humanity wading the river, so full of music."

HARPER'S WEEKLY.

SEPTEMBER 27, 1862.]

613

THE REBEL ARMY CROSSING THE FORDS OF THE POTOMAC FOR THE INVASION OF MARYLAND.—[SEE PAGE 618.]

For four days, Confederates forded the Potomac's waist-deep waters. The pontoon bridge in the background is likely from the engraver's imagination.

"Yankee Doodle." All the men are apparently jolly. I, at least, did not feel very jolly, though I imagine some of them contemplated the serious side of the situation. While I was deeply interested in the movement, and believe it would ultimate in a great advantage to our cause, yet I could not for the life of me suppress a feeling of sadness as I beheld this vast concourse of humanity wading the river, so full of music and apparently never once thinking that their feet (many of them) would never press the soil on the south side of the Potomac again. . . . About noon, as I now remember the hour, it came the turn of the Texas brigade to cross over. In we bulged, our bands playing, and the boys yellin', as jolly as any who had gone before or any who came after us.

CORPORAL AUSTIN C. STEARNS

13TH MASSACHUSETTS INFANTRY, HARTSUFF'S BRIGADE

Survivors of John Pope's ignominious failure at Second Manassas in late August, Stearns and his comrades trudged east, back toward Washington, D.C. The air of defeat hung heavy about the Massachusetts troops; they were demoralized, rain soaked, and often jeered by McClellan's men along the way.

PRIVATE ALEXANDER HUNTER

17TH VIRGINIA INFANTRY, KEMPER'S BRIGADE

An Alexandria native, Private Hunter recalled that Robert E. Lee's invasion force was little more than a ragtag band of undernourished, unwashed men. Their appearance prompted a Frederick, Maryland, woman to remark, "There is not a scarecrow in the corn-fields that would not scorn to exchange clothes with them."

We were wet through to the skin, and as no fire was allowed, we huddled together and tried to keep ourselves warm; at length a hay-stack was discovered and it was soon confiscated to make bedding for soldiers. The morning dawned bright but cold, and we were allowed to build fires and cook our food and dry ourselves, which we were not long in doing.

The army was falling back, for we had heard the rumbling of teams and artilery all the morning; about noon the order came for us to join in the moving mass. We marched along through Fairfax C. H., and late at night, hungry, tired, and very cross, we drew our weary selves up on to what some of the boys called Halls Hill, one of the slight elevations out-lying the fortifications of Washington. The next week was one of the most disagreeable weeks of all my army life. Sorely smarting under our recent defeat, tired, hungry and cold, and lying on the site of one of McClellan old camps but, added to our discomfort, without tents, or blankets, [and] some of the boys without coats, made it indeed a week long to be remembered, and one that tried our patience to the utmost.

On the 8th we struck up the refrain of "Maryland, My Maryland!" and camped in an apple orchard. We were hungry, for six days not a morsel of bread or meat had gone in our stomachs—and our *menu* consisted of apples and corn. We toasted, we burned, we stewed, we boiled, we roasted these two together, and singly, until there was not a man whose form had not caved in, and who had not a bad attack of diarrhoea. Our under-clothes were foul and hanging in strips, our socks worn out, and half of the men were bare-footed, many were lame and were sent to the rear; others, of sterner stuff, hobbled along and managed to keep up, while gangs from every company went off in the surrounding country looking for food. . . . Many became ill from exposure and starvation, and were left on the road. The ambulances were full, and the whole route was marked with a sick, lame, limping lot, that straggled to the farm-houses that lined the way, and who, in all cases, succored and cared for them. . . .

In an hour after the passage of the Potomac the command continued the march through the rich fields of Maryland. The country people lined the roads, gazing in open-eyed wonder upon the long lines of infantry . . . and as far as the eye could reach, was the glitter of the swaying points of the bayonets. It was the first ragged Rebels they had ever seen, and though they did not act either as friends or foes, still they gave liberally, and every haversack was full that day at least. No houses were entered—no damage was done, and the farmers in the vicinity must have drawn a long breath as they saw how safe their property was in the very midst of the army.

DOCTOR LEWIS H. STEINER
INSPECTOR, U.S. SANITARY COMMISSION

A native of Frederick, Steiner was a Baltimore medical school professor when he was appointed to the U.S. Sanitary Commission at the beginning of the war. While stationed in his hometown, Steiner heard early reports of the Confederate crossing into Maryland and witnessed the panic that ensued.

Friday, September 5. . . .
Along the road, at different stopping-places, reports reached us as to the numbers of the Confederates that had crossed into Maryland. The passengers began to entertain fears that the train would not be able to reach Frederick. These were, however, quieted by a telegram received at a station near Monrovia, which announced the road open. Arriving at 12 o'clock, M., I found the town full of surmises and rumors. Such information had been received by the Post Quarter Master and the Surgeon in charge of Hospital, that they were busy all the afternoon making arrangements to move off their valuable stores.

This hat insignia was worn by officers of the U.S. Sanitary Commission, an organization charged with overseeing the general health of Union soldiers.

The citizens were in the greatest trepidation. Invasion by the Southern army was considered equivalent to destruction. Impressment into the ranks as common soldiers, or immurement in a *Southern* prison—these were not attractive prospects for quiet, Union-loving citizens!

Towards nightfall it became pretty certain that a force had crossed somewhere about the mouth of the Monocacy. Telegrams were crowding rapidly on the army officers located here, directing that what stores could not be removed should be burned, and that the sick should as far as possible be sent on to Pennsylvania. Here began a scene of terror seldom witnessed in this region. Lieut. Castle, A. Q. M., burned a large quantity of his stores at the depot. Assist. Surg. Weir fired his store-house on the Hospital grounds and burned the most valuable of his surplus bedding contained in Kemp Hall, in Church street near Market. Many of our prominent citizens, fearing impressment, left their families and started for Pennsylvania in carriages, on horseback, and on foot. All the convalescents at the Hospital that could bear the fatigue, were started also for Pennsylvania, in charge of Hospital Steward Cox. The citizens removed their trunks containing private papers and other valuables from the bank-vaults, under the firm belief that an attack would be made on these buildings for the sake of the specie contained in them.

COLONEL JOSEPH J. BARTLETT
BRIGADE COMMANDER, ARMY OF THE POTOMAC

Following the defeat at Second Manassas, the demoralized Federals found reason to cheer in September when the popular general George McClellan took command of the now-consolidated Union forces. As the news spread around the camps, Bartlett, leading a brigade in Henry W. Slocum's division of the VI Corps, witnessed the depth of the soldiers' affection for the man they would follow into battle.

I was congratulating my Quartermaster upon his success in getting his last load of shoes for the barefooted men of the four regiments of my command, when through the clear air of the bright September day come from our right a steadily-increasing volume of sound, which swept down upon us as a great wave. My own troops took it up and sent it onward to the left with their strong voices, until it died away again in the far distance. There certainly had been no victories won for which to cheer. There was no voicing of this great shout, yet, when questioned, the soldiers said: "McClellan is again in command." They did not know, for it was impossible for them to know, it as a fact. Still, they persisted in that answer. I went immediately to corps headquarters, where many of the General officers were paying their respects to our stanch and soldierly commander, Gen. Wm. B. Franklin, and they knew nothing more about it than I did. I told them what the soldiers said, and a general discussion was lanched upon similar events occurring within the recollection of more than one old campaigner; but Gen. Franklin had received no order to that effect, or intimation that the army would move. It was more than an hour after this before he received an order that Gen. George B. McClellan had been restored to the command of the Army of the Potomac and the defenses of Washington. This was accompanied with an order from Gen. McClellan, assuming command, and for the Sixth Corps to move at 3 o'clock, by the Long Bridge, through Washington, on the road to Tennallytown. Not all the Quartermasters of divisions and brigades had been so fortunate as mine in getting the necessary outfit for their suf-

fering commands; but the two orders were received with enthusiastic cheers along the whole line, and the camps were all bustle and cheerful excitement from that moment until the heads of our columns drew out on the road toward Long Bridge. Bands played, then men stepped out with that veteran swing which is only acquired by troops after long and continuous campaigning, and the Army of the Potomac seemed to be itself again.

It was nearly 10 o'clock at night when we passed McClellan's house on H street, Washington, the whole command singing, as those who had preceded us had done, "McClellan is our leader, he is gallant and strong. For God and our country we are marching along."

The crowds upon the streets cheered us; ladies from windows and balconies waved handkerchiefs and flags. Even the despairing patriot officials of Washington seemed hopeful and buoyant once more, as they saw the old Army of the Potomac again starting to the front under its real and loved commander, throwing itself between their threatening and enterprising enemy and the spoils of office, to which they clung so fondly.

Dubbed the Young Napoleon early in the war, General George McClellan, a brilliant military organizer and administrator, held the unflagging respect and loyalty of those he commanded, sentiments not shared by official Washington. By the summer of 1862 the 35-year-old soldier's career had been blemished by his lackluster performance in the Peninsula campaign, and it was with grave doubts that President Lincoln reconfirmed McClellan as the commander of the Army of the Potomac, saying, "If he can't fight himself, he excels in making others ready to fight."

PRIVATE EDWARD A. MOORE
ROCKBRIDGE (VIRGINIA) ARTILLERY, J. R. JONES' DIVISION

Bivouacked after crossing the Potomac River, Private Moore and his messmates, defying Lee's orders against leaving camp, eagerly ventured into Frederick, seeking whatever creature comforts the town could provide.

*I*n a day or two we were approaching Frederick City. Strict orders had been issued against foraging or leaving the ranks, but Steve Dandridge and I determined to take the bit in our teeth and endeavor to do the town for one day at all hazards. Knowing the officers and provost-guards would be on the alert and hard to evade

"Here we found O'Rourke, an Irishman of our company, who had a talent for nosing out good things—both solids and liquids."

after the town was reached, we concluded, in order to be safe from their observation, to accomplish that part of our plan beforehand. A field of corn half a mile from the city afforded us good cover till well out of sight. Then, by "taking judicious advantage of the shrubbery," we made our way into a quiet part of the city, and, after scaling a few picket fences, came out into a cross-street remote from the line of march. Steve was the fortunate possessor of a few dollars in greenbacks, my holdings being of a like sum in Confederate scrip. . . .

We soon found a nice little family grocery-store; that is, one kept by a family, including among others two very comely young women. Here we found O'Rourke, an Irishman of our company, who had a talent for nosing out good things—both solids and liquids. We were served with a good repast of native wine, bread, butter, etc.; and, in case we should not have leisure for milder beverages, had a canteen filled with whiskey. . . .

About four P.M. I met Joe Shaner, of Lexington, and of our battery, on the street. His gun having met with some mishap the day previous, had fallen behind, and had now just come up and passed through the town. Joe was wofully dejected, and deplored missing, as one would have imagined, the opportunity of his life—a day in such a city, teeming with all that was good. But little time now remained before evening roll-call, when each must give an account of himself. He was hungry, tired, and warm, and I felt it my duty to comfort him as far as possible. I asked him how he would like a taste of whiskey. "It's just what I need," was his quiet reply, and before I had time to get the strap off of my shoulder he dropped on one knee on the curb-stone and had my canteen upside down to his mouth, oblivious of those passing by. He had no money, but, being a messmate, I invested the remnant of my change for his benefit, but found it necessary to include a weighty watermelon, to make out his load to camp. . . .

The sun was now setting; camp was two miles away. Thither I set out, cheered by the assurance that, whatever punishment befell, I had had a day. Arriving there, my apprehensions were relieved, possibly because

offenses of the kind were too numerous to be handled conveniently. . . .

We spent two or three days in a clean, fresh camp in this fertile country, supplied with an abundance of what it afforded. At noon each day apple-dumplings could be seen dancing in the boiling camp-kettles, with some to spare for a visitor, provided he could furnish his own plate.

GENERAL ROBERT E. LEE
COMMANDER, ARMY OF NORTHERN VIRGINIA

Lee brought his army into Maryland in large part to spare a ravaged northern Virginia another campaign and to garner provisions for his men. As the following proclamation shows, Lee also hoped to capitalize on the kindred sentiments that he and his countrymen believed lay waiting in the hearts of Marylanders.

Headquarters Army of Northern Virginia
Near Fredericktown, Md., September 8, 1862.
To the People of Maryland:
It is right that you should know the purpose that brought the army under my command within the limits of your State, so far as that purpose concerns yourselves. The people of the Confederate States have long watched with the deepest sympathy the wrongs and outrages that have been inflicted upon the citizens of a commonwealth allied to the States of the South by the strongest social, political, and commercial ties. They have seen with profound indignation their sister State deprived of every right and reduced to the condition of a conquered province. Under the pretense of supporting the Constitution, but in violation of its most valuable provisions, your citizens have been arrested and imprisoned upon no charge and contrary to all forms of law. The faithful and manly protest against this outrage made by the venerable and illustrious Marylander, to whom in better days no citizen appealed for right in vain, was treated with scorn and contempt; the government

"Our army has come among you, and is prepared to assist you with the power of its arms in regaining the rights of which you have been despoiled."

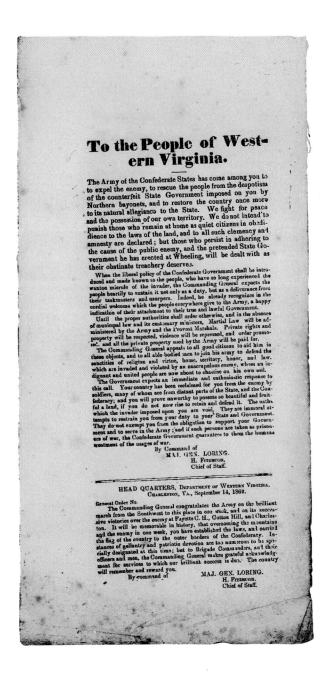

To the People of Western Virginia.

of your chief city has been usurped by armed strangers; your legislature has been dissolved by the unlawful arrest of its members; freedom of the press and of speech has been suppressed; words have been declared offenses by an arbitrary decree of the Federal Executive, and citizens ordered to be tried by a military commission for what they may dare to speak. Believing that the people of Maryland possessed a spirit too lofty to submit to such a government, the people of the South have long wished to aid you in throwing off this foreign yoke, to enable you again to enjoy the inalienable rights of freemen, and restore independence and sovereignty to your State. In obedience to this wish, our army has come among you, and is prepared to assist you with the power of its arms in regaining the rights of which you have been despoiled.

This, citizens of Maryland, is our mission, so far as you are concerned. No constraint upon your free will is intended; no intimidation will be allowed within the limits of this army, at least. Marylanders shall once more enjoy their ancient freedom of thought and speech. We know no enemies among you, and will protect all, of every opinion. It is for you to decide your destiny freely and without constraint. This army will respect your choice, whatever it may be; and while the Southern people will rejoice to welcome you to your natural position among them, they will only welcome you when you come of your own free will.

R. E. Lee,
General, Commanding.

As Robert E. Lee moved into Maryland, troops of the Department of Southwestern Virginia, led by Major General William W. Loring, drove two Federal brigades from Union-held Charleston in western Virginia on September 13. The Federals were forced to retreat toward the northwest, up the Kanawha River valley. A day later, General Loring issued this communiqué to the people of the region, similar in spirit to Lee's Maryland proclamation.

CAPTAIN WILLIAM W. BLACKFORD

STAFF, MAJOR GENERAL
J. E. B. STUART

Eager to reciprocate the hospitality of the Frederick townspeople, General Jeb Stuart, the flamboyant cavalier, hosted a ball at Urbana, several miles southeast of Frederick. Blackford, an engineer officer on Stuart's staff, described the event, thereafter referred to as the Sabres and Roses Ball, as one they would long remember.

While at Urbana our life at headquarters was a delightful one, an oasis in the war-worn desert of our lives. There was nothing to do but await the advance of the great army preparing around Washington, and though constant vigilance was necessary, General Stuart like a good soldier knew how to improve the passing hour in the enjoyment of the charming society the country round afforded. Our horses stood saddled day and night, and Stuart and his staff slept in the open air in the shady yard of the residence of Mr. Cocky, with clothes, boots, spurs and arms on, ready for instant action, but with these precautions we enjoyed the society of the charming girls around us to the utmost. One hour's acquaintance in war times goes further towards good feeling and acquaintanceship than months in the dull, slow period of peace. This no doubt makes a military people like the French call it "Merry War."

It was the 11th of September before we were disturbed in our enjoyment of these scenes and pleasant associations at Urbana. One bright event occurred of which I must say something as illustrative of the life

Despite the cordiality shown the Army of Northern Virginia by many citizens of western Maryland, Unionist sympathies still prevailed in the region. Farther north, the reaction to Lee's Maryland proclamation was more pronounced, as seen in the September 27 issue of Harper's Weekly (right), featuring cartoons lampooning Lee's purported intent to liberate Maryland from the yoke of Union oppression.

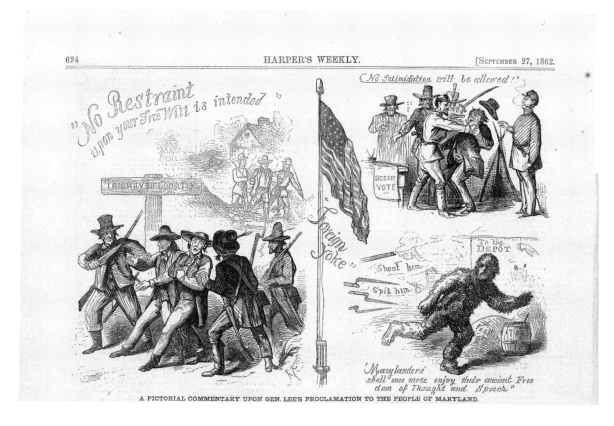

A PICTORIAL COMMENTARY UPON GEN. LEE'S PROCLAMATION TO THE PEOPLE OF MARYLAND.

"Like a flock of angels in their white dresses assembled around the stretchers, they bent over the wounded men, dressing their wounds and ministering to their wants, with their pretty fingers all stained with blood."

we led with the dashing and brilliant leader of our cavalry. A rosy light hovers around it still, illuminating the vista of dark and lowering clouds of war overhanging the past. General Stuart was fond of dancing, and in return for the hospitality we had received he determined to give a ball. On the edge of the village stood a large, vacant building which had been in peace times used as a female academy, and the staff was soon busied in having a large room prepared there. The walls were decorated with regimental Confederate flags collected from the regiments around, an army band furnished the music, and lovely moonlight lit the beauty and fashion of the country on their way as they assembled in response to our invitation. The officers came prepared for any emergency, fully armed and equipped, picketing their horses in the yard and hanging their sabres against the walls of the dance hall. As the delightful strains of music floated through the vacant old house, and the dancing began, the strange accompaniments of war added zest to the occasion, and our lovely partners declared that it was perfectly charming. But they were destined to have more of the war accompaniment than was intended by the managers, for just as everything had become well started and the enjoyment of the evening was at its height, there came shivering through the still night air the boom of artillery, followed by the angry rattle of musketry. The lily chased the rose from the cheek of beauty, and every pretty foot was rooted to the floor where music had left it. Then came hasty and tender parting from tearful partners, buckling on of sabres, mounting of impatient steeds, and clattering of hoofs as the gay cavaliers dashed off to the front.

The ladies could not be persuaded to believe that they were not tak-

ing a last farewell of those who would sleep that night in bloody graves, but being assured that it was probably only a night attack on the outposts to feel our position, and that we might all return to finish the evening, and being influenced possibly by that curiosity which the dear creatures are said to possess, they at last agreed to await our return.

McClellan's advance guard had struck our outposts, but after a sharp skirmish they withdrew for the night and we hastened back "covered with glory," at least in the ladies' eyes. Dancing was resumed and was at its height again when, alas, it was doomed to a final interruption. Heavy tramping of feet in the passage attracted the attention of the lady who was my partner, standing at the time next the door of the ballroom. Looking out, she clasped her hands and uttered a piercing scream. The scream brought all the dancers trooping out to see what was the matter now, and there on stretchers the wounded were being carried by to the vacant rooms upstairs.

It was no use talking to them of any more dancing that night. There, like a flock of angels in their white dresses assembled around the stretchers, they bent over the wounded men, dressing their wounds and ministering to their wants, with their pretty fingers all stained with blood. One handsome young fellow, as he looked up in their faces with a grateful smile, declared that he would get hit any day to have such surgeons to dress his wounds. All that was left for us now was to escort the "lovely angels" home by the light of the moon and to bid a last, tender farewell to them and to the happy days we had spent among them, for we knew that the morrow would bring again war's stirring scenes around us.

SERGEANT J. J. MCDANIEL
7TH SOUTH CAROLINA INFANTRY, KERSHAW'S BRIGADE

Having enjoyed a respite from hostilities, Lee's army began its westward move from the outskirts of Frederick on September 10, passing through largely Unionist counties. As they marched along, McDaniel and his fellow soldiers were treated to an ambivalent welcome. They exchanged taunts with pro-Northern Marylanders, yet were surprised by a sympathizer's unexpected act of kindness.

As we passed through Frederick City, great demonstrations were made by friends and foes—some ladies were bringing pails of water to quench the thirst of the soldiers—some milk—some bread—some waved handkerchiefs and Confederate flags, while others waved Union flags from windows and held their noses as we passed—some crying, while our bands were playing and the troops cheering. In passing through this exciting scene, a Georgia Major, inspired in part by the occasion, and in part by liquor, was riding along our lines speaking. He was calling the attention of the citizens to "the grand invincible army of the South;" in passing our Brigade, he said, "I'm a Georgian, but I give to South Carolina the honor of beginning this struggle for liberty." We gave him a cheer and he passed on. After passing the city we took the Hagerstown road and traveled that to Middleton. . . . At the towns we passed in this section, the Union sentiment seemed greatly to predominate. Women, with Yankee effrontery from their windows, would make remarks of ridicule, but were always badly cut by a soldier's wit. One asked why our soldiers were so dirty and ragged. She was answered, "Our mammas always taught us to put on our worst clothes when we go to kill hogs." Another wanted to know why so many of us were barefooted. She was answered: "We wore out our shoes running after the Yankees." But I must say in justice to Maryland, we have some warm friends, even in these Union Counties through which we passed. An old man was seen to pull off his shoes and give them to one of our barefooted soldiers, and ride off in his socks.

LIEUTENANT WILLIAM M. OWEN
WASHINGTON (LOUISIANA) ARTILLERY

Lieutenant Owen served as adjutant of a reserve artillery battalion made up of four batteries of the famed Washington Artillery of New Orleans. Attached to General Longstreet's command, the battalion set out for Hagerstown on September 10.

The 10th of September was a bright, beautiful day, and the army of Lee, with bands playing and colors flying, marched through Frederick. The citizens crowded the streets and windows to see the troops pass. Ladies were demonstrative, and waved their handkerchiefs; but the men looked coolly on as though afraid to express their feelings either way. The artillery boys marched in front of their batteries and sang their choruses, led by Lieut. Frank McElroy.

The army passed through in good order, and all in the merriest and jolliest mood possible, indulging occasionally in good-natured chaff, as was their wont. Any peculiarity of costume or surroundings of any person was sure to bring out some remark that would set whole regiments in a roar. On a small gallery stood a buxom young lady, with laughing black eyes, watching the scene before her; on her breast she had pinned a small flag, the "stars and stripes." This was observed, and some soldier sang out, "Look h'yar, miss, better take that flag down; we're awful fond of charging breast-works!" This was carried down the line amid shouts of laughter. The little lady laughed herself, but stood by her colors.

Members of the Washington Artillery of New Orleans boasted their own insignia—a gold pin featuring crossed cannons, a stylized lion's head, and the motto Try Us.

Confederates marching through Frederick call a halt on Market Street in this rare photograph taken from an upper window of J. Rosenstock's store. "They were the dirtiest men I ever saw," a local woman noted, "a most ragged, lean and hungry set of wolves. Yet there was a dash about them that the northern men lacked."

PRIVATE IVY W. DUGGAN

15th Georgia Infantry, Toombs' Brigade

Taking heart from what he saw as his regiment marched into Hagerstown, Duggan, a schoolteacher from Washington County, Georgia, noted fervent displays of secessionist sentiments among many of the women and children of the town, feelings shared but necessarily kept secret by the men, who were more liable to censure by Federal authorities. Overall, Lee's men found Hagerstown to be a pro-Southern haven compared with the more Unionist countryside.

There is secession here. I was not a little surprised at the enthusiasm, shown by many of the citizens as our brigade passed along the streets, while the excellent band of the second Georgia, discoursed sweet music. What a number of ladies plainly showed by smiles, the waving of flags, handkerchiefs &c., one expressed in words, "I am a rebel, every inch of me," and I assure you she felt what she said. We have often heard little children, whose words were difficult to understand, "Hurrah for Jef. Davis!" "Hurrah for Stonewall Jackson!" "Hurrah for Gen. Lee!" We have frequently observed that the women and children manifest more secession feelings than the man; and it is easily accounted for since they are less subject to be punished by the Federals. One lady, from whom I procured a map of the country, said, "You must not tell where you got it." I asked the reason, and she replied, "They made father swear." And that young lady's father had sent me to his daughter, that I might get the map, which he would not bring me himself. Perhaps he feared some one would see him and report. He was quite a gentleman, well posted, and a rebel too. As I walked the street alone one morning, an old lady, after voluntarily proposing to give me breakfast; said, "We are cowed down. We are not allowed to act or speak. All news, favorable to the Confederacy, is kept from us, and every battle reported a victory, while we are continually told that the rebellion is almost crushed out. These are dark days, and we are glad to see you come. After a secession victory, we can scarcely whisper to a friend, or smile at one across the street; without being reported as rejoicing over a Union defeat." I do not say that anything like a majority of the people of Hagerstown are Secessionists, but I do say there are many who are thoroughly so; and when, for the first time, they saw a victorious rebel army enter their streets, many were overjoyed, cast off all restraints, and exhibited the most enthusiastic demonstrations.

That many more would have shown similar feelings, had not prudence taught them that they might be called to answer for such conduct, before an enemy who regards neither mercy nor justice, I sincerely believe. Hagerstown is but five miles from the Pennsylvania line, and we were confidently assured that there are a few very strong Secessionists over the line.

This pass, issued by General Toombs during the Rebel occupation of Hagerstown, authorized two residents to move through Confederate lines.

"Who that was present will ever forget the cheerful welcome received as the heavy columns of troops passed through Frederick City."

General McClellan reaches for the hand of a child thrust up to greet him as he rides through Frederick on Dan Webster, his powerful dark bay. "The whole population turned out, wild with joy," a Federal officer wrote. "When McClellan appeared, the crowd became so demonstrative that we were forcibly brought to a halt."

ANONYMOUS
35TH MASSACHUSETTS INFANTRY, FERRERO'S BRIGADE

Although the residents of Frederick had hardly suffered under the brief Confederate occupation, people turned out in numbers to welcome McClellan and his men as liberators as they passed through town on September 12. As this writer records, the warm reception gave the troops of the Army of the Potomac a boost in morale even if it was, for some, tempered by thoughts of the fighting that lay ahead.

Who that was present will ever forget the cheerful welcome received as the heavy columns of troops passed through Frederick City, flags and handkerchiefs waving, and friendly faces greeting the soldiers from all sides! . . .

At a corner of the streets General McClellan with his staff reviewed the troops, and cheer after cheer rent the air as the regiments passed. This welcome from patriotic Marylanders made the soldiers feel as if they were to fight upon their own soil, and greatly inspirited the army unused to such moral support. The song of "Maryland, My Maryland," was ever after a Union song. Our regiment sang together "Marching Along" and "Old John Brown," with grand effect, as we swung through the streets; but when we halted for a few moments in the outskirts, some of the cynical elders of the brigade suggested: "Save your breath, boys; you'll need it ahead there!" Too true! for we never sang together on the march afterwards, we had no heart for it, it seemed like tempting evil fortune.

CORPORAL WILLIAM B. WESTERVELT
27TH NEW YORK INFANTRY, BARTLETT'S BRIGADE

Less eager to impress the citizenry than were the Confederates, Federal troops passing through Frederick and other Maryland towns in pursuit of Lee were often prone to take liberties. New York native and veteran Westervelt, who would shortly find himself fighting at South Mountain, seized the opportunity for a sumptuous repast, and would later write, "This was, I believe, the only time that I went into a fight with a full stomach."

About noon we reached Jefferson, just as the people were returning from church. As our line halted a few minutes, I slipped into one of the houses just as the family were sitting down to their noonday meal, and with the modesty that characterizes an old campaigner, I took the only vacant chair at the table, and invited myself to dinner. It was well I did, for the old gentleman failed to invite me, and even seemed to ignore my presence after being seated. After waiting patiently until he had helped the whole table including himself, I quietly exchanged my empty plate for one he had just filled and placed in front of a dudish-looking young man who seemed to be the quest of his daughter. Picking up a knife and fork I commenced my dinner. A smile passed around the table at my monumental cheek; but with perfect gravity and without speaking a word, I continued to devour everything eatable that came within my reach, knowing that minutes were precious. I listened for our bugle to sound the advance, and took no notice of the muttered imprecations from the "nice young man" on my right, who seemed to have lost his appetite at the time he lost his plate. I did not even notice the muttered sounds that came from the old gentleman at the head of the table, that I imagined sounded very much like "hog." Having no time for anything but the work before me, it received my undivided attention for about fifteen minutes. As my breakfast had been taken at daylight, and had consisted of one hard tack and a quart of coffee, I was then in good condition to astonish the old gentleman and his family with my gastronomic feat. In fact, I almost astonished myself.

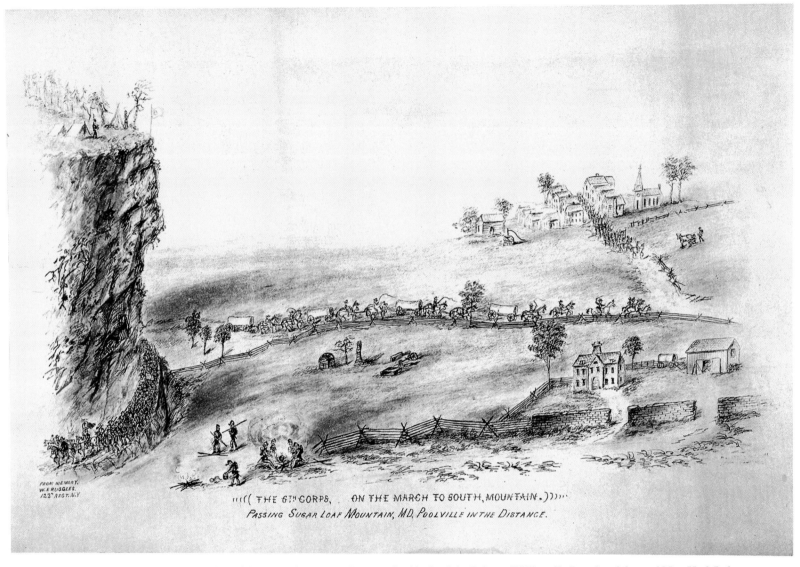

A column of the VI Corps, part of the left wing of the Federal army, trudges west in this sketch by Private William E. Ruggles of the 122d New York Infantry.

LIEUTENANT SAMUEL E. PITTMAN

STAFF, BRIGADIER GENERAL ALPHEUS S. WILLIAMS

The lost copy of General Lee's orders made its way up the chain of command and finally reached George McClellan, who exultantly proclaimed, "Here is a paper with which if I cannot whip Bobbie Lee, I will be willing to go home." The two soldiers from the 27th Indiana Infantry who found the orders were both wounded four days afterward at the Battle of Antietam.

In a correspondence with General Colgrove some years ago upon this subject, he wrote as follows:

"When the Twelfth Corps halted at Frederick, it stacked arms on the ground that Gen. Hill's command had occupied the evening before, and I had not yet dismounted when First Sergt. John M. Bloss (afterwards Captain) and Private B. W. Mitchell, both of Co. F of my regiment, brought to me the now famous Order No. 191 of Gen. Lee.

"The Sergeant stated that it had been found by Mitchell near where the regiment stacked arms. It was wrapped around three cigars, and Mitchell said it was the same shape when he picked up the little package. It seemed to have dropped from someone's vest or side pocket."

Gen. Colgrove then goes on to say that he immediately carried the order to our headquarters and delivered it to me; that I immediately identified the signature of Col. R. H. Chilton, Lee's Assistant Adjutant General. As a rule written orders of a commanding officer are signed with the name of such commanding officer by his Adjutant General, thus this Order No. 191 was signed "By command of Gen. R. E. Lee, R. H. Chilton, Assistant Adjutant General."

Before the war I was teller of the Michigan State Bank, and R. H. Chilton at the same time was a paymaster in the U.S. Army, stationed at Detroit. His bank account was kept at our bank, and a bank teller

becomes more or less an expert as to signatures; therefore, when some one among those present raised the question that perhaps it was a ruse de guerre, I was able to assert that I was familiar with Col. Chilton's signature and that this signature on the order was genuine.

Taking Colgrove with me, I immediately reported to Williams with the document, and he directed me to lose no time in placing it in Gen. McClellan's possession. I requested permission to take it in person, but the General objected, as orders were momentarily looked for to move on after Lee; therefore I could not be spared.

I then dispatched the document, accompanied by a note to Gen. McClellan's Assistant Adjutant General, sending it by a trusty courier on duty at our headquarters, with instructions to ride fast, and it was in McClellan's possession or at his headquarters with no delay whatever.

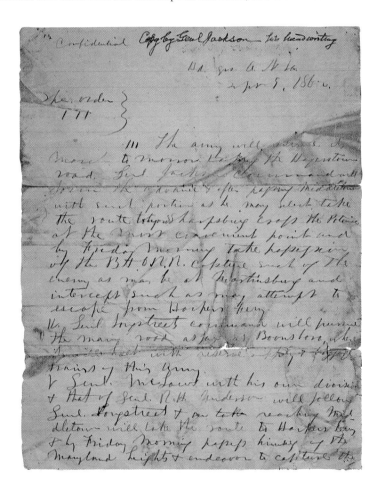
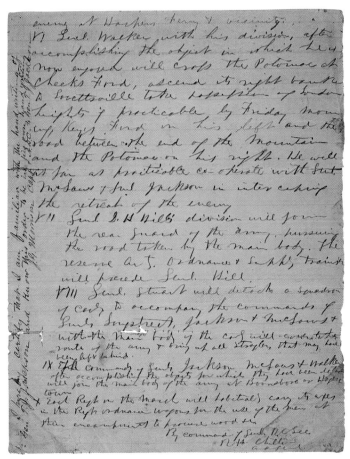

The "lost orders" were probably the set intended for General D. H. Hill, but having already received a copy from Jackson rendered in Stonewall's own hand (above), Hill had no knowledge of the duplicate set that somehow got left behind when the Confederates departed Frederick.

South Mountain

The first crisis of General Robert E. Lee's daring invasion of Maryland came on September 14, when advance elements of three of General George McClellan's Federal corps arrived at South Mountain, an extension of the Blue Ridge Mountains stretching roughly 50 miles from the Potomac River northward into Pennsylvania. Lee, counting on McClellan to move slowly, had divided his army since crossing the Potomac a week before, leaving only a single division, commanded by D. H. Hill, to hold the passes snaking through South Mountain. Six divisions under Stonewall Jackson were 15 miles to the southwest, laying siege to Union-held Harpers Ferry; the remaining two Confederate divisions under Longstreet were strung out to the northwest between Boonsboro and Hagerstown.

The usually dilatory McClellan, however, had moved westward from Washington to meet the Confederate invasion faster than Lee had anticipated. By the morning of Sunday, September 14, lead elements of three Federal corps were advancing on the roads leading to South Mountain. A swift breakthrough would give McClellan a chance, as he said, "to whip Bobbie Lee," smashing first one part and then another of the Confederate army.

Alerted to his danger, Lee fired off messages instructing Longstreet to hurry back southward and urging Jackson to capture Harpers Ferry with all possible speed and also join up. To the small force he had nearby—some of Jeb Stuart's cavalry and D. H. Hill's brigades—Lee issued a do-or-die order: Turner's Gap, the main pass through South Mountain, "must be held at all hazards."

The battle got under way in earnest about 9:00 a.m. when Union general Jacob Cox, deciding to outflank the Confederates holding Turner's Gap, sent his 3,000-man division from Jesse Reno's IX Corps onto the Old Sharpsburg Road leading to Fox's Gap just to the south. After a bitter, bloody two-hour fight, the Federals managed to rout the Confederate blocking force—General Samuel Garland's 1,000-man brigade—from its defensive positions, killing Garland in the process. The North Carolinians, demoralized by the loss of their leader, fell back toward Fox's Gap.

Now in command of the situation, Cox's Federals moved north along a ridge road toward their main objective, Turner's Gap. But with success in sight, the Federals were slowed by a makeshift defensive line cobbled together around a couple of guns by a desperate D. H. Hill. Then they were stopped entirely by fresh Rebel brigades that had just arrived from the rear. Suddenly pressed by the Confederates, Cox pulled back before Fox's Gap and waited for reinforcements.

It was not until midafternoon that the first of the remaining three divisions of the IX Corps arrived to support Cox. Meanwhile D. H. Hill's line had been bolstered by his three remaining brigades and, shortly afterward, by two more from Longstreet. Wasting little time, the Confederate commander hurled his troops at the stalled Federals. Badly managed, the counterattack failed; but two more brigades from Longstreet's corps arrived to prevent any decisive breakthrough by the Federals.

More Federal attacks followed. By 4:00 p.m. Hooker's I Corps had finally come up and started to advance, intending to approach Turner's Gap by a sweep around the Confederate left. After a bitter fight, the divisions

of Generals John Hatch and George Meade eventually outflanked the lone Rebel brigade under Robert Rodes defending the northerly ridges, then also pushed back some of Longstreet's men who moved up to help.

The commander of the IX Corps, General Reno, had no sooner come on the scene to direct the renewed assault of Rodman's and Sturgis' divisions than a bullet cut him down not far from the spot where General Garland had been killed. Carried off down the mountain, Reno died within the hour. He was the highest-ranking Federal officer to fall during the campaign.

As a diversion for the attacks on the Rebel flanks, General John Gibbon's brigade was ordered to march straight up the National Road into Turner's Gap. Gibbon, fighting hard, neared the crest but was stopped there by Alfred Colquitt's brigade, which was securely positioned behind boulders and stone walls.

At this point, just as Meade and Hatch seemed about to rout the still badly outnumbered Confederate defenders at the northern end of the line, darkness descended and put an end to the fighting. Lee had lost more than 2,000 men, but his force remained intact behind the South Mountain barrier.

While this daylong battle was going on, another Union force, the VI Corps under General William Franklin, attacked Crampton's Gap seven miles to the south—but only after wasting most of the day in reconnaissance and deployment. Finally, around 4:00 p.m., the Federals launched a mass head-on charge that quickly broke Colonel William Parham's Virginia brigade and two cavalry regiments under Colonel Thomas Munford, who were holding the gap. Confederate reinforcements—General Howell Cobb's brigade—climbed the western slope, only to be swept up in the rush to the rear. But Franklin failed to follow up his victory. He told his men to make camp instead of pushing forward six miles farther, as ordered by McClellan, to help the embattled garrison at Harpers Ferry.

Without Franklin's aid, badly led by the seemingly befuddled Colonel Dixon Miles, and staring down the barrels of Jackson's guns that virtually ringed the town, the defenders of Harpers Ferry shortly gave up, surrendering on the next day, September 15. Into Confederate hands fell 73 artillery pieces, 13,000 small arms, and 12,500 men, the largest capitulation of Federal forces during the war. The surrender also allowed Jackson to start northward along the Charles Town Turnpike to join up with Lee.

For his part, Lee decided to abandon South Mountain and retreat westward, reuniting his army near the small Maryland town of Sharpsburg. There he drew up his divisions on an undulating ridge behind a lazy watercourse called Antietam Creek. McClellan followed, but slowly; his first divisions only reached the east side of the creek on the afternoon of the 15th. Then McClellan paused again, spending an entire day deploying his army—allowing Lee, now reinforced by Jackson, to prepare for what one Wisconsin officer foresaw would be "a great enormous battle, a great tumbling together of all heaven and earth."

At South Mountain, the opening IX Corps attack crushed the Rebel right at Fox's Gap. But tardy Union reinforcements gave D. H. Hill time to bring up more brigades, allowing him to fend off repeated assaults. Franklin's VI Corps routed the Confederates at Crampton's Gap, but his failure to pursue doomed any attempt to defeat Lee's army in detail.

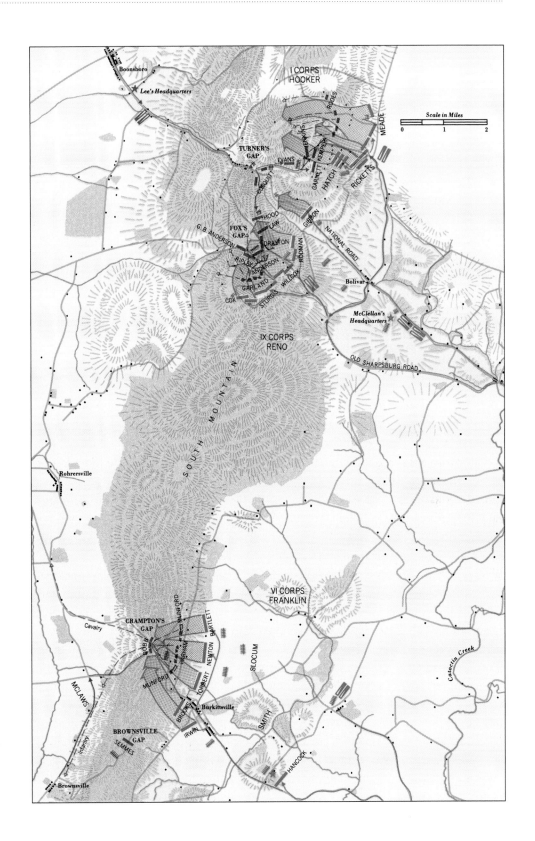

MAJOR GENERAL DANIEL H. HILL

DIVISION COMMANDER,
ARMY OF NORTHERN
VIRGINIA

Left to guard the passes over South Mountain, Hill was probably a little concerned on September 14 when the Federals showed up looking for a fight. But this fearless, battle-hardened West Pointer could not help but be impressed by the sight of his vast enemy deploying to drive him off the mountain.

LIEUTENANT COLONEL RUTHERFORD B. HAYES

23D OHIO INFANTRY,
SCAMMON'S BRIGADE

After a year of largely undistinguished service in western Virginia, the future president and his regiment spearheaded Jacob Cox's attack on the Rebel right at Fox's Gap. Here Hayes describes being wounded while leading the charge against the Confederates.

The marching columns extended back far as eye could see in the distance; but many of the troops had already arrived and were in double lines of battle, and those advancing were taking up positions as fast as they arrived. It was a grand and glorious spectacle, and it was impossible to look at it without admiration. I had never seen so tremendous an army before, and I did not see one like it afterward. For though we confronted greater forces at Yorktown, Sharpsburg, Fredericksburg, and about Richmond under Grant, these were only partly seen, at most a corps at a time. But here four corps were in full view, one of which was on the mountain and almost within rifle-range. The sight inspired more satisfaction than discomfort; for though I knew that my little force could be brushed away as readily as the strong man can brush to one side the wasp or the hornet, I felt that General McClellan had made a mistake, and I hoped to be able to delay him until General Longstreet could come up and our trains could be extricated from their perilous position.

I soon began to fear we could not stand it, and again ordered a charge; the enemy broke, and we drove them clear out of the woods. Our men halted at a fence near the edge of the woods and kept up a brisk fire upon the enemy, who were sheltering themselves behind stone walls and fences near the top of the hill, beyond a cornfield in front of our position. Just as I gave the command to charge I felt a stunning blow and found a musket ball had struck my left arm just above the elbow. Fearing that an artery might be cut, I asked a soldier near me to tie my handkerchief above the wound. I soon felt weak, faint, and sick at the stomach. I laid down and was pretty comfortable. I was perhaps twenty feet behind the line of my men, and could form a pretty accurate notion of the way the fight was going. The enemy's fire was occasionally very heavy; balls passed near my face and hit the ground all around me. I could see wounded men staggering or carried to the rear; but I felt sure our men were holding their own. I listened anxiously to hear the approach of reinforcements; wondered they did not come. . . .

The firing continued pretty warm for perhaps fifteen or twenty minutes, when it gradually died away on both sides. After a few minutes' silence I began to doubt whether the enemy had disappeared or whether our men had gone farther back. I called out, "Hallo Twenty-third men, are you going to leave your colonel here for the enemy?" In an instant a half dozen or more men sprang forward to me, saying, "Oh no, we will carry you wherever you want us to." The enemy immediately opened fire on them. Our men replied to them, and soon the battle was raging as hotly as ever. I ordered the men back to cover, telling them they would get me shot and themselves too. They went back and about this time Lieutenant Jackson came and insisted upon taking me out of the range of the enemy's fire. He took me back to our line, and feeling faint, he laid me down behind a big log and gave me a canteen of water, which tasted so good. Soon after, the fire having again died away, he took me back up the hill where my wound was dressed by Dr. Joe. I then walked about half a mile to the house of Widow Kugler. . . .

I omitted to say that a few moments after I first laid down, seeing something going wrong and feeling a little easier, I got up and began to give directions about things; but after a few moments, getting very weak, I again laid down. While I was lying down I had considerable talk with a wounded soldier lying near me. I gave him messages for my wife and friends in case I should not get up. We were right jolly and friendly; it was by no means an unpleasant experience.

When his men began to falter at Fox's Gap, Brigadier General Samuel Garland of Virginia (left) rode forward to steady his soldiers. Just as one of his colonels warned him of the danger, the brigade commander was mortally wounded. Shown below is the sword and scabbard presented to him by the Lynchburg Home Guard, a militia company he organized in 1859.

"I could see dimly through the dense sulphurous battle smoke and the line from Shakespeare's Tempest flitted across my brain: Hell is empty and all the devils are here."

PRIVATE FREDERICK C. FOARD
20TH NORTH CAROLINA INFANTRY, GARLAND'S BRIGADE

After Garland's men finally broke and ran, Colonel Duncan McRae, Garland's successor, tried to stem the rout, but the battered brigade had seen enough fighting for the day. Foard had just returned to the ranks after recovering from a wound received in June. In late 1863 Foard transferred to the cavalry; he was captured the following summer but escaped and served until the war's end.

At last the enemy charged us three lines of battle deep. We resisted stubbornly retarding their progress in our front but being unopposed in the intervals between the regiments they advanced more rapidly and got around both of our flanks and were about to completely surround us which compelled a hasty and precipate retreat with the sure alternative of death or capture.

As I pulled my trigger with careful aim throwing a musket ball and three buck shot into them at not more than twenty yards distant I could see dimly through the dense sulphurous battle smoke and the line from Shakespeare's Tempest flitted across my brain: Hell is empty and all

the devils are here. Before I could reload our line broke on both sides of me and it was a sharp run until we had extracted ourselves from the flanking columns. Just as our line broke Jimmie Gibson from Concord, one of General Hill's old Davidson students was shot down. Texas Dan Coleman so called to distinguish him from another Dan Coleman, who on account of his courage and great strength had been detailed to the ambulance corps, and Jimmie were great friends. Jimmie exclaimed, "Great God, Dan don't leave me." Dan ran back in face of the enemy's fire, took Jimmie on his shoulder the enemy's line being not 10 yards distant and ran out with him. . . .

My bayonet was fixed for hand to hand work and in running through the laurel bushes my bayonet caught in the bushes above my head, threw the butt of my gun between my feet and I fell sprawling. Just then the man next to me was shot through the head and fell across me. I had to roll his dead body off of me before I could get up. . . .

The Chaplain of one of our regiments was conspicuous for a pair of bear skin leggings probably the only pair of their kind in either army which he continually wore in camp and on the march. The parson who with a prescience born of more than mortal wisdom quickly discerned it was impossible for us to withstand the enemy's onslaught, insured his own safety by flight. Those bear skin leggings could be seen bounding over the tops of the laurel bushes like a kangaroo. McRae who was always facetious exclaimed in a voice that could be heard above the din of battle "Parson—Parson—God damn it, come back here; you have been praying all your life to get to heaven and now that you have a chance for a short cut you are running away from it."

Situated on the fence-lined Old Sharpsburg Road at Fox's Gap, the Wise farm (above) saw some of the hottest action on September 14. After the Yankees ruined his well by throwing a couple of Rebel corpses in it, the farm's owner tossed in over 60 more when the Federals offered him a dollar each to dispose of the bodies on his land.

PRIVATE GEORGE L. WAKEFIELD
9TH NEW HAMPSHIRE INFANTRY, NAGLE'S BRIGADE

One of the greenest units on the field at South Mountain was Wakefield's regiment, fresh from home just 20 days before. After supporting a battery through most of the afternoon, it climbed the mountain shortly before dusk and was ordered to clear out the last Rebels. Wakefield passed unscathed through this baptism but was wounded two years later. He ended the war as a sergeant.

When we got to the stone wall on the side of the mountain,—where the rebels retreated just as we were about to climb over the wall, which was very high—Colonel Fellows turned to the men and said, "I want every man of the Ninth New Hampshire to follow me over that wall. Now, men of the Ninth, is the time to cover yourselves with glory—or disgrace! Any man that does not cross this wall I will report to his state."

The rebels on the other side of the wall were armed with long knives, carried in their belts, which they doubtless intended to use on us; but Colonel Fellows called their attention to our sabre bayonets, and the sight of these and our fellows all scrambling over the wall was too much for the doughty rebels, who turned and fled up the mountain as if for their lives, with the Ninth in hot pursuit.

As we neared the top of the mountain we came to a rail fence and stone wall combined, beyond which was an open field (Wise's). The rebels were just getting over the fence when we received our first order to fire. We halted for a moment and fired, and if it was our first attempt, hit the mark.

There is one incident which will recall to the boys' minds the whole affair as above written, and that is the rebel who was "shot on the wing," and who got his feet so locked in the fence rails that he could go neither forward nor backward, but sat there on the fence bolt upright,—stone dead, though the boys thought him only sullen because he did not answer when they spoke to him.

Colonel Enoch Q. Fellows (left) began the war in August 1861 as commander of the 3d New Hampshire and participated in the Federal campaign along the South Carolina coast. In June 1862, at the request of the governor of his state, he resigned to take charge of the 9th New Hampshire, one of the new regiments called up by Lincoln that summer. But the Maryland campaign proved to be his last. On November 12 he resigned, citing his bad health and the conviction that he had already done his duty.

PRIVATE OTIS D. SMITH
6TH ALABAMA INFANTRY, RODES' BRIGADE

The first reinforcements to come to the relief of D. H. Hill's battered soldiers on South Mountain were the remaining three brigades of his division. While two of the brigades were thrown into the fray at Fox's Gap, Rodes' Alabamians were ordered to the left to defend against the Federal I Corps assault on Turner's Gap. Wounded and captured during the fight, Private Smith was later exchanged but saw only rear-area duty for the rest of the war.

Our brigade, still under . . . Gordon, occupied a narrow precipitous ridge on the extreme left of our line. Here an amusing incident occured. Our line was formed immediately in front of a little one roomed hut, on the crest of the ridge. The hut was occupied by an old woman of ample proportions and her brood of white haired children. Standing in the doorway, she barred all entrance of soldiers or officers, seeking water. Glaring through her immense steel-bowed spectacles, she denounced all comers as "low down thieving rebels." The soldiers cheered vociferously at each outburst of her wrath. Attracted by the uproar . . . Gordon rode up with his staff. Raising his hat in the most courtly manner, he said with the greatest politeness and deference, "My dear madam, fighting will begin in five minutes. Your life and that of your children are in imminent peril. You must leave here at once." The old woman, with arms akimbo, her eyes blazing with wrath replied, "I know what you want, you thieving rebels, you want to get me out of my house, and come and steal all I've got. I won't go, so there! I'll die fust!" The soldiers yelled "Go it old lady! Hold the fort! Bully for you!" &c. . . . Gordon retreated, amidst the ill-concealed laughter of his staff, for once speechless, utterly discomforted. I never knew the fate of this mountaineer Spartan mother, as at that moment my company was ordered to the foot of the mountain as skirmishers. We reached our position just as the enemy's line of skirmishers, a full regiment, extending beyond our right and left, came out of a field of corn, which had concealed them. As they advanced, in perfect line, with neat uniform, and glistening bayonets, they were an imposing and beautiful sight. Notwithstanding their overwhelming numbers, our men, a hundred yards back in the bushes, pluckily held their ground. As the enemy mounted the fence we fired, and dropped a score or more. The whole line dropped back into the corn. But discovering the smallness of our force, advanced, with a rush. To prevent capture we fell back as rapidly as possible, firing at every favorable opportunity. Their fire was terrific. The pat, pat, of the bullets against the rocks sounded like hail. When we had nearly reached our line of battle, three others and myself occupied a covert, protected by two large trees in front, and huge boulders on each side. From this vantage ground we checked the line in our immediate front, but did not notice that the enemy had passed us on either side. One of our men in the rear called to us, "Come out of there or you will be gobbled up." The warning came too late. As we attempted to crawl out through the thick bushes, a storm of bullets poured upon us. My three companions were killed instantly, and I was severely wounded in two places. . . .

. . . As I lay on the ground, faint from loss of blood, the Federal Gen. Reynolds, in command, stopped near me and questioned me as to the numbers and disposition of our forces. My reply not proving very satisfactory he said, "You seem to be a pretty intelligent man to know so little," taking me for an officer. I replied "I am only a private, and know nothing. If I did do you think I ought to tell you?" He smiled, called to his staff surgeon and told him to do what he could for me. He dressed my wounds as well as he could, and gave me a stiff drink of fine French brandy. The General, about to ride on, turned and said, "Is there anything else I can do for you?"

Emboldened by the brandy, I asked, "Can't you send me to the foot of the mountain? I don't want to die up here among these rocks." He hesitated a moment, then called two litter bearers, who took me to a camp of the wounded. There I lay on the bare ground for three days. But my good fortune still followed me. The surgeon in charge of the field-hospitals, a burly, bluff, Englishman, shared his meals with me, or rather gave me what he and his servant did not eat. I fared pretty well on the scraps, and had plenty of good strong coffee.

SERGEANT ASHBALA F. HILL
8TH PENNSYLVANIA RESERVES, MAGILTON'S BRIGADE

Hill's regiment was part of a division under George Meade that formed the right wing of Hooker's attack on Turner's Gap. Advancing uphill in the fading light, Meade's command lost 392 men to the Rebels firing on them from behind the cover of trees and boulders. The division would lose nearly 500 more at Antietam, including Hill, who was severely wounded and discharged in December.

We pressed the rebels closely. They stood awhile, loading and firing, but at last began to waver. Directly in front of the right of our regiment, they gave way; and several companies from the right—ours among them—pressed forward, becoming detached from the regiment. We soon found ourselves thirty or forty paces ahead of the regiment, having gained the flank of the Seventeenth South Carolina. We were within twenty or thirty steps of them, directly on their left, and they did not see us; then we mowed them down. Poor fellows! I almost pitied them, to see them sink down by dozens at every discharge! I remember taking deliberate aim at a tall South Carolinian, who was standing with his side to me loading his gun. I fired, and he fell into a crevice between two rocks. Step by step we drove the rebels up the steep side of the mountain. By moving a little to the left, I reached the spot where I had seen the rebel fall. On my arrival thither, he arose to a sitting posture, and I was convinced he was not dead yet. I inquired whether he was wounded, and he very mournfully nodded assent. The blood was flowing from a wound in the neck. He also pointed to a wound in the arm. The same bullet had made both wounds; for at the time I fired, he was in the act of ramming a bullet home—his arm extended vertically. He arose to his feet, and I was pleased to find him able to walk. I informed him that, in the nature of

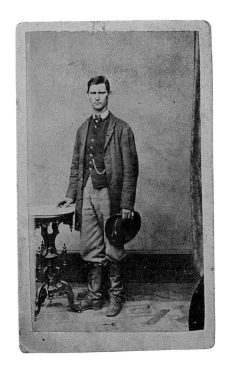

As Willcox's division approached the mountain to support the attack on Fox's Gap, the "enemy sent their shell amongst us thick and fast," recalled Private Frederick Pettit (left) of the 100th Pennsylvania. Willcox's two brigades headed up the slope, but the Rebels had had ample time to bolster their defenses, and the Federals advanced "through a shower of musket balls." None struck Pettit that day, but on July 9, 1864, in the trenches around Petersburg, a sharpshooter's bullet killed him as he sat writing a letter to his sister.

"There, scarcely ten paces from me, stood a great grim rebel, just on the point of bringing his gun to an aim—right at *me*, too."

PRIVATE PHILIP F. BROWN
12TH VIRGINIA INFANTRY, PARHAM'S BRIGADE

Outnumbered 12 to 1 by Franklin's VI Corps massing to the east, the Confederates holding Crampton's Gap managed to delay an assault with aggressive artillery fire that convinced the tentative Federal commander that he faced a much larger force. Captured along with 400 others when the attack finally came, Brown was paroled 12 days later. He received a medical discharge in January 1863.

things, he was a prisoner; and I sent him to the rear, under charge of one of the boys.

Having done so, I threw myself upon the ground, and crawled among the rocks to a position fifteen paces in advance of the company, with the intention of taking some unwary rebel by surprise, and getting a fair shot at him. Cocking my rifle, I abruptly arose from my position, which was protected by a rock three feet high. Oh horror! there, scarcely ten paces from me, stood a great grim rebel, just on the point of bringing his gun to an aim—right at *me*, too, and his dark eyes scowled fiercely upon me from beneath the broad brim of a large ugly hat. Now it is sheer nonsense to talk about taking a cool aim under such circumstances. Therefore, with a little more agility than I had ever before exhibited, I blazed away at random, and dropped behind the rock—every hundredth part of a second seeming like an age; for I felt sure that the rebel bullet would catch me yet, ere I could drop behind my redoubt. A bullet tipped the rock above my head as I dropped.

Step by step, the rebels retired. I waited at my new position till the line came up. Our boys had just reached me, when Dave Malone was struck in the head by a bullet, and he fell back, quivering and gasping for breath. He soon expired. After the battle he was buried in that wild, lonely mountain—where he fell.

As we decended the mountain, we could see, in the distance clouds of dust rising above the trees on the several roads leading to this point. Such an ominous sight made us feel that in a few hours a battle would be fought.

. . . We were deployed eight feet apart, in order to extend our line as far as possible. We were behind a rail fence, with just enough distance from the road to lie down at full length, and rest our rifles on a low rail, where good aim could be taken. I suppose we were in position nearly an hour before the enemy's advance column appeared in our front, about two hundred yards distant, was another rail fence a freshly fallowed field lying between us. We had strict orders, not to fire until the enemy was in good rifle range.

For fully ten or fifteen minutes after arriving at the point mentioned, they hesitated to make a charge on us. Finally, a great cheering, as if greeting some welcome re-inforcements, swelled along the line, and over the fence they clambered, and started for us at double quick time. When they had advanced about fifty yards, a deadly rifle fire hurled them back, leaving a line of killed and wounded. By the time they reached the point from which they started, another volley was poured into them. From these two opposite points, a desultory fire was kept for some time. Then another great cheering (more fresh

Mortally wounded near the Wise farmhouse after sundown on September 14, Jesse L. Reno (above) was one of three Federal major generals killed during the campaign. As he was being carried to the rear, Reno, convinced he had been felled by friendly fire, gasped to General Willcox: "I am killed. Shot by our own men."

troops) and over the fence they came again.

I was in the act of firing my rifle when the cheering commenced; and, seeing an officer with his hat lifted on the point of his sword, as he mounted the fence, I took deliberate aim, but the smoke of my rifle prevented my seeing what effect it had. I do know, however, that they moved only a few feet before they doubled back, and kept up their fire from behind the fence.

In the meantime, a battery of artillery, in our rear was delivering a plunging fire of shot and shell into their ranks. Their force outnumbered our own so greatly, that while we were holding them back in our front, they had lapped around our right and left for some distance; when at a given signal, they made a desperate rush upon our line. Though we popped our rifles as rapidly as possible, it seemed evident that we would soon be overwhelmed.

When they were about twenty yards distant, I was shot in the left arm, about three inches below the elbow, the bullet passing between the two bones, then through the elbow joint, and lodged in the muscle of the arm. I do not know whether it was the excitement, or what, but I felt no more pain at the time, than if a brush had hit me, but the blood trickling to my finger tips, and the utter uselessness of, or inability to move the arm, made me realize that it was broken, and, before the enemy reached the fence, I pulled myself into the road.

At this moment, Cobb's Georgians came to our relief, and enabled all who could, to escape, for they halted the enemy at the fence from which we had, only a few minutes before, been firing at them. While lying in the wheel rut of this road, with the Yankee guns not more than ten feet to my left, my face resting on my bloodcovered hand, I could not help thinking of the shocking sights seen after the battle of Manassas, for, should a battery of artillery, or a squadron of cavalry, move, I would be ground or trampled into an unrecognizable mass.

For fully ten minutes the bullets were hissing near my ears, and, as soon as the enemy crossed over this road, I held my shattered arm in my right, and took refuge in an old cooper shop near the roadside, where a number of Federal soldiers were making good use of several barrels of fresh cider. I passed by them, and seated myself on the back sill feeling quite faint from the loss of blood.

I was not there more than a minute when one of the number brought me a tin cup of the cider, addressing me as "Johnnie." He seemed very much interested in my condition, and insisted on going with me, to have my wound attended to. I was utterly amazed at this mark of kindness, and I soon followed him over the field, where many evidences of the effectiveness of our fire was seen.

COLONEL JOSEPH J. BARTLETT
BRIGADE COMMANDER, ARMY OF THE POTOMAC

A lawyer from New York, Bartlett enlisted at the first call for troops in 1861 and saw action in all but one of the campaigns in the eastern theater. At Crampton's Gap he led one of the brigades that chased the Rebels off the mountain. As a division commander at war's end, he received the surrendered arms of Lee's army at Appomattox.

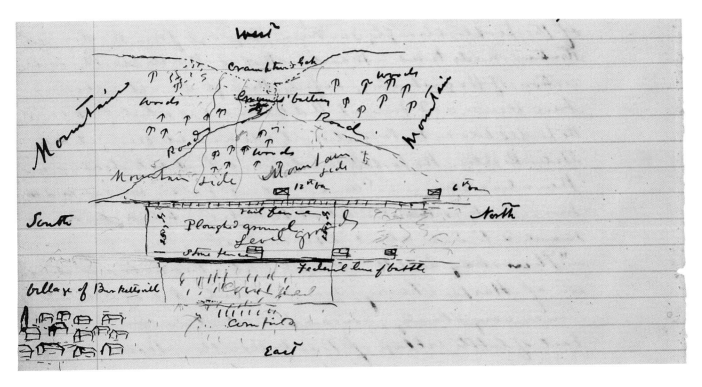

Private George S. Bernard, another member of the 12th Virginia wounded and captured at Crampton's Gap, drew this map of the battlefield as part of his diary. Marked with flags are the positions of the troops before the Federal charge, including Bernard's regiment in the center, deployed behind a rail fence.

Every regiment prepared, the men took an extra tug at their waist-belts, and at the concerted signal the entire command rose upon their feet and giving a ringing cheer rushed forward. The enemy was well prepared to receive us, and poured in our faces a terrible fire from behind the wall, the trees and rocks on the mountain, and a stone house on the right of the 96th Pa., which was the right of the line. There was not a falter in our ranks, or a shot fired from them, and comrades were falling at every step. At last the stone wall was reached, the enemy's line broken, the stone house captured, with its garrison, and the enemy were in rout flying up the mountain side. Then our lines, in perfect order, opened their fire, and in pursuit passed on up the steep mountain, loading and firing as they went. Torbert with his gallant Jerseymen had also carried his front, and was pressing them closely up the mountain on the left. The fiercest part of the struggle was on the right, in front of my line, which is plainly shown in the losses sustained by the regiments composing it. About half way up the mountain above us a wood road ran diagonally down its side, into which

reinforcements were pouring with the old rebel yell, but the line of blue kept struggling upward, firing and loading as rapidly as they could under such difficulties.

Our fire here was very effective. Each bullet must hit either a tree, a rock or a man, for they could not go over the mountain. The enemy, however, were firing over us, and our loss was very little, although two of our bravest and most gallant officers were wounded when we received the first fire from the reinforcements in the wood road (Col. Rod Matheson, 32d N.Y., and Maj. Lemon, of the same regiment; and both these noble soldiers died of their wounds). The 18th N.Y. and the 32d N.Y. . . . together with the 96th Pa., on their right, were directly in front of this newly-developed strength of the enemy, and if they now faltered the victory would be lost. Maj. McGinnis, of the 18th, said to me: "Colonel, my men are out of cartridges." I replied: "Never mind, Major; push on; we have got 'em on the run. The regiments each side of you have got ammunition, and are using it." The gallant Major, smilingly, encouraged his men and pushed vigorously onward.

PRIVATE RANDOLPH A. SHOTWELL

8TH VIRGINIA INFANTRY, GARNETT'S BRIGADE

After a forced march of some 20 miles and an exhausting climb up the west side of South Mountain at Turner's Gap, Garnett's men had no sooner deployed on the Confederate left than they were hit hard by one of the last Federal I Corps attacks. The darkness that saved them also compounded the confusion in their ranks, and the withdrawal down the mountain was anything but orderly. Shotwell, like many of his comrades, had long since worn out his shoes.

All, except those gallant fellows who lie upon their faces with outstretched arms, pointing with their bayonets, as it were, even in death, at the enemies of their country—all, except those patient sufferers, who lie among the rocks and bushes awaiting death, or perchance shuddering at the thought of the surgeon's knife, and mournfully listening to the retiring footsteps of their comrades, as they march away amid the gloom. Occasionally the agonized cry of "water, water! kill me or give me a drink of water!" startled the night air. I would much rather have remained, to fight if need be all next day,

BATTLE OF SOUTH MOUNTAIN—FRANKLIN'S CORPS STORMING CRAMPTON'S PASS.—Sketched by Mr. A. R. Waud.—[See Page 683.]

This engraving from the October 25, 1862, issue of Harper's Weekly takes license by depicting the Confederate troops making their stand at Crampton's Gap as a formidable, densely packed force (on the left). In reality they were undermanned and loosely spaced, and eventually they were routed, as shown in the distance.

than to abandon the field and our wounded to the foe, to say nothing of the dreadful night-marching. Oh, the torture of that night! Already I had marched quite sixteen miles since dawn, including the fatiguing toil up the mountain, and, as usual, the intense excitement of the battle speedily gave way to extreme relaxation and lassitude which seemed to deprive me of the last particle of strength, rendering each step more difficult than the last. One who has never experienced the relaxation, which follows the tense excitement of a fiercely contested battle, in a young, nervous, and excitable person, can have but little idea of my real condition that night.

My comrades, of course, soon outstripped me in the descent of the precipitous mountain-side, leaving me to stumble and stagger as best I could among the sharp rocks, stumps, fallen timber, briar thickets, and every other imaginable torture for naked feet. Twice I fell head-long, and had to spend half an hour hunting for my scattered gun, bayonet, hat, etc., etc., for the night was very dark. Half way down, I met with by far the worst mishap of all—equivalent, indeed, to a severe gunshot wound.

The slope of the mountain was cleared and cultivated part of the way to the top, and a field enclosed by a stone fence lay across my line of retreat. I clambered on the rude rock wall to sit for a moment's rest. Down in the valley below lay the village of Boonsboro, with numerous flashing lights, while amid the great canopy of darkness could be heard the distant rumbling of wagons and artillery, and the murmur and clank of battalions of soldiers in motion. "No time to lose sitting here," thought I, and easing myself over the wall I threw the whole weight of my body supplemented by 100 pounds of gun and baggage upon my left foot.

Horror! The bare skin and flesh gave way—as if cut by a knife—to the sharp edge of a grey slate rock sticking perpendicularly in the ground, or else the broken bottom of a large glass bottle! It was too dark to determine which. The leap downward from the wall gave a descent of some four feet squarely upon this keen edge, and the result was a terrible gash, two inches in length, diagonally across the hollow of the foot and fully an inch and a quarter deep! It was worse than having stepped upon the upright edge of an axe, for *it* would have made a clean gash whereas this thing mangled the flesh and filled it with gravel and scales of slate. So acute was the pain that I ran some distance down the mountainside in a sort of frenzy.

Private Alfred Turner, shown in this rare "charge bayonets" photograph, was a member of the 4th North Carolina Infantry, part of George B. Anderson's brigade. Heavily engaged at Fox's Gap, the brigade fell back to the west with the rest of the Rebel defenders, but Turner fell into Yankee hands at Boonsboro, probably as a straggler. Exchanged two months later, Turner apparently had had his fill of the war—he never returned to duty.

" 'This must be Mount Ararat, up above the world so high, like a diamond in the sky.' "

SERGEANT CHARLES C. CUMMINGS
17TH MISSISSIPPI INFANTRY, BARKSDALE'S BRIGADE

McLaws' division, the northern arm of the three-pronged pincer converging on Union-held Harpers Ferry, encountered the only serious resistance from the Federal garrison when the Rebels were forced to fight for control of Maryland Heights. On September 13, after being stymied by strong enemy defenses, the Confederates, including Cummings' regiment, took possession of the heights when the Federals gave up the fight and fell back to the town.

About nine o'clock on the morning of the 13th of September we took position after an all night's climb up the Heights. Our position under Barksdale we thought the harder part, as we had to climb great bowlders piled one above the other in careless confusion. When in the greatest peril there is always some wag to think up funny things. Eb Robinson, of my company, said: "This must be Mount Ararat, up above the world so high, like a diamond in the sky." Bill Day, the Irish wag, replied: "No, there ain't ary rat here; it is too high and dry."

. . . While I was myself considerably shaken at the idea of scrambling over great bowlders, having to place our guns on them and climb up to them in the charge, one of the boys halted, when, looking up, he saw the muzzles of the enemy's guns pointing down at us and turned pale and said he could go no farther; but a cry from a skulker in our rear, who had weakened and turned back, showed that those who were not well up in line were in more danger than we who were doing our duty. They were overshooting us. I called my comrade's attention to this, and we soon made a final lunge upward and found that the gallant charge of the Carolinians, led by their gamecock Kershaw, crawling through the abatis of timber in front of the fort (the Federal leader being wounded), had demoralized the opposing force, and the Federals were fleeing down the mountain side into the ferry, where the whole

Nestled in a spectacular setting, Harpers Ferry could also boast of its strategic location. Situated at the convergence of the Potomac and Shenandoah Rivers and at the site of a Baltimore & Ohio Railroad bridge, it was a vital link in the North's east-west communications. At the same time, Confederates bent on invasion had to have Harpers Ferry to secure a supply line back into Virginia. In this 1862 image taken before the siege, the Potomac flows past Harpers Ferry (right) to its confluence with the Shenandoah River just beyond the town. Crossing the Potomac are the railroad bridge and a half-finished pontoon bridge that would be used by the Federals who abandoned Maryland Heights (left). The promontory to the right, Loudoun Heights, was left undefended by the Federals and became an artillery platform during the siege for John Walker's Confederates.

twelve thousand were caught in the garrison. . . .

I asked of General Barksdale the privilege of taking a squad and following the Federals down the mountain side to see that they were well corraled into the ferry, which we did till we came to an open spot of cleared land where there was a spring and could see that they were "all in." But about this time their battery spied us over there and began dropping shells uncomfortably close to us. There was then a scattering out in my force, and we made it back to safety.

I then climbed a tall pine overhanging the river, threading the cañon away down below, and viewed the twelve thousand men stacking their arms, a most magnificent sight from a view commanding, it seemed to me, all of what is now West Virginia. Jefferson long ago went on record as saying that it was worth a visit from the Old World across the waters, to enjoy this scene from Maryland Heights.

One of Barksdale's men who helped oust the Yankees from Maryland Heights, Sergeant John C. Lowe of the 13th Mississippi (above), lost his left arm at Antietam a few days later and was captured. Exchanged shortly afterward, he was discharged in April 1863 and returned home to Lauderdale, Mississippi.

CAPTAIN EDWARD H. RIPLEY
9TH VERMONT INFANTRY

A member of the Harpers Ferry garrison, Ripley, along with the rest of the hapless Federals in the town, probably shared the same sentiment as their nemesis, Stonewall Jackson, who once remarked that he would rather "take the place 40 times than undertake to defend it once." In May 1863, four months after his exchange, Ripley became colonel of the regiment.

No sooner had dawn broken on Sunday morning than our last hope fled as we saw the rebels had, during the night, been working on Loudon Heights and were now plainly visible in two places on the crest, from which it seemed almost possible to hurl hand grenades down upon us. Quickly our guns on Camp and Cemetery Hills opened an ineffectual fire on them, but they could not reach them, and the batteries seemed to hope to frighten the enemy off with a big noise. The wicked waste of ammunition went on for hours unchecked. Major Stowell and I lay and watched them with our glasses, uneasily, but could as yet detect no guns. Wearisomely our shells lifted themselves in their futile flight up the side of the mountain, seeming always to fall short and provoke no attention. At about one o'clock we were again watching the Rebel working parties, when suddenly we saw one, two, three, half a dozen puffs of smoke burst out in their centre. We jumped to our feet, and shouted, "Our guns have at last got the range and will drive them out."

As suddenly, in the centre of White's brigade, lying at our feet, there was a crash, then another, and another, and columns of dirt and smoke leaped up as though a dozen vigorous volcanoes had broken forth. Stowell caught the situation quicker than I, and exclaimed, "Good God! It's their guns!" In an instant the bivouac of White's brigade took on the appearance of an overturned beehive. Artillery, infantry, and cavalry were mixed in an absurd mêlée, at which one could not help laughing as the panic increased. We settled ourselves down again and watched. The Rebel batteries were forced into furious play, and as the fugitives came streaming toward us, the shells pursued them with fiendish accuracy. All at once one dropped in my company's street, which changed my point of view, and let all the humor out of it. It was time to be taking care of ourselves. In a cool and quiet way the companies fell in, and marched deliberately up over the crest of the hill and lay down, where the shells skipped over our heads into the valley beyond. Here we felt comfortable, but only for a moment, and for the last time in Harper's Ferry. We lay thus peering over at Loudon with occasional anxious scannings of the front at our left, where we could see the Rebel lines moving in and out of the fringe of wood and new batteries getting into position. To our dismay straight behind us, we heard a new uproar. Across the valley, not eight hundred yards away, where the Shepherdstown Pike skirted the woods, was an appalling long bank of smoke. In an instant the air seemed alive with bursting shell. Our old Belgians were not good for such a range. We were between two fires where there was not shelter for a rabbit. . . .

For a space of time that seemed interminable we did the best we could by moving over from one slope to another, out of the frying-pan into the fire. Whichever slope we were on, we wished it were the other one.

Fate had not been kind to Colonel Dixon S. Miles (left) since the outbreak of war. Drugged from medication for dysentery at First Manassas, he had been accused of drunkenness and had been made one of the scapegoats for the Federal defeat. Thus, despite long service in the Regular Army, his next assignment was command at Harpers Ferry—uneventful duty until the Rebels showed up. The shell that mortally wounded him shortly after he chose to surrender probably spared him a court-martial.

PRIVATE JOHN H. WORSHAM
21st Virginia Infantry, Johnson's Brigade

The Yankee capitulation at Harpers Ferry yielded an incredible bounty: The Confederates gained not only prisoners and weapons but also a treasure-trove of provisions, as well as luxuries, that left many a hard-bitten Rebel wide-eyed with wonder. Afraid that looting might break down discipline among his troops, Stonewall Jackson quickly issued orders to prevent it. But this stricture failed to stop some, like Private Worsham, from at least giving it a try.

Some of the headquarters folks had offered to feed a horse for me if I would get one. My opportunity had come. Making my way to the fortifications, I clambered over them and saw that the Yankees had stacked their arms and were parking their artillery and wagons. I was surrounded at once and plied with all kinds of questions as to what Jackson would do with them. Since I did not know anything about the terms of surrender, I could tell them nothing. I took a Colt army pistol from one of them and, buckling it around my waist, went on my way looking for a horse. . . .

I approached a line of tents that looked as if they were abandoned. Going among these I was delighted by the sight of as fine a horse with equipment as I had ever seen. He was tied to a stake near a tent, and my heart fairly leaped to my throat as I went to him, untied and mounted him! As I started off, a Yankee colonel came from a tent, addressed me very politely, and inquired what I intended to do with his horse. I replied that I was very much obliged to him and would take good care of him for Harper's Ferry's sake. He asked me to stop, which I did. He came forward and told me that probably I did not know the terms of the surrender: General Jackson had allowed the officers to retain their arms, horses, equipment, and private baggage, and he added that he had no fear of my taking his horse after learning the terms. I sadly turned the horse's head toward the stake, rode him to it, and fastened him. The colonel invited me into his tent to take lunch, as he called it; yet it was a big dinner for an old Confederate. He also placed on the table several bottles, from which I might help myself. I disliked the losing of the horse but could not take him after the terms were made known to me. Indeed, the behavior of the officer so impressed me that it would have saved the horse if the terms had not been known!

LIEUTENANT WILLIAM M. LUFF

12TH ILLINOIS CAVALRY

Among those Federals bottled up in Harpers Ferry were 1,500 cavalrymen who had no intention of falling into Rebel hands. With the reluctant blessing of Colonel Miles, they slipped across the Potomac pontoon bridge into Maryland on the night of September 14. The troopers finally made their way to safety, but not before running into a column of wagons strung out along the road from Hagerstown carrying Longstreet's reserve ammunition supply.

One of the units that broke out from Harpers Ferry, the 8th New York Cavalry, carried this flag during their harrowing ride north to Pennsylvania, and safety.

As the advance of the column approached the pike, the rumbling of wheels in the distance toward Hagerstown was heard. The sound indicated the approach of artillery or wagons. It was an anxious moment; but Colonel Davis (Eighth New York) and Lieutenant-Colonel Davis (Twelfth Illinois), who were at the head of the column, were equal to the occasion. They promptly decided to surprise the enemy and capture the guns or wagons, whichever they should prove to be.

. . . All was done in silence, and it was still too dark for our troops, concealed in the timber which skirted the road, to be seen.

The approaching column proved to be a train of army wagons (ninety-seven in number), loaded principally with ammunition and escorted by infantry,—four or five men accompanying each wagon, with a detachment of cavalry in the rear.

When the head of the train came up it was halted, and the guard ordered to surrender, which it did without a shot being fired on either side.

Captain William Frisbie (Eighth New York Cavalry) was then ordered to take the train, turn it on the Greencastle pike, and run it through to that place at the rate of eight miles an hour. . . .

While Captain Frisbie was holding the train and disarming the prisoners, the Rebel officer in charge of the escort came up and demanded of the teamster, in no gentle tones, by what authority he stopped the train. The teamster pointed to his captor, with the remark, "The woods are full of Yanks!" The Rebel officer had the temerity to turn upon the Captain and roughly demand *his* authority. The Captain replied, "By the authority of an officer of the United States Army!" The Rebel put his hand on his revolver; but seeing the force by which he was surrounded, was convinced that resistance was hopeless, and in his turn surrendered, and joined his comrades in the corner of the fence. The train was immediately started forward, the foremost wagons being turned to the right, driven a short distance over a dirt road to the Green-

castle turnpike, and then driven northward on that road at a rapid rate.

As each wagon successively reached the point where Colonel Davis was posted, it shared the fate of its predecessors. Its escort was noiselessly captured, and, with scarcely another halt or check of the column, the whole train was transferred to the Greencastle road and travelling northward faster than a wagon train ever moved before.

The capture was effected so quietly that after the foremost wagons had been taken and turned toward Greencastle the escorts of the remainder were in complete ignorance of what had taken place until they reached the point where the change of direction was made, and they too passed into the service of the United States Army. A change of governments was probably never more quietly or speedily effected. . . .

As the sun rose, bright and warm, the scene upon the pike was very enlivening. The long train of heavily loaded wagons rumbling over the hard smooth road as rapidly as they could be urged forward, enveloped by throngs of cavalry-men with a solid column in their rear, the clouds of dust, the cracking of whips, the cries of the drivers, and the shouts of officers and men, formed a striking contrast to the long march in the silence and darkness of the previous night.

"They were silent as ghosts; ruthless and rushing in their speed; ragged, earth-colored, dishevelled, and devilish, as though they were keen on the scent of the hot blood."

The youngest officer on Stonewall Jackson's staff, 23-year-old Lieutenant Henry Kyd Douglas (above) was a native of nearby Shepherdstown whose familiarity with the area proved immensely valuable to his commander. During the march from Harpers Ferry to Sharpsburg, Douglas scribbled this short note to his father.

CAPTAIN EDWARD H. RIPLEY
9TH VERMONT INFANTRY

A scant two months after their mustering in and with scarcely a shot fired in action, Captain Ripley and the rest of his regiment surrendered at Harpers Ferry. The men were paroled the next day and sent to Annapolis, Maryland, minus their guns. Before leaving, however, they were obliged to stand aside as their captors pushed past them toward Sharpsburg. Months later, waiting to be exchanged in Chicago, the Vermonters were put to work guarding Rebel prisoners.

That night I lay beside the Charlestown Pike and watched until morning the grimy columns come pouring down from the pontoons. It was a weird, uncanny sight, and drove sleep from my eyes. It was something demon-like, a scene from an Inferno. They were silent as ghosts; ruthless and rushing in their speed; ragged, earth-colored, dishevelled, and devilish, as though they were keen on the scent of the hot blood, that was already steaming up from the opening struggle at Antietam, and thirsting for it; their sliding dog-trot was as though on snow-shoes. The shuffle of their badly shod feet on the hard surface of the Pike was so rapid as to be continuous like the hiss of a great serpent, broken only by the roar of the batteries, as they came rushing by on the trot, or the jingling of the sabres of the cavalry. The spectral, ghostly picture will never be effaced from my memory.

With the two armies massing around their town, residents of Sharpsburg flee westward toward the Potomac River, where bluffs along its banks offer protection from the shells that will soon fill the air. Some residents left for distant towns within the first week or so of the Confederate invasion, but by Sunday, September 14, when the first Rebel cavalry showed up, the roads out of town were fast filling up with troops, making flight from the area a much more difficult proposition. The remaining townspeople found what shelter they could. Some escaped to the river, while others sought refuge in the nearest stone cellar.

MAJOR HEROS VON BORCKE
STAFF, MAJOR GENERAL J. E. B. STUART

As Sharpsburg and the surrounding fields and woods filled up with Rebels on the 16th, the area soon became an irresistible target for Federal gunners across Antietam Creek. Major von Borcke, a Prussian volunteer, was in town that day acting as Stuart's liaison to General Lee, who had set up his headquarters just west of Sharpsburg. By the early evening a full-scale artillery duel was raging.

Sharpsburg is a pretty little village of perhaps two thousand inhabitants. It presented, during these memorable September days, a busy scene of military life. Waggon-trains blockaded its streets, artillery rattled over its pavements, orderlies were riding up and down at full speed. The house of Dr G., one of the largest in the place, was situated just opposite the principal church, and was still occupied by his hospitable family, who awaited with an indifference peculiarly American the momentous events that were so close upon them. About 11 A.M. the enemy began to throw shells into the town, which, being aimed at the church steeple, fell all around their dwelling in such perilous proximity that I felt it my duty to order the ladies into the cellar, as the safest place of refuge. This order they obeyed, but, impelled by feminine curiosity, they were running up-stairs every five minutes to witness the effect of the cannonade. I had frequent occasion during the war to observe how much stronger is curiosity with women than the fear of danger. Accordingly, while the fire was every moment growing hotter, it was not long before the whole of Dr G.'s family were again assembled in the room I occupied. All at once, while they were looking out of the windows at some wounded men carried by, a shell fell with a

The first Federal officer to die at Antietam was Colonel Hugh W. McNeil (above) commander of the 13th Pennsylvania Reserves, nicknamed the Bucktails for their distinctive cap ornament. McNeil was shot down at dusk on September 16 during a firefight between Seymour's brigade and Rebel skirmishers in the East Woods.

terrific crash through the top of the building, and sent them in precipitate flight to the security of the vaults. About noon the bombardment became really appalling, and the explosion of the innumerable projectiles stunned the ear. Still deeming it obligatory on me to remain at my post, I was seated on the sofa engaged in writing in my journal, when a shell, piercing the wall of the room a few feet above my head, covered me with the debris, and, exploding, scattered the furniture in every direction. At the same moment another missile, entering the upper part of the house, and passing directly through, burst in the courtyard, killing one of our horses, and rendering the others frantic with terror. Regarding further exposure of my own life and the lives of my couriers as now unnecessary, I gave orders for our immediate departure; but it was not easy, amid the blinding dust and smoke out of doors, to find my horse, nor, after I had found him, to get into the saddle, so furiously did

he rear and plunge, as if fully conscious of the danger of his situation.

In the street there was the greatest confusion. Dead and wounded, men and horses lay about in every direction, in the midst of waggons and ambulances overturned in the hurry and anxiety of everybody to get out of the village, where cannonballs whizzed incessantly through the air, and pieces of bursting shells, splinters of wood, and scattered fragments of brick were whirled about in the dense cloud of powder-smoke that enveloped all things.

The Bloodiest Day

The Army of the Potomac began its massive onslaught against Lee's outnumbered forces at dawn on September 17. McClellan intended to launch a series of blows, beginning on the north and extending southward along the front of the Confederate line. As fog hugged the valley of Antietam Creek, the three divisions of Joseph Hooker's I Corps—which had crossed to the west bank of the stream the day before—swept south against the Confederate left, where Stonewall Jackson's men waited near the little church of a pacifist sect called the Dunkers. Behind Hooker, Joseph Mansfield's XII Corps crossed the stream and prepared to advance in the second wave.

As hundreds of shells from the opposing batteries shrieked and roared overhead, Hooker's troops encountered stiff resistance from Jackson's line. George Meade's and

Federal soldiers pose on the hotly contested Burnside Bridge in this postbattle photograph taken from the wooded bluff on the west bank of Antietam Creek. From this position, General Toombs' Georgians held the bridge for hours, picking off Federals emerging from the tree line beyond the field on the far bank.

James Ricketts' divisions emerged from the cover of the woods that ringed farmer David Miller's Cornfield, only to be savaged by the volleys of Alexander Lawton's Confederate division, which anchored Jackson's right.

At 7:00 a.m., an hour and a half into the fight, the wavering Rebel line at the Cornfield's southern edge was shored up by Harry T. Hays' Louisiana brigade, nicknamed the Tigers, who were in turn brought to a standstill near the East Woods by the last reserves of Ricketts' Federal division. In 15 minutes of combat the Louisianans lost 323 of 500 men; Yankee losses were equally horrific. North and west of the Cornfield, Abner Doubleday's division was gaining ground against Jackson's left, where the fence-lined Hagerstown pike led past the Cornfield's western edge. With the hard-fighting midwesterners of John Gibbon's Iron Brigade in the vanguard, the Yankees cleared the ravaged Cornfield and pushed into the open field beyond, headed for the center of Jackson's line at the Dunker Church.

At the moment that Gibbon's spearhead began to falter, the Federals were hit on the right by a daring counterattack from William E. Starke, who had assumed command of two brigades when division commander John R.

Jones was wounded. Emerging from the cover of the West Woods, Starke was shot dead in the forefront of the charge. But his soldiers gained the rail fence along the Hagerstown pike and poured round after round into the Yankee formations. The Federals stood their ground. The Rebels recoiled into the West Woods and again Hooker's corps rolled forward, toward the Dunker Church.

With the Confederate left threatening to collapse, Jackson committed his last reserves —John Bell Hood's division. Battling with characteristic ferocity, Hood's men, including the Texas Brigade, shoved the Federals back across the Cornfield. The Rebels' success cost them dearly, however, with the 1st Texas sustaining the highest casualty rate—more than 82 percent—of any unit of the entire war. Hood had brought Hooker's offensive to a halt, but he was unable to do more. Now Mansfield's 7,200-man XII Corps moved through the East Woods to the battlefield, and the Southerners had to rally to confront this new threat.

Though a veteran with decades of service, Mansfield had never led troops in battle, and most of his men were raw recruits. Consequently, the regiments of the XII Corps failed to form a proper line of battle and advanced in a chaotic jumble. The unwieldy column was caught in a cross fire between Jackson's troops and several brigades of D. H. Hill's division. Mansfield was mortally wounded, and the leading elements of his corps were brought to a standstill at the Cornfield's eastern edge. Lashing out from amid the chaos, George S. Greene led XII Corps brigades in a charge that routed two of Hill's brigades. He drove westward almost to the Dunker Church before the Confederates rallied and repulsed the charge.

By 9:00 a.m. the Federal assaults had ground to a halt. Hooker was wounded, Mansfield dying, and thousands of men had fallen without any appreciable gain. Watching from his headquarters at the Philip Pry house on the eastern bluff of Antietam Creek, McClellan was now relying on Edwin V. Sumner's II Corps to break the impasse. With McClellan holding back one division as a reserve, Sumner had led two divisions across the stream in preparation for an assault on the now-depleted center of the Confederate line. But rather than coordinate the movements of his subordinates, Sumner impetuously joined John Sedgwick's division in a charge on the West Woods. The rest of his force veered off to the left toward a sunken farm lane that was being defended by elements of Longstreet's corps.

Pushing past the Dunker Church and into the West Woods, Sumner and Sedgwick at first met light resistance from the Rebel batteries atop a ridge called Nicodemus Hill. Fixated on the guns, Sumner was unaware of the crisis looming on his left until it was too late. Seizing the opportunity to flank the advancing Yankees, Jubal A. Early (who had taken over for the wounded Lawton) and Lafayette McLaws hurled their divisions on the naked left of Sedgwick's division. Unable to deploy their three brigades into an effective front, the Yankees were sent reeling from the West Woods with heavy losses.

While Sedgwick's division was meeting with disaster, French launched the first of three successive assaults on the Confederate center, where the Sunken Road provided a natural trench for the Rebel defenders. Wave after wave of Union troops charged forward, only to be mowed down by their hidden enemy. Hill's and Longstreet's men mounted

several counterattacks but were unable to drive back French's soldiers. It was noon before Sumner's remaining division, led by Israel B. Richardson, arrived and swept the Rebels from the Sunken Road, now a corpse-strewn "bloody lane." Though stretched to the breaking point, Lee's center managed to hold along the Hagerstown pike.

Shaken by the carnage and loath to renew the assault in the northern portion of the field, McClellan yet hoped that his left wing, the IX Corps, now under Ambrose E. Burnside, would fulfill his directive to cross Antietam Creek and strike Lee's understrength southern flank. But throughout the morning Burnside had been stymied in his efforts to charge across the southernmost of the three bridges spanning the creek. Despite his vast superiority in numbers, Burnside did not get his troops across the bridge until nearly 1:00 p.m. Once they gained the west bank, however, his divisions rolled forward, fighting their way up the bluffs to the outskirts of Sharpsburg. Once again, disaster loomed for Lee's army. But the Federals were stymied. Burnside's delays had given A. P. Hill time to march his division north from Harpers Ferry, where it had been occupied in paroling captured Yankees. Covering 17 miles in eight hours of forced marching, Hill arrived in the nick of time. By 4:00 p.m. his troops had succeeded in halting Burnside's advance.

Lee's embattled line had held, though at great cost. McClellan, unwilling to risk his last reserves in another attack, was content to maintain his bridgehead on the west bank of Antietam Creek. By late afternoon the fighting was all but over, as both armies, bloodied and dazed by the terrible slaughter, prepared for what many thought would be a resumption of the battle on the morning of September 18.

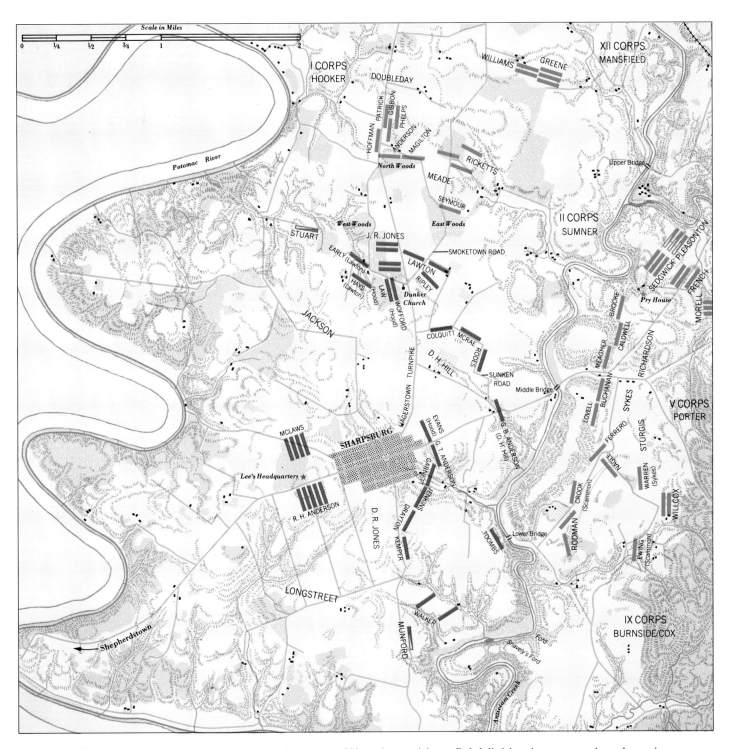

By dawn on September 17, Lee's army was arrayed north and east of Sharpsburg, with two Rebel divisions in reserve and another on its way from Harpers Ferry. Two Federal corps, the I and XII, had crossed over Antietam Creek the night before and had taken position to open the battle.

ANONYMOUS
RESIDENT OF SHARPSBURG

The artillery exchanges that began on September 16 resumed at first light on the morning of the 17th. The unnamed author of this account, a black serving woman at a tavern in Sharpsburg, remained in town during the battle despite the rain of Federal shells that overshot the Confederate lines and landed amid the streets and houses throughout the day.

General Lee come to the house early the next morning. He was a fine-lookin' man, and he was the head general of 'em all in the Rebel army, you know. Our old boss was a Democrat, too; so he gave the general his breakfast. But while the officers was eatin' there in the dining-room a shell come right thoo the wall and busted and scattered brick and daubin' all over everything. There was so much dirt you could n't tell what was on the table. I was bringin' in coffee from the kitchen and had a cup and saucer in my hand. I don't know where I put that coffee, but I throwed it away, and we all got out of there in a hurry.

I went out to the gate. An old colored man was comin' down the pavement with an iron pot on his head. He said the Yankees had got the Rebels on the run, and there'd be fightin' right in the town streets. He was goin' to get away, and he was carryin' that pot so he'd have somethin' to cook in.

Pretty soon I was back workin' in the kitchen, but the soldiers told me I'd better get out, and then all of us in the house went into the cellar. We carried boards down there and spread carpets on 'em and took chairs down to set on. There was seven or eight of us, white and black, and we was all so scared we did n't know what we was doin' half the time. They kept us in the cellar all day while they was fightin' backwards and forwards. My goodness alive! there was cannon and everything shootin'. Lord 'a' mercy, man! we could hear 'em plain enough. The cannon sounded jest like thunder, and the small-arms the same as pop-guns. Sometimes we'd run up and look out of a window to see what was happening, but we did n't do that often—not the way them guns was firin'.

CAPTAIN WILLIAM W. BLACKFORD
STAFF, MAJOR GENERAL J. E. B. STUART

The engineer officer on Stuart's staff, Captain Blackford spent most of the day on the far left of the Confederate line along with two-thirds of the Rebel cavalry. Although Stuart's three cavalry brigades saw little action, his horse artillery under Major John Pelham wrought havoc on the Federals all through the battle from its positions atop Nicodemus Hill and Hauser's Ridge.

Between our cavalry lines and the enemy stood a handsome country house in which, it seems, all the women and children in the neighborhood had assembled for mutual protection, not thinking that part of the country would be the scene of conflict. Between us and the house was a roughly ploughed field. When the cannonade began, the house happened to be right in the line between Pelham's battery and that of the enemy occupying the opposite hills, the batteries firing clear over the top of the house at each other. When the crossing shells began screaming over the house, its occupants thought their time had come, and like a flock of birds they came streaming out in "Mother Hubbards," and even less, hair streaming in the wind and children of all ages stretched out behind, and tumbling at every step over the clods of the ploughed field. Every time one would fall, the rest thought it was the result of a cannon shot and ran the

Major John Pelham (left), commander of the three batteries of General Stuart's horse artillery, directed the cannon fire that took a heavy toll in the Union ranks on the northern end of the battlefield. Though the "boy major" was barely 24 when he fought at Antietam, he had already distinguished himself for his uncanny ability to place his guns where they could be used to maximum effect, often without bothering to wait for orders.

faster. It was impossible to keep from laughing at this sudden eruption and impossible to persuade them to return. I galloped out to meet them and represented to them that they were safe, probably, where they had been, but it was no use; so swinging up before and behind as many children as my horse could carry, I escorted them to our lines and quieted the fears of the party, assuring them that they were not in danger of immediate death. Seeing what was going on, the batteries on each side ceased firing until the little party was disposed of.

Photographed just a few days after the battle, Sharpsburg's now-quiet Main Street was used by Confederate troops moving up to the front from the Potomac River fords.

"Every one dropped whatever he had in his hands, and looked around the group to see whose head was missing."

PRIVATE WILLIAM F. GOODHUE
3D WISCONSIN INFANTRY, GORDON'S BRIGADE

Just over a month after taking heavy losses at the Battle of Cedar Mountain, Gordon's brigade was ready to go into action again. Late on September 16 the brigade, along with the rest of the XII Corps, forded Antietam Creek and took up position behind the I Corps, where they bedded down to await the dawn.

It was in the grey of early morning when the Sergeant Major, walking rapidly along the line of sleeping men, awakened us with a gruff voice to roll call. I arose from my greensward bed with a feeling of numbness in my left side, caused by the pressure of my cartridge box against it all night, for we had slept accoutred for the battle which we were certain would occur with the daylight. Even as the roll was being called the musket fire of the picket lines commenced quite briskly, and mounted orderlies came galloping along the lines seeking the regimental commanders for whom they had orders. Behind us we could hear the continuous whinney of artillery horses and the braying of mules hauling the ammunition wagons, all expecting their morning feed, which a very few received. Looking along the line I saw the men wiping the moisture from their muskets, for the dew had been heavy, and just now there was considerable fog. Others were changing their gun caps or adjusting a knapsack, putting canteen and haversack well behind, to give free access to the cartridge box. Others were munching hardtack, and some were smoking. Several of my comrades, with canteens, had gone for water, with the evident intention of making coffee, while others had made little fires for cooking breakfast, taking rails from an adjacent fence for the purpose; when suddenly and sternly came the order to get back into the ranks.

. . . The premonitions of battle were growing stronger, and the expected breakfast was soon forgotten. The symptoms of an impending battle had been apparent for more than 24 hours, and we knew that the culmination of another great tragedy was at hand. How pallid were the faces of all, with unkempt hair, thus giving them the appearance almost, of wildmen. They did not have the rosy hues of days in the past when arising from the clean and restful bed under the home roof, yet these men standing in battle-line were scarcely old enough to be men and voters at home. They had grimy, sallow features and muscular bodies, lean and gaunt as hounds . . . for this was their third campaign since the spring flowers had bloomed.

CAPTAIN J. ALBERT MONROE
BATTERY D, 1ST RHODE ISLAND LIGHT ARTILLERY, DOUBLEDAY'S DIVISION

The Rebels were first to go into action on the morning of the 17th, unleashing their artillery as soon as they could make out targets in the early-morning fog. Monroe, who held temporary command of all four batteries in Doubleday's division, had his hands full providing close support for the attacking infantry.

We were awakened before daylight by the cook, who had brought up a pail of steaming coffee, some johnny-cakes and "fixins," together with cups, plates and other table ware. A blanket was spread on the ground for a table-cloth, on which was placed the breakfast, and the officers gathered around it on their haunches. It was the early gray light that appeared just before the sun rises above the horizon, and we could little more than distinguish each other. We had not half finished our meal, but it had grown considerably lighter, and we could see the first rays of the sun lighting up the distant hilltops, when there was a sudden flash, and the air around us appeared to be alive with shot and shell from the enemy's artillery. The opposite hill seemed suddenly to have become an active volcano, belching forth flame, smoke and scoriae.

The first shot apparently passed directly through our little breakfast party, not more than a foot or two above the blanket, and it struck the ground only a few feet from us. Every one dropped whatever he had in his hands, and looked around the group to see whose head was missing. So suddenly did the firing commence and so rapidly did shot follow shot, I felt lost for an instant.—I never knew how the others felt,—but I at once ordered Hugh Rider, my groom, to give me my mare, who was hitched only about ten feet distant, and by the time he got her to me I had fully recovered from my surprise.

FRANK H. SCHELL

SPECIAL ARTIST, FRANK LESLIE'S ILLUSTRATED NEWSPAPER

Schell contributed some 200 drawings to Leslie's Illustrated over the course of the war. But his written accounts were also highly valued. This one describes the opening attack by the Federal I Corps. Schell's vantage point was the Pry house (below) on the east side of Antietam Creek, where McClellan had his headquarters. Major General Fitz-John Porter commanded the V Corps, most of which stood idle on the east side of the Antietam for the entire day.

I saw near McClellan's headquarters at Pry's farm, on a bare hill beyond it, a group of dismounted officers. I climbed to the hilltop, and the group resolved itself into Generals McClellan, Fitz-John Porter, and other officers to me unknown. Aids and couriers were coming and going with fidgety hurry, bringing reports and taking orders. There were moments of impressive silence as, with suppressed mental excitement, all eyes were fired in one direction—toward the distant point to the right.

The positions of the Confederate artillery as a whole, and even some of the guns, could be distinctly seen; but, as yet, the whereabouts of the infantry could only be inferred from the dull gray mantles of smoke spreading along the ground, or rising in thin strata from the recesses of the east wood.

I joined the group about the commanding general, who was anxiously scanning through his field glass the situation to the right, across the Antietam. Looking more to the left, the thick west wood, with its dark, broad front so clearly emphasized by the little white Dunker church, was clearly in view along its entire extent upon the Hagerstown turnpike.

General McClellan suddenly lowered his glass, and, with a few animated words and expressive gestures, called Porter's attention to something that caused an immediate ferment of buzzing excitement throughout the group and a close scrutinizing of the bit of woodland,

for the time being, the focus of such absorbing interest.

I leveled my glass in the general direction and saw innumerable glints of light reflected from a long line of gun-barrels at the edge of the wood, which quickly passed to a great field of tall corn above the top of which the coruscating line began to advance, and a corresponding, though more ragged line, to recede from near its opposite end.

Soon, out rushed a broken Confederate force from the corn-field across the open ground toward the Dunker church wood, into which, after some halting and sporadic firing in vain resistance, it finally disappeared from view.

But onward through the ripened corn the Yankee line pushed its way; its position and direction beautifully indicated by the National and regimental colors gaily waving above the corn-stalks, and by the sparkling flashes from gun-barrels and bayonets.

We saw that there was trouble in preserving the alignment amid the obstructions, for there were short halts and a perceptible loss of momentum as the line neared the outer limit of the corn-field.

Who, that stood upon the hilltop there, could ever forget the soul-racking suspense, the burning anxiety, the heart thumps of those history-making moments, all watching closely the advancing wall of battle and wondering what would be the outcome of that early dash upon the hidden enemy's stronghold in the gloom of the west wood?

On the morning of the 17th, McClellan and his staff moved into the Pry house (right) after the owner, Philip Pry, and his wife and four sons were removed to nearby Keedysville. When Pry returned four days later he found his once-prosperous 125-acre farm in ruins. Union soldiers had cleaned out most of the crops and livestock, losses from which the family never fully recovered.

Federal I Corps Attack: East Woods and Cornfield

While Lee was completing his deployments on the afternoon of September 16—placing Jackson on the Confederate left, north of Sharpsburg, and Longstreet in the center—McClellan moved at last. The Federal commander ordered Hooker's I Corps to cross Antietam Creek still farther to the north; he then sent Mansfield's XII Corps across the creek's upper bridge to support Hooker. The Federal attack, with Hooker leading, would hit Jackson's flank at dawn the next morning.

Precisely as ordered, Hooker sent his corps forward at 6:00 a.m. Abner Doubleday's division marched south through the morning mist on the Federal right, with Ricketts' division on the left and Meade's troops in the center. Almost immediately, however, as Doubleday's columns emerged from a stand of trees later dubbed the North Woods, more than a dozen Rebel guns under Major John Pelham atop Nicodemus Hill opened a furious and deadly fire on the advancing Federals. These guns were joined by Stephen D. Lee's four batteries positioned in front of the Dunker Church. Hooker's guns blasted back, his massed batteries firing from a ridge behind the North Woods and four batteries of big 20-pounders shooting from across Antietam Creek. "Each discharge was at first discernable," a Union colonel later recalled, "but after a little grew so rapid from all the guns brought into play from both sides that it became one prolonged roar."

Under this cannonade, the Federals continued forward. Truman Seymour's brigade of Meade's division on the Union left drove to the southern edge of the East Woods, where it ran into the far right of the Confed-

erate line held by Trimble's brigade, led that day by Colonel James A. Walker. After a deadly exchange of fire, the Federals were forced to take cover back in the woods.

At almost the same moment, Ricketts' lead brigade under Abram Duryée pushed forward to the northern edge of the soon-to-be-infamous Cornfield. After two Federal batteries brought up in support sent a few rounds of canister into the Cornfield, Duryée's men advanced into the head-high corn. They emerged from the south side of the field only to be raked by volleys from a brigade of Georgians commanded by Marcellus Douglass.

The fight continued as the two brigades, less than 200 yards apart, hammered each other; then the skirmish intensified as Seymour's troops rushed to aid Duryée's men and Walker's already bloodied brigade moved west to reinforce the Georgians. "They stood and shot each other," said New York soldier Isaac Hall, "till the lines melted away like wax." Still more Union troops entered the cauldron, William Hartsuff's brigade arriving to back up Duryée and Seymour.

At 6:45 a.m. Walker's Confederate brigade pulled back, having lost 228 of its nearly 700 men. But Douglass' troops held on—and were reinforced at the last minute by the Louisiana Tigers. The Tigers charged straight ahead, driving the Federals back across the Cornfield with what one Union officer later called "the most deadly fire of the war." Then it was the Tigers' turn as the Federals rolled a battery right into the Cornfield and pounded the Louisianans at point-blank range. As the Tigers staggered back, the last of Ricketts' brigades, under William Christian, came up

and charged into the body-strewn field. By 7:00 a.m. the bloodletting had finally forced a stalemate. Both Ricketts' Federal and Lawton's Rebel divisions had been reduced to human wreckage, and neither would see more action that day.

While the slaughter in the East Woods and the Cornfield was going on, Doubleday's division on the Federal right was fighting its way down both sides of the Hagerstown Turnpike. Gibbon's brigade, despite heavy flanking fire from John R. Jones' Confederates, gained a foothold in the West Woods and then advanced farther down the pike, forcing back two Virginia brigades led by Colonel Andrew Grigsby. Quickly, however, another threat appeared as the two remaining brigades from Jones' division, led by General William Starke, rushed from the woods and took cover behind a rail fence bordering the west side of the pike. From there they emptied a murderous fire into the Federal vanguard only 30 yards away. The Federals swiftly wheeled to meet the threat; and shortly two regiments of Gibbon's Iron Brigade were firing on the flank and rear of the Rebel troops, killing Starke and making a grim scene of grotesquely tangled corpses along the rail fence.

With the Confederates now falling back on both sides of the turnpike, Gibbon's men, followed by the brigades of Marsena Patrick and Walter Phelps, surged toward the small white building called the Dunker Church. At this desperate moment, Jackson's main reserve, John Bell Hood's division, stormed past the church and then fanned out. William Wofford's Texas brigade rushed toward the

southern edge of the Cornfield, and Evander
Law's headed for the East Woods. At the
same time D. H. Hill's division marched at a
double-quick past the Roulette and Mumma
farms to support Hood's counterattack. The
Federals, reeling backward, were saved by
one of Meade's brigades.

Posted behind a fence at the northern
edge of the Cornfield, Meade's men loosed
point-blank volleys at Wofford's oncoming
troops. The Rebels were also greeted by a
hail of canister from guns Gibbon had brought
into play, and they were taken in the flank
by Federal infantry along the pike. By 7:30
Hood's assault had come to a halt, some of
his regiments all but annihilated. Back in
the cover of the West Woods, a fellow officer asked Hood, "Where is your division?"
"Dead on the field," Hood replied.

After an opening artillery exchange at dawn, Hooker
drove his corps south through the East Woods, across
the Miller farm, and along the Hagerstown Turn-
pike. A horrific seesaw fight ensued, as Stonewall
Jackson countered each Federal thrust with fresh
brigades. By 7:30 a.m. both commands were bloody
wrecks, with little gain to show for their losses.

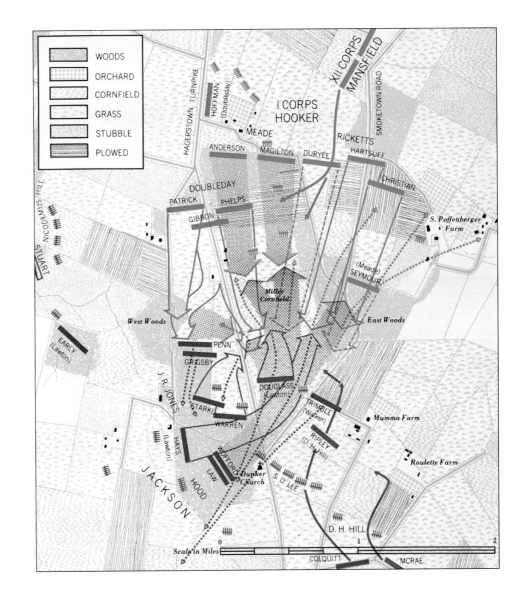

PRIVATE ISAAC G. BRADWELL
31ST GEORGIA INFANTRY, DOUGLASS' BRIGADE

After the battle opened with the firefight in the East Woods, Hooker ordered in the brigade of General Abram Duryée. Waiting for the Federals along the southern edge of the Miller farm Cornfield were Georgians under the command of Colonel Marcellus Douglass. Although Private Bradwell himself was on medical leave during the battle, his comrades in the 31st Georgia related to him the details of the bloody exchange that followed.

Then a grand sight met their eyes. The number of regimental standards floating in the morning air indicated the immense numbers of the advancing enemy. It was a wonderful sight. The remnant of our regiment formed in an apple orchard on the right of the brigade to assist in holding back the hosts of the enemy. Colonel Douglass, fearing the result of an attack by so large a force on his weak brigade, ran from regiment to regiment exhorting the men not to fire until the enemy reached the fence and began to get over it—to shoot low and make every bullet count.

On they came, crashing down the rank growth of corn, while Hardaway's Battery in rear of our line on a little hill mowed them down with grape and canister, and Stuart's light battery enfiladed their ranks. Wide gaps were torn in the blue lines, but they continued to come on until they reached the fence and began to get over in great disorder. This was the signal for the Confederates to open. The volley made them stagger and hesitate, but the second line came up, and, despite the fire of the Confederates, they came over and advanced slowly, step by step, and finally halted only a few feet in front of the Confederates, where they kept up the fight for a short while and began gradually to fall back to the fence. When they reached this, they broke in a disorderly mass toward the woods, while the Confederates helped them on by cheering and yelling. . . .

. . . When the fugitives reached the woods they were met by fresh troops, and their ranks were reformed and beaten into shape for a new effort. And then, after some delay, they came into the open field again with their "huzzas," and the Confederate batteries began their deadly work, while every man in our thin ranks lay low with his gun ready to do or die; and as the enemy approached the fence they opened on them with a fire so destructive that they broke immediately to the protection of the woods. . . .

There is only a man every ten feet or more to resist the last and greatest effort of the enemy. Heavy reenforcements have been sent into the woods. These come forward in such numbers that the few Confederates defending the position are beaten back step by step to the reserve line.

CAPTAIN JAMES COOPER NISBET
21ST GEORGIA INFANTRY, J. A. WALKER'S BRIGADE

To the right of Douglass, Colonel James A. Walker's brigade met a brigade of Pennsylvanians led by General Truman Seymour (below) on the farm of Samuel Mumma. Although it cost Walker heavily, he eventually drove Seymour back into the East Woods, but the Rebels were soon compelled to retire. Captain Nisbet describes the heavy toll taken on the Georgians.

Lieutenant Colonel Glover discovered a fence in front of the 21st Georgia with a rock underpinning, and obtained permission to advance his regiment there, which was in rifle range of the woods in front. Just at daylight the enemy advanced in heavy force and drove in our skirmishers. Their line of battle then advanced to the edge of the woods. We opened fire on them. In the course of two or

Truman Seymour, who led a brigade of Pennsylvanians at Antietam, graduated from West Point in 1846 and saw action in the Mexican War. He took part in the Peninsula campaign, Malvern Hill, Second Manassas, and—with great distinction—Turner's Gap. In 1863 he was severely wounded in the attack on Battery Wagner near Charleston, South Carolina, and subsequently transferred to duty in Florida. He retired from the army in 1876 and moved to Italy, where he died in 1891.

"Did you ever hear the wh'st-wh'st, the zip-zip of rifle balls as they passed your head? You don't hear the one that hits you."

Thomas Coke Glover was a successful physician in Campbell County, Georgia, when the war broke out. But instead of signing up for duty as a surgeon he organized his own company of volunteers, which became part of the 21st Georgia. He had been promoted to major by the time of Antietam, where he was severely wounded, and to lieutenant colonel in 1864. On September 19 of that year he was killed at Winchester, Virginia.

that our rock ledge was a dangerous point to tackle. They did not come out of the woods any more in our front. We lay behind the fence about one hour, watching the battle rage, our men firing sometimes to their right and left, but the distance was too great, we thought. Lieutenant Colonel Glover at length informed Colonel James A. Walker, commanding the brigade, that the 21st Georgia could no longer be effective in its position, as the enemy could not be reached. He received permission to change front forward on the left, swinging around into the

three hours the enemy twice brought up fresh troops against us but they melted away.

Whilst lying behind this low, loose-rock foundation I was near a red-headed, white-eyed fellow of my company. He would say each time he turned over from his back to shoot: "I got another of the 'Blue Bellies,' that time!"

I said: "Take care, Smith, they'll get you."

He had taken about twenty shots when a ball glanced through a crack in the rocks and struck him in the stomach. He fell over, calling lustily for the litter-bearers, saying: "I'm shot through the paunch."

I noticed blood in front and rear as the litter-bearers took him up. I picked up his rifle and shot the cartridges that remained in his box. That was the only time I fired a rifle at anybody during the war, except at Kennesaw Mountain. I used my Colt's navy pistol sometimes at close quarters.

Did you ever hear the wh'st-wh'st, the zip-zip of rifle balls as they passed your head? You don't hear the one that hits you.

The enemy discovered that three of their lines had melted away and

Much depleted by the summer campaign, the 12th Georgia of Walker's brigade was down to 100 men and commanded by a captain, James G. Rodgers (above). Captain Rodgers first had the fingers of his left hand shot off and then took a round in the thigh before a fatal bullet in the back of his head killed him instantly.

Smoketown road, so as to get on the flank of the fellows fighting Lawton's Brigade. . . .

Our Lieutenant Colonel Glover was shot through the body as the order for us to advance was sent down the line. I took command, being the senior officer present. I instructed the regiment to go at double quick, open order, until they got to the fence across the Smoketown road. As soon as we left the rock fence our object was divined. The enemy in the woods in our front opened on us and the left regiment, fighting Lawton's Brigade, commenced to fire at us left-oblique. A number of our men were hit.

As I threw my leg over the top rail of the last fence, a minnie ball went through the rail, the folds of my blanket and oil cloth, striking me squarely on the sword clasp. I fell into the road unconscious, lying upon elevated ground. I recovered my senses in a few minutes and the men seeing the earth around me cut by the bullets, called to me: "Crawl down here, Captain."

I crawled down to where the men were firing through the rail fence. Just as I got there Lieutenant John Wesley Blevins, a gallant soldier of my company, was shot through the shoulder and fell. I helped him up and told him where he would find our surgeons. . . .

Captain M. T. Castleberry of Company "C," started to ask me about Blevins' wound; a ball went into his mouth, and through his head. He fell against the fence, his head lying low and bent back. I pulled him around so as to elevate his head and put a cartridge box under it. As I did so, I heard our boys crying out: "They are running!" Looking over the fence I saw that the Yankee line was falling back into the woods. I sent word to Lawton's right regiment that we were going to advance in their front. I then ordered the 21st forward.

When we reached the woods the enemy was gone. We pressed forward through the woods until we were near its extremity. Mansfield's Corps could be seen advancing.

Private Albert W. Dyer (right) was the 19-year-old clerk of Company E, 13th Massachusetts Infantry. Along with the 12th Massachusetts, which fought at its side, the regiment was still licking its wounds from Second Manassas when Private Dyer and his comrades were caught up in the slaughter at Antietam.

PRIVATE GEORGE KIMBALL
12TH MASSACHUSETTS INFANTRY, HARTSUFF'S BRIGADE

One of the hardest hit Federal units during the battle was Private Kimball's regiment, which had already lost its first commander, Colonel Fletcher Webster, at Second Manassas. First thrown into confusion by the wounding of General Hartsuff, the 12th, along with the rest of the brigade, finally got moving, only to be savaged by Rebel artillery. When they emerged from the East Woods and Cornfield they ran head-on into Harry Hays' Louisiana Tigers.

We gain the crest of the little ridge. Our main line has not yet fired a shot. Being now upon open ground, high enough to afford a view of our surroundings, what a scene is that which opens up about us! Directly in front, not more than one hundred yards away, is "Stonewall" Jackson's whole division moving toward us. With their saucy battle flags gayly floating above them, these gray-clad heroes present a magnificent spectacle. To their left, in more scattered order, behind fences and rocks and trees, are Hood's men. Farther still in the same direction are Stuart's batteries, pouring a heavy cross fire upon the little knoll upon which we are standing.

The painting below depicts the 12th Massachusetts Infantry in action at Antietam, where it lost 224 out of 334 men in less than an hour. Artist Richard Holland, who served with the 9th Massachusetts Light Artillery, incorporated the state (left) and national colors, which had been carried into battle by the regiment that day.

We comprehend the situation at a glance and open and receive a storm of leaden missiles. How terrible is the shock and how our men go down! What screams and groans follow that first volley! Then we load and fire at will as rapidly as we can. Our officers cry, "Give it to them, boys!" and the men take up the cry, too. There is a pandemonium of voices as well as a perfect roar of musketry and a storm of bullets. Shells are bursting among us, too, continually. In the wild excitement of battle I forget my fear and think only of killing as many of the foe as I can. The tall soldier at my side, who had told me on the march that he felt as though he was to be hit in this battle, has already fallen. He lies at my feet with a mortal hurt. His brother drags him back a few paces and then returns to his place in the ranks. A few moments more and my brother, too, is wounded, though not so badly. When I have assisted him to a stump a short distance in the rear he creeps up behind it and

This Alexander Gardner photograph (right), taken two days after the battle, looks north from a position just south of the Smoketown road and encompasses much of the open, gently rolling Miller farm property. Barely visible as a white streak at the base of the distant North Woods lies the blood-soaked Cornfield. The guns and men arrayed in the foreground were part of Captain Joseph Knap's Pennsylvania battery, which provided artillery support during the XII Corps attack.

Private Thomas Taylor of the 5th Louisiana was wounded in the knee and permanently crippled during the duel between the Louisiana Tigers and Ricketts' brigade. Though Stonewall Jackson regarded the Louisiana brigade—made up of a hodgepodge of nationalities—as "foreigners," their prowess in battle was undeniable. The Tigers suffered more than 60 percent casualties during the fight.

tells me to "go back and give it to them."

Our ranks are terribly broken now, but the line is kept up and we fight on. Our Second Lieutenant has gone to the rear, his right shoulder being torn from its socket by a piece of shell. Lieut. White remains still. His eyes glow with the joy of battle, and he seems to be everywhere imparting courage and stimulating the efforts of his men. By-and-by he is struck again. A piece of shell has stripped the flesh from the upper part of one of his arms. The shock is severe enough to throw him to the ground, but he quickly rises again and his voice is heard as before above the din of battle. I look at his face to see if he shows evidences of pain and am met with a cheery smile. By this time our ranks

have become fearfully decimated, and the Lieutenant begins moving those who are yet in line up nearer the colors. "Let us die under the flag, boys!" he cries.

Incidents of the fight are happening every moment. My ramrod is wrenched from my grasp as I am about to return it to its socket after loading. I look for it behind me, and the Lieutenant passes me another, pointing to my own, which lies bent and unfit for use across the face of a dead man. A bullet enters my knapsack just under my left arm while I am taking aim. Another passes through my haversack, which hangs upon my left hip. Still another cuts both strings of my canteen, and that useful article joins the debris now thickly covering the ground. Having

lost all natural feeling I laugh at these mishaps as though they were hugh jokes, and remark to my nearest neighbor that I suppose I shall soon be relieved of all my trappings. A man but a few paces from me is struck squarely in the face by a solid shot. Fragments of the poor fellow's head come crashing into my face and fill me with disgust. I grumble about it as though it was something that might have been avoided. My supply of cartridges is exhausted and I seek for more among the cartridge boxes of the dead. Many others are doing the same, and nearly everybody has had experiences similar to mine. There are but few of us left now. The enemy's line, which looked so magnificent when we opened fire upon it, seems as ragged as our own.

"There was, on the part of the men, great hysterical excitement, eagerness to go forward, and a reckless disregard of life, of every thing but victory."

MAJOR RUFUS R. DAWES
6TH WISCONSIN INFANTRY, GIBBON'S BRIGADE

About the time that Hartsuff's Union brigade pushed into the Cornfield, Gibbon got his brigade moving south along both sides of the Hagerstown pike with the 6th Wisconsin in the lead. Under constant artillery fire, Major Dawes and his mates fended off three Rebel brigades before being driven back by Hood's attack.

The regiment continued moving forward into a strip of woods, where the column was deployed into line of battle. The artillery fire had now increased to the roar of an hundred cannon. Solid shot and shell whistled through the trees above us, cutting off limbs which fell about us. In front of the woods was an open field; beyond this was a house, surrounded by peach and apple trees, a garden, and outhouses. The rebel skirmishers were in this cover, and they directed upon us a vigorous fire. But company "I" deployed as skirmishers, under command of Captain John A. Kellogg, dashed across the field at a full run and drove them out, and the line of the regiment pushed on over the green open field, the air above our heads filled with the screaming missiles of the contending batteries. The right of the regiment was now on the Sharpsburg and Hagerstown Turnpike. The left wing was obstructed in its advance by the picket fence around the garden before mentioned. As the right wing passed on, I ordered the men of the left wing to take hold all together and pull down the fence. They were unable to do so. I had, therefore, to pass the left wing by the flank through a gate with the utmost haste, and form again in the garden. Here Captain Edwin A. Brown, of company "E," was instantly killed. There is in my mind as I write, the spectacle of a young officer, with uplifted sword, shouting in a loud imperative voice the order I had given him, "Company 'E,' on the right by file into line!" A bullet passes into his open mouth, and the voice is forever silent. I urged the left wing forward with all possible speed. . . . We climbed the fence, moved across the open space, and pushed on into the corn-field. The three right companies of the regiment were crowded into an open field on the right-hand side of the turnpike. Thus we pushed up the hill to the middle of the corn-field.

At this juncture, the companies of the right wing received a deadly fire from the woods on their right. To save them, Colonel Bragg, with a quickness and coolness equal to the emergency, caused them to change front and form behind the turnpike fence, from whence they returned the fire of the enemy. Meanwhile, I halted the left wing, and ordered them to lie down on the ground. The bullets began to clip through the corn, and spin through the soft furrows—thick, almost, as hail. Shells burst around us, the fragments tearing up the ground, and canister whistled through the corn above us. Lieutenant Bode of company "F" was instantly killed, and Lieutenant John Ticknor was badly wounded. Sergeant Major Howard J. Huntington now came running to me through the corn. He said: "Major, Colonel Bragg wants to see you, quick, at the turnpike." I ran to the fence in time to hear Bragg say: "Major, I am shot," before he fell upon the ground. I saw a tear in the side of his overcoat which he had on. I feared that he was shot through the body. I called two men from the ranks, who bundled him quickly into a shelter tent, and hurried away with him. . . .

. . . While this took place on the turnpike, our companies were marching forward through the thick corn, on the right of a long line of battle. Closely following was a second line. At the front edge of the corn-field was a low Virginia rail fence. Before the corn were open fields, beyond which was a strip of woods surrounding a little church, the Dunkard church. As we appeared at the edge of the corn, a long line of men in butternut and gray rose up from the ground. Simultaneously, the hostile battle lines opened a tremendous fire upon each other. Men, I can not say fell; they were knocked out of the ranks by dozens. But we jumped over the fence, and pushed on, loading, firing, and shouting as we advanced. There was, on the part of the men, great hysterical excitement, eagerness to go forward, and a reckless disregard of life, of every thing but victory. . . .

The Fourteenth Brooklyn Regiment, red legged Zouaves, came into our line, closing the awful gaps. Now is the pinch. Men and officers of New York and Wisconsin are fused into a common mass, in the frantic struggle to shoot fast. Every body tears cartridges, loads, passes guns, or shoots. Men are falling in their places or running back into the corn. The soldier who is shooting is furious in his energy. The soldier who is shot looks around for help with an imploring agony of death on his face. After a few rods of advance, the line stopped and, by common impulse, fell back to the edge of the corn and lay down on the ground behind the low rail fence. Another line of our men came up through the corn. We all joined together, jumped over the fence, and again pushed out into the open field. There is a rattling fusilade and loud cheers. "Forward" is the word. The men are loading and firing with demoniacal fury and shouting and laughing hysterically, and the whole field before us is covered with rebels fleeing for life, into the woods. Great numbers of them are shot while climbing over the high post and rail fences along the turnpike. We push on over the open fields half way to the little church. The powder is bad, and the guns have become very dirty. It takes hard pounding to get the bullets down, and our firing is becoming slow. A long and steady line of rebel gray, unbroken by the fugitives who fly before us, comes sweeping down through the woods around the church. They raise the yell and fire. It is like a scythe running through our line. "Now, save, who can." It is a race for life.

Alfred R. Waud probably based this sketch, Skirmish between the Brooklyn 14th and 300 Rebel Cavalry, *on exaggerated accounts from Federal soldiers. As part of Phelps' brigade, the New Yorkers were in the thick of the fight—but no Rebel cavalry was ever in their vicinity. Collided bullets (lower left), found in the Cornfield, bear witness to the storm of metal that filled the air over the Miller farm.*

Skirmish between the Brooklyn 14th and 300 Rebel Cavalry

CAPTAIN JAMES M. GARNETT

STAFF, COLONEL ANDREW J. GRIGSBY

In 1903 Garnett wrote an account of the battle at Antietam for the Baltimore Sun. In it he recalled General William Starke leading his Louisiana brigade and that of Colonel E. T. H. Warren to reinforce the beleaguered troops of Grigsby's brigade, who were hard pressed by the assault of Gibbon's Federals.

*t came at once and raged furiously both on the right and left of the Hagerstown turnpike . . . Our two little brigades in the front line, about 400 men, resisted as long as it was possible—I cannot remember just how long—but presently Colonel Grigsby said to me: "Go to General Starke and tell him that unless I receive reinforcements I cannot hold this line much longer." I hurried back to the edge of the woods, found General Starke (General J. R. Jones having been stunned by the explosion of a shell very early in the morning and carried off the field), and delivered the message.

The words had barely escaped my lips when I saw the front line falling back and said to General Starke: "There they are, coming back now, General." He immediately ordered the Louisiana Brigade and Taliaferro's Brigade to rise and move forward, which they did in gallant style at a right oblique, and he himself led them, but he had not more than reached the fence along the Hagerstown road when he fell, pierced by three musket balls and survived but an hour. . . .

Colonel Grigsby rallied the men of the front line at the edge of the

William E. Starke was a successful cotton broker in New Orleans when the war broke out. He began his service as an aide to General R. S. Garnett, and after being cited twice for bravery during the Seven Days' Battles, attained the rank of brigadier general in August 1862. After Starke died at Antietam, his body was returned to Richmond, where he was buried next to his son, who had fallen at Seven Pines.

Two days after the battle, dead Confederates, probably from Starke's brigade, remain

...ell along a fence line on the west side of the Hagerstown pike. After rushing forward to stem Doubleday's advance, the Rebels were caught in a cross fire that took a heavy toll.

woods, where they resisted a while longer, those on the left shooting from a ledge of rocks and some straw stacks in rear of a farmhouse. But increasing numbers forced them from this position and all of the men that could be rallied withdrew across a small stream and took position about half-way up the hill beyond, in front of another farmhouse—Hauser's, I think it must have been—where they stayed.

The enemy came into the woods and even to the ledge of rocks and straw stacks above mentioned, but did not venture across the little stream.

PRIVATE LAWRENCE A. DAFFAN
4TH TEXAS INFANTRY, WOFFORD'S BRIGADE

As Lawton's situation grew desperate, the general sent a respectful but urgent message to Hood, whose division was being held in reserve: "General Lawton sends his compliments with the request that you come at once to his support." Hood responded by sending two brigades, one under Wofford, the other under Law, charging toward the Cornfield and the East Woods around 7:00 a.m.

Then the Texas Brigade was ordered to charge; the enemy was on the opposite side of this stubblefield in the cornfield. As we passed where Lawton's Brigade had stood, there was a complete line of dead Georgians as far as I could see. Just before we reached the cornfield General Hood rode up to Colonel Carter, commanding the Fourth Texas Regiment (my regiment), and told him to front his regiment to the left and protect the flank. This he did and he made a charge directly to the west. We were stopped by a pike fenced on both sides. It would have been certain death to have climbed the fence.

Hays' Louisiana Brigade had been in on our left, and had been driven out. Some of their men were with us at this fence. One of them was a better soldier than I was. I was lying on the ground shooting through the fence about the second rail; he stood up and shot right over the fence. He was shot through his left hand, and through the heart as he fell on me, dead. I pushed him off and saw that "Seventh Louisiana" was on his cap.

The Fifth, First and Eighteenth Georgia, which was the balance of my brigade, went straight down into the cornfield, and when they struck this cornfield, the corn blades rose like a whirlwind, and the air was full.

LIEUTENANT COLONEL PHILLIP A. WORK
1ST TEXAS INFANTRY, WOFFORD'S BRIGADE

A former member of the Texas Secession Convention, Work led his regiment into the Cornfield, where in less than a half hour 80 percent of his men would be killed or wounded. Work resigned for medical reasons in January 1864, but he later raised a company for service in Texas.

The 1st Texas encountered and entered a patch of green corn in an old clover field. Pursuing the Federals through it to near the farther (North) side a Federal battery came in view on a slight eminence at the distance of from seventy-five to one hundred yards beyond it, and it being evident that it was limbering up and in the act of withdrawing, the regiment, of its own notion and of one accord, unheeding the reiterated command to Forward, Load and Fire at Will, came to a halt and began shooting down horses and artillerists with the hope and expectation of capturing it, unmindful of the fleeing

Georgian William T. Wofford set aside his law practice to raise a company that fought with distinction in the Mexican War. When his state seceded, he became colonel of the 18th Georgia and commanded the Texas Brigade at Antietam. Wofford—"one of Georgia's best soldiers," according to Lee—soon rose to brigadier general and earned laurels at Chancellorsville, Gettysburg, and the Wilderness.

The flag of the 1st Texas, now partially restored, was badly tattered when Private Samuel Johnson of the 9th Pennsylvania Reserves picked it up in the Cornfield.

Federal infantry in our immediate front who had taken refuge behind a tumbled-down rock fence just at the outer (Northern) edge of the corn patch and was pouring a galling and deadly fire into its ranks.

At this juncture, it becoming manifest that the left wing of the regiment was being fired upon from the left and rear, I sent Adjt. Shropshire to Col. Wofford, commanding the 18th Georgia regiment on my left, requesting him to move up his regiment if possible to an alignment of the left of the 1st Texas. Very soon afterwards I sent Amos G. Hanks, a private of Co. "F," upon the same errand, and following him sent Private Hicks. None of these returned. Nor, as I afterwards learned, did either reach Col. Wofford. Shropshire and Hicks were killed and Hanks lost a leg.

Just as messenger Hicks had left me on his mission, Major Matt Dale, commanding the right wing, came to me at my station at the center and reported that nearly every man of the right wing had been shot down, killed or wounded, and not a man would be left alive unless we withdrew at once. The roar all about us of nearby small arms and of artillery more distant was so deafening that the Major, in making his report, had to place his mouth to my ear. Just as he concluded and whilst we still were standing breast to breast, he with his right side and I with my left towards the front, he was stricken by a bullet, straightened, stiffened and fell backwards prone upon the ground, dead.

Immediately thereafter—scarcely a minute—Capt. John R. Woodward, acting Major, in command of the left wing, came to me with a like report as to that wing. As the regiment no longer had the ability either to advance or resist attack effectively, and in addition, as its line of retreat was in momentary danger of being cut off by the Federals who were firing into our left from the rear, I directed Capt. Woodward to retire the left and myself proceeded to withdraw the right wing.

Falling back to the Southward limit of the corn patch, I directed the few who had emerged from the corn to rally upon a squad of perhaps thirty men who were gathered about a Confederate battle flag some thirty to forty yards to the Northwest of us and resisting the advance of Federal infantry, whilst I remained to forward on others as they might appear from without the corn. Just as the few had started for the battle-flag mentioned, Captain Woodward cried out substantially, "The flags, the flags. Where are the flags? The bearers are shot down and I'll get them," and suiting the action to the word, rushed back into the corn to recover them. He had proceeded but a short distance when he came face to face with the advancing enemy, and returned without them.

Captain Houston B. Lowrie of Company C, known as the Orange Grays, of the 6th North Carolina Infantry, was killed during Colonel Evander Law's charge through the Cornfield on the morning of September 17.

BUGLER JOHN COOK

BATTERY B,
4TH U.S. ARTILLERY,
DOUBLEDAY'S DIVISION

Cook's battery, commanded by Captain Joseph B. Campbell, slowed the surge of Hood's Confederates through the Cornfield by firing at short range into the Rebel ranks. For his actions that morning and later at Gettysburg, the 15-year-old Cook was awarded the Medal of Honor, largely on the recommendation of Lieutenant James Stewart, who was himself twice breveted for gallantry.

General Gibbon, our commander, had just ordered Lieutenant Stewart to take his section about one hundred yards to the right of the Hagerstown Pike, in front of two straw stacks, when he beckoned me to follow. No sooner had we unlimbered, when a column of Confederate infantry, emerging from the so-called west woods, poured a volley into us, which brought fourteen or seventeen of my brave comrades to the ground. The two straw stacks offered some kind of shelter for our wounded, and it was a sickening sight to see those poor, maimed, and crippled fellows, crowding on top of one another, while several stepping but a few feet away, were hit again or killed.

Just then Captain Campbell unlimbered the other four guns to the left of Stewart, and I reported to him. He had just dismounted, when he was hit twice, and his horse fell dead, with several bullets in its body. I started with the captain to the rear and turned him over to one of the drivers. He ordered me to report to Lieutenant Stewart and tell him to take command of the battery. I reported, and, seeing the cannoneers nearly all down, and one, with a pouch full of ammunition, lying dead, I unstrapped the pouch, started for the battery, and worked as a cannoneer. We were then in the very vortex of the battle. The enemy had made three desperate attempts to capture us, the last time

coming within ten or fifteen feet of our guns. It was at this time that General Gibbon, seeing the condition of the battery, came to the gun that stood in the pike, and in full uniform of a brigadier-general, worked as a gunner and cannoneer. He was very conspicuous, and it is indeed surprising, that he came away alive.

BRIGADIER GENERAL JOHN GIBBON

BRIGADE COMMANDER,
ARMY OF THE POTOMAC

Gibbon's expertise in artillery—he once taught the subject at West Point and had served in various batteries before the war—served him well at Antietam. His performance there would earn him a promotion to division commander. After further distinguished service and wounds at two battles, he would be given a corps to command. Gibbon later saw action in the Indian Wars, during which he received his third wound.

We knew but little of what was going on beyond our immediate vicinity. We were in the hottest of hornet's nests and had all we could do to attend to what was in our front whilst the sounds of a severe battle reached our ears from all directions. Bullets, shot and shell whistled and screamed around us, wounded men came to the rear in large numbers, and the six Napoleon guns of Battery "B" hurled forth destruction in double rounds of canister as the enemy in increased numbers rushed forward to capture the guns. He seemed to be making headway against our troops in the cornfield to our left and the piece on the pike was firing in that direction. The gun was on a part of the road which sloped towards us and every time it went off it recoiled a great distance down the slope. In the midst of this pandemonium I happened to look at this gun and noticed that the cannoneers had

"General Gibbon, seeing the condition of the battery, came to the gun that stood in the pike, and in full uniform of a brigadier-general, worked as a gunner and cannoneer."

carelessly allowed the elevating screw to run down and every time the piece was fired its elevation was increased until now its missiles were harmlessly thrown high over the heads of the enemy in its front. I yelled to the gunner to run up his elevating screw, but in the din he could not hear me. I jumped from my horse, rapidly ran up the elevating screw until the nozzle pointed almost into the ground in front and then nodded to the gunner to pull his lanyard. The discharge carried away most of the fence in front of it and produced great destruction in the enemy's ranks as did the subsequent discharges, and at one of these, a sergeant of the battery (Mitchell) was badly hurt by the gun running over him in its recoil. The enemy got so close to the battery in his desperate attempts to capture it, that the pieces were double-shotted with canister before which whole ranks went down, and after we got possession of the field, dead men were found piled on top of each other.

LIEUTENANT COLONEL ADONIRAM J. WARNER
10TH PENNSYLVANIA RESERVES, ANDERSON'S BRIGADE

As Hood's men emerged from the northern edge of the Cornfield they were greeted by volleys from two of Meade's brigades, one now led by Robert Anderson, who replaced the original commander, wounded at Turner's Gap. During the battle Colonel Warner's pelvis was shattered by a bullet, but he had his men put him back on his horse so he could rally his regiment before seeking medical attention.

The rebel skirmishers were driven back and our columns deploying into line one after another pushed rapidly on . . . Our Div.—the Penna. Res. were lying yet just under a little rise of ground not far in front of our starting point. The rebel artilery played furiously on our advancing lines and got a pretty good range on us while lying in column awaiting orders, but the ground rose a little on three

sides and it was hard to throw shell just where we were. Some few were wounded, however, but no one at this time could shrink from his post. The wounded began to come back from our front. The fire now was deadly and terrific; one awful hour of musketry told the unmistakeable nature of the conflict. Minni bullets flew thick back even to us. These terrible missles are the ones that do the work in close engagements. The smoke began to arise thick and heavy: There was also some fog in the air, and nothing definite could be seen where the fight was raging. What minutes these were to us! We knew into this chasm where leaped innumerable hissing leaden messengers of death filling the air like hail we must in a moment plunge! Just here a man from Wisconsin with his bowels all open lay calmly waiting his end. He had been struck by a shot and brought back so far and left by a tree to die. He gave his name and the name of his parents and them to know that he had done his duty. He did not groan nor murmured, but ordered what was going on as one unconcerned for himself, but soon turned over and died. This incident our men looked on without emotion apparently, for such is the feeling at such a time. Aye, into that cloud of battle smoke where amid the searing roar of arms thousands were going down already in dreadful struggle, we must follow! . . . Not many stragglers were coming back though a few under one pretense or another and some of them too wore shoulder straps! The wounded began to come by scores. I tried to make myself useful by stopping those who had no wounds to run away and leave their comrades.

Our men were driving the rebels. It was evident. But our turn soon came. We moved forward as we were in column at double quick, over a clear space where the fire of the rebel artillery could sweep us. Some few were struck, but not many. Reaching lower ground just before we came to a cornfield where the fighting was terribly raging, we deployed in a line. . . . Already now the First Brig. were entering the cornfield—that dreadful cornfield that will ever be known as the scene of the most deadly strife that took place on that day. We were now on ground strewn thick with our own and the rebel dead. . . . Our division moved on through the cornfield over the slain and the dying. The carnage had already been fearful here but the conflict was by no means over. The rebels met our lines firmly and the strife raged more savagely than ever. The sounds were unbroken. Artillery roar was almost drowned by the deafening thunder of small arms. Battle never raged fiercer than on this field at this time.

Amid the mountains of debris found on the battlefield were a Union knapsack, a bayonet, and this Zouave jacket from the 5th New York—a V Corps unit that was held in reserve through all the fighting at Antietam. The jacket may have been a trophy carried to Antietam by someone in the Texas Brigade, which crushed the 5th New York at Second Manassas 18 days earlier.

CAPTAIN J. ALBERT MONROE
Battery D, 1st Rhode Island Light Artillery, Doubleday's Division

When Captain Monroe brought up his battery into the Cornfield after the Rebels had fallen back, he was appalled by the carnage. By midmorning, both Hooker's and Jackson's commands ended up virtually where they had started at dawn, with little but a field of bloody bodies to show for their efforts. Nearly a third of Hooker's I Corps was killed or wounded, and Jackson's corps fared even worse.

We had an easy time until about ten o'clock, when General Gibbon rode up to me and said: "Here, Captain; your men are good and fresh; General Hooker wants to see you." I thought it pretty cool, this reference to the fresh condition of the men, for they had had but little sleep for several nights, and they had been hard at work since early daylight, for after working the guns they were kept busy replenishing the ammunition chests and at other necessary work; besides, we were very short-handed, owing to heavy losses in previous actions. First directing Lieutenant Fisk to limber the pieces, I reported to General Hooker, whom I found at the point where a little while after he received the severe wound that incapacitated him for further service that day. Said he:

"Captain, you see that cornfield; the second one, I mean?"

"Yes, sir."

"You see the one beyond that?"

"Yes, sir."

"Well, I want you to go through the second one into the ploughed ground, and into the cornfield beyond, if you can get there. Now go and look out for your support; you will find some infantry there to support you."

The bullets were right thick where he gave me the order, for the position was an exposed one, just such as one would expect to find General Hooker in. On the right was the Hagerstown turnpike, leading to Sharpsburg, running southerly and parallel with the line of vision. . . . The Dunker church was in plain sight, and down to that point our troops, apparently, had driven the enemy into or across the turnpike. As far as the church the ground appeared to be a descending plain of cultivated land, beyond which it seemed undulating and uncertain in character.

. . . Over this space the two lines had been putting forth all their energies since early light, and the ground was strewn with dead and wounded horses and men, clothing, knapsacks, canteens, muskets and side arms broken and twisted in every imaginable manner. The blue and the gray were indiscriminately mingled, either motionless and life-less, or dragging their bleeding forms along in search of some less ex-posed situation. And there were those whose life-blood was fast or slowly ebbing away, with only strength sufficient to raise a supplicating arm for assistance or relief. The stretcher-bearers were straining every nerve to succor the helpless wounded, but it would have required a force in itself equal to a small army to have immediately removed them all; nor would their situation have been materially improved by re-moval, except that they would have been carried from the midst of the noise and excitement of the field, for the hospitals were crowded to repletion, and hundreds were waiting their turns for the care of the surgeons. . . .

Unless under great excitement horses will not step on the bodies of men, either alive or dead, but when attached to a battery they may go so close as to cause further injury to the wounded or mutilation to the dead by passing the wheels over them; so we picked our way carefully, avoiding running over the bodies strewn around on every hand, and looking out for the wounded. At one point we were moving along quite briskly, when a poor wounded fellow, clad in the dingy yellow, the "butternut," as we called it, so common to the uniforms of the rebel soldiers, with a countenance expressive of all the terror of one who expected no consideration, raised himself on one elbow and cried out, "O, don't run over me!" I said, as some of the men quickly but careful-ly removed him aside, "You shan't be hurt, my man," and an expres-sion of relief and gratitude overspread his face that spoke more plainly and loudly than would have a thousand words of thanks.

"Unless under great excitement horses will not step on the bodies of men, either alive or dead, but when attached to a battery they may go so close as to cause further injury to the wounded."

Major General Joseph Hooker commanded his I Corps skill-fully, but without reinforcements he could achieve no better than a standoff at the Cornfield. Within months President Lin-coln placed him at the head of the Army of the Potomac, which he masterfully restored after its defeat at Fredericksburg only to lead it into the debacle at Chan-cellorsville in May 1863.

Federal XII Corps Attack: East Woods to Dunker Church

Held in reserve during Hooker's assaults, the 7,200 men of General Joseph Mansfield's XII Corps advanced about 7:30 a.m. to renew the attack on the Confederate left. The corps contained many raw units, however, and getting them ready proved to be a painfully slow operation. Moreover, Mansfield was himself new to battle, in his first field command at the age of 58. Fearing that his untested units might panic and run, he bunched his troops in tight, unwieldy columns, ideal targets for enemy fire. While trying to untangle the confusion, Mansfield was shot in the chest and mortally wounded. Immediately Brigadier General Alpheus S. Williams, the leader of one of the XII Corps' two divisions, took command and managed with surprising speed to get the Federal brigades in line of battle and moving forward.

First to hit the Confederates was Samuel Crawford's brigade from Williams' division, which advanced toward the dreaded Cornfield—only to be savaged by the remnants of Hood's troops in the East Woods and then turned back by Roswell Ripley's brigade, which had moved up from the Mumma farm into the Cornfield. The battle lines in fact had hardly changed since Hooker's initial attacks had begun two hours before. Confederates still clung to the Cornfield and the nearby East Woods. The West Woods were occupied by remnants of Lawton's and Jones' Confederate divisions. The Cornfield especially was a ghastly charnel house, with hundreds of shattered corpses sprawled amid the stubble. Hundreds more wounded men writhed in agony as the fighting once more raged around them.

Stopped at first, General Williams countered by pushing George Gordon's brigade on the Union right into the pasture north of the Cornfield, where it was quickly caught up in a vicious firefight with Ripley's Confederates. D. H. Hill, meanwhile, rushed his last two brigades into action, sending Alfred Colquitt's men to bolster Ripley's and Garland's brigades—now under Duncan McRae—into the East Woods. At the same time General George Greene launched his Union division into the East Woods, where the brigades led by Hector Tyndale and Henry Stainrook shifted the weight of numbers back in favor of the Federals.

The Confederates held firm at first, peppering the ranks of the oncoming Federals with fire; but then disaster struck. McRae's North Carolinians, many of them still shaken by the death of their original leader, Samuel Garland, at South Mountain three days before, overheard one of their officers yelling in alarm, "They are flanking us! See, yonder's a whole brigade!" Shortly one of McRae's regiments panicked, then the entire brigade. "In a moment the most unutterable stampede occurred," recalled McRae, who watched in astonishment as his line melted away and vanished from the field.

The sudden retreat created a dangerous gap in the Confederate defense, and into it charged Greene's Federals. A descendant of Nathanael Greene, a distinguished general of the American Revolution, George Greene spurred his men forward, driving the Rebels from the East Woods and, supported by Gordon's brigade, forcing them to fall back from the Cornfield. With the Confederate flank

broken wide open, the Federals advanced along both sides of the Smoketown road, driving fast toward the Dunker Church.

The lead regiment, the 102d New York, moved so fast, in fact, that Greene had to ride forward and order the troops to pause while he brought up supporting artillery. "You are bully boys," he cried, "but don't go any farther!" Then, with the guns firing, the Federals charged once more. S. D. Lee's Confederate batteries were driven from the strategic high ground to the east of the church, a main objective of the Union attacks all morning.

The Federals, now in control of the narrow battlefield east of the Hagerstown Turnpike, seemed to have cracked Jackson's defenses. Some Union troops had even gotten into the West Woods—although largely by mistake. These were Pennsylvanians from Crawford's brigade who got separated from Williams' division and found themselves in the woods almost at the Dunker Church's front door.

The situation looked so promising for the Federals that General Hooker, riding forward to get parts of his I Corps moving again, was convinced that the Union troops were about "to drive the rebel army into the Potomac or destroy it." Hooker's efforts were frustrated when he was hit in the foot by a Confederate sharpshooter's bullet and, faint from pain and loss of blood, had to be carried to the rear.

In fact this second Federal assault, for all of Greene's efforts, was running out of steam. Hooker's I Corps was badly scattered. The XII Corps had also become disorganized after the hard fighting and swift advance; it had suffered 25 percent casualties. Worse, Greene's regiments were running out of ammunition

and faced increasingly heavy fire from Confederates hidden in the West Woods.

Realizing he had to regroup, Greene halted his advance on the eastern edge of the
high ground 200 yards from the church and
sent men back to round up more ammunition. Soon the firing on both sides subsided
and a partial lull descended on the field—
where more than 8,000 Americans, about
half Union and half Confederate, had already
been wounded or killed in the three hours
since 6:00. But the fighting was far from over
as another massive assault, this time by the
Federal II Corps, was about to begin.

*After confusion and delays Mansfield's XII Corps
finally got moving just as Hooker's Federals were
falling back. With only the shattered units from the
earlier fight to oppose the advance, D. H. Hill
rushed three brigades into the Federals' path. After
a brief standoff the Rebels broke, and Greene's division swept forward to the open ground in front of
the Dunker Church. Unsupported and low on
ammunition, the Yankees pulled up and a brief
lull settled over the battlefield.*

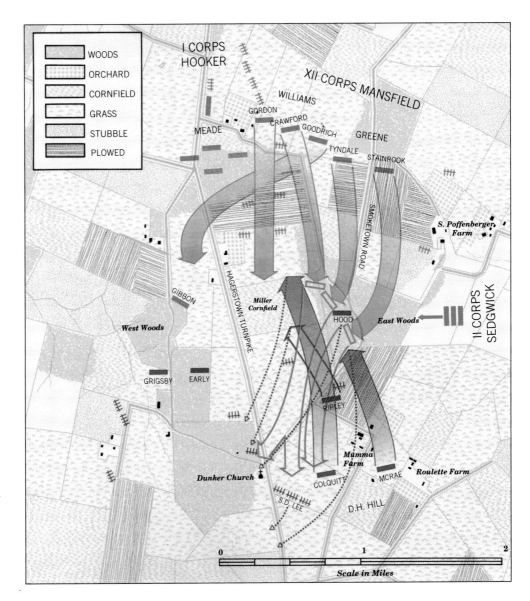

LIEUTENANT JOHN M. GOULD

10TH MAINE INFANTRY, CRAWFORD'S BRIGADE

As the lead elements of the Federal XII Corps laboriously readied themselves for the advance, Lieutenant Gould stood by helplessly as his commander, General Mansfield, galloped along the front ranks and drew fatal fire from the Rebels in the East Woods.

The enemy fell back as we approached. On arriving at the fence, we opened fire, and then rushed into the woods for such cover as the trees, &c., offered. The enemy also was well scattered through the woods, behind numerous ledges, logs, trees and piles of cord wood, a few men only being east of the Smoketown road, which at that time was not fenced.

The fire of the enemy was exceedingly well aimed; and as the distance between us was only about one hundred yards, we had a bloody time of it.

We had fired only a few rounds, before some of us noticed Gens. Mansfield and Crawford, and other mounted officers, over on the Croasdale Knoll, which, with the intervening ground was open woods. Mansfield at once came galloping down the hill and passed through the scattered men of the right companies, shouting "Cease firing, you are firing into our own men!" He rode very rapidly and fearlessly till he

reached the place where our line bent to the rear. . . . Captain Jordan now ran forward as far as the fence, along the top of the ledge behind which his division was sheltered, and insisted that Gen. Mansfield should "Look and see." He and Sergt. Burnham pointed out particular men of the enemy, who were not 50 yards away, that were then aiming their rifles at us and at him. Doubtless the General was wounded while talking with Jordan; at all events he was convinced, and remarked, "Yes, you are right." He then turned his horse and passed along to the lower land where the fence was down, and attempted to go through, but the horse, which also appeared to be wounded, refused to step into the traplike mass of rails and rubbish, or to jump over. The General thereupon promptly dismounted and led the horse into Sam Poffenberger's field. I had noticed the General when he was with Crawford on the Croasdale Knoll, and had followed him with my eye in all his ride. Col. Beal was having a great deal of trouble with his horse, which

was wounded and appeared to be trying to throw the Colonel, and I was slow in starting from the Colonel to see what Mansfield's gestures meant. I met him at the gap in the fence. As he dismounted his coat blew open, and I saw that blood was streaming down the right side of his vest.

The General was very quick in all his motions and attempted to mount as soon as the horse had got through the fence; but his strength

Major General Joseph Mansfield (above), a 40-year Regular Army veteran, had lobbied tirelessly for a field command. When it finally came, it lasted only two days. In this sketch showing the deployment of Williams' division, Alfred Waud indicated Mansfield's position—just left of the two mounted officers— though the general had already been mortally wounded and carried off by the time the battle line had fully deployed as shown.

The drum shown above was cut down to size so it could be carried by Thomas Floyd, a drummer boy with the 125th Pennsylvania, of Crawford's brigade.

was evidently failing, and he yielded to the suggestion that we should take him to a surgeon. . . . We then got a blanket and other men, and I started off ahead of the re-formed squad to find a Surgeon.

The road had appeared to be full of ambulances a half hour before, but all were gone now and we carried the General clear to Sam Poffenberger's woods. . . . an ambulance was found and two medical officers, just inside the woods, a few steps north of where Sam Poffenberger's gate now hangs. . . . The younger doctor put a flask to the General's mouth. The whiskey, or whatever it was, choked the General and added greatly to his distress. We put the General into the ambulance and that was the last I saw of him.

PRIVATE W. R. HAMBY
4TH TEXAS INFANTRY, WOFFORD'S BRIGADE

Although they fought with tenacity, Hood's shot-up regiments were no match for the renewed Federal advance, and even with reinforcements from D. H. Hill they were forced to fall back. Following the battle, Private Hamby was detailed to nurse the wounded who were taken back to Winchester, Virginia. In November Hamby received a medical discharge for an untreatable hernia.

The Texas Brigade was now only a skirmish line; in fact, all of the Confederates on this portion of the field scarcely covered a fourth of the Federal front. It was yet early in the morning, although the battle had been hot and furious for some hours. In addition to the infantry and artillery on front and flanks, the heights

above the Antietam were crowned with long-range batteries that poured a merciless fire; while the fresh troops of the Union forces seemed inexhaustible as they were thrown upon the fragments of the Confederate lines. The earth and sky seemed to be on fire, and it looked like here would be the Thermopylie of the Texas Brigade. With sublime courage the 1st Texas held their advanced position in the cornfield against overwhelming numbers, and retired only to escape annihilation. . . . Many of the men had exhausted their ammunition and supplied themselves from the cartridge boxes of the dead and wounded around them. They were holding a position they knew they could not maintain; yet men never fought better, and withdrew only to keep from being surrounded. Falling back slowly below the crest of the hill, the line moved through the field, crossed the pike, and took position in the woods near the church. The 4th Texas was then ordered up through the woods west of the pike near the edge of the field on the north, where they remained about an hour defiantly waving their flag over empty muskets, when they were ordered to rejoin the other regiments of the brigade.

Born in Alabama but raised in Texas, Private William Smith, a member of the 4th Texas Infantry, survived the Battle of Antietam unscathed. But his luck ran out a year later, when he was killed at Chickamauga.

PRIVATE CALVIN LEACH

1ST NORTH CAROLINA INFANTRY, RIPLEY'S BRIGADE

First to reinforce Hood's men was Roswell Ripley's brigade of Georgians and North Carolinians. Many of Ripley's soldiers carried muskets that fired buck-and-ball loads whose shotgunlike effects took a heavy toll in wounded Federals, including the two Indiana soldiers who had found Lee's lost orders on the way to Antietam. Leach survived the battle, only to be killed at Bethesda Church on May 30, 1864.

Soon in the morning the fireing commenced, and very soon our Reg was under fire the balls whisin over us and wounding and killing many of our brave boys Here our gallant and much loved capt Boushell got severely wounded in the mouth and had to be carried off the field. Olso Lieut Peden was wound.

We were ordered by the left flank and were very soon into the engagement. I commenced loading and shooting with all my might but my gun got chooked the first round, and I picked up the gun of one of my comrades who fell by my side and continued to fire. Here I could see the second line of battle of the enemy and when their men would fall, the rest would close in and fill their places. Their first line was lying by a fence and I could see the old "Stars & Stripes" waving over them I fired as near as I could aim at the men around the flag I do not know whether I killed any one or not.

During this time our Reg got cut up very severely, and the Reg was ordered to retreat back when we met reinforcements comeing in and I was glad to see them for I was nearly tired to death, not having hardly any thing to eat for 4 or 5 days. we then marched up on a hill out of danger of the balls where we stacked arms and rested awhile. . . .

We received more amunition and was ordered back to our position a line of battle. . . . I often looked at the sun and longed for night to come so the fireing would cease.

As we marched back to our position Gen Lee met us and sayed "Go in cheerfull boys they are driving them back on the right and left and we need a little help in the center."

The 3d North Carolina Infantry, commanded by Colonel William DeRosset (left), lost 299 of 520 men at Antietam, including DeRosset who was severely wounded in the hip and subsequently discharged. More than 20 years later, DeRosset still vividly recalled the day: "Having been shot down as the movement began, as I was carried from the field, [I] had the satisfaction of seeing as grand a charge, by my regiment . . . as any made upon an enemy anywhere."

PRIVATE WILLIAM F. GOODHUE

3D WISCONSIN INFANTRY, GORDON'S BRIGADE

General Alpheus Williams' first act after taking charge of the Federal XII Corps was to shift units to the right to bolster Hooker's position. One brigade marched off to the West Woods while General Gordon's brigade headed into the Cornfield to confront Ripley's Confederates and resume the slaughter. Gordon's command suffered more than 600 casualties but refused to budge even after the Rebel line was reinforced with Alfred Colquitt's brigade.

In this din and swirl of cannon shot, we hear but scarcely heed the flying bullets from the enemy's pickets. They too are firing at random in the mist. About 200 yards to our right we could just discern a house, stacks and a well of water, where later the wounded men of both armies crowded about for water. Before us is a cornfield. . . . Its yellow tassels drooping with the night's heavy dew. To our right the trees surrounding the Dunkard Church can be dimly seen. . . .

To the left may be seen dark masses of foliage, but the enemy is not discernable. Suddenly, in our rear, cannon boom from our batteries, which have taken position, their shots by the score, passing over us. It seemed as though we could almost touch them in their hurried sweep. We felt, however, this was a waste of ammunition, and that

"The smoke coming from the artillery hung heavily over the fields, and as the sunlight pierced it, the grayish tints disappeared, and there was left a blue sulphurous tinge, the incarnate color of battle."

all was at random in the fog.

. . . One of the men, who had been looking intently at the cornfield, bringing himself to "attention" quietly said: "boys, here they come!" At this instant there are bursting volleys of musketry on the left, followed by long rattling rolls of musketry from the extended lines of troops. Further yet to the left there is seen a ribbon-like continuation of sounds similar to the flutter of a flag in the breeze. The fire of the enemy mingles with our own, and the roar of musketry is incessant. Heavy and successive discharges of artillery are almost deafening. Amid this din we could faintly hear the command: "Attention!" which we quickly obeyed. The fog was now vanishing, but the smoke coming from the artillery hung heavily over the fields, and as the sunlight

pierced it, the grayish tints disappeared, and there was left a blue sulphurous tinge, the incarnate color of battle.

Our attention was now drawn to the cornfield in which we saw several conical shapes dancing above the tasseled stalks. Eagerly we watched them as they came, when, suddenly, as if by magic, the corn disappeared, and a long line of confederate gray covered our entire front! The conical forms we saw in the cornfield, were the tops of confederate battle-flags, now plainly seen, scarcely a hundred yards away. Amid the deafening roar about us, I heard a voice behind me shouting: "Ready! Aim! Fire!" and the crash of our guns was like a blow on an anvil, nearly four hundred guns were discharged upon the instant, cutting down men in great numbers in the advancing line.

TWENTY-SEVENTH INDIANA.   THIRD WISCONSIN.
BATTLE OF ANTIETAM. (BY F. R. GARDNER.)

In this soldier drawing from the 27th Indiana's regimental history, General Gordon's brigade pushes forward across the Miller farm after the collapse of Mc-Rae's North Carolina brigade initiated a general Confederate retreat. On the left is the East Woods and in the distance the burning Mumma farmhouse. Although crudely rendered, the two field pieces on the right illustrate the role of close support the artillery played on both sides.

CAPTAIN ROBERT G. SHAW

2D MASSACHUSETTS INFANTRY, GORDON'S BRIGADE

After serving for a time on Gordon's staff, Captain Shaw rejoined his regiment before the battle. Advancing across the Miller farm, he encountered the pitiful scene described below. Later in the battle, a spent ball struck him in the neck, but it left nothing more than a bruise.

The Brigade advanced through a cornfield in front, which, until then, had been occupied by the enemy; it was full of their dead and wounded, and one of our sergeants took a regimental colour there, belonging to the Eleventh Mississippi. Beyond the cornfield was a large open field, and such a mass of dead and wounded men, mostly Rebels, as were lying there, I never saw before; it was a terrible sight, and our men had to be very careful to avoid treading on them; many were mangled and torn to pieces by artillery, but most of them had been wounded by musketry fire. We halted right among them, and the men did everything they could for their comfort, giving them water from their canteens, and trying to place them in easy positions. There are so many young boys and old men among the Rebels, that it seems hardly possible that they can have come of their own accord to fight us, and it makes you pity them all the more, as they lie moaning on the field. . . .

The wounded Rebels were always as surprised and grateful as men could be at receiving attention from us, and many said that all they wanted was to get into our hospitals, and wished they had never fired a shot at us. One boy, seventeen or eighteen, told Morse he had only left North Carolina three weeks ago, and how his father and mother grieved at his going.

Among the dead from Ripley's brigade was 18-year-old Private William E. Newlin, of the 1st North Carolina Infantry. Newlin, who attended the Hillsborough Military Academy, served as a drillmaster before being drafted in July 1862.

The saddle at left belonged to Captain John D. Woodbury of Battery M, 1st New York Light Artillery, which saw heavy action all morning near the center of the XII Corps battle line. This type of saddle, which had been designed by General McClellan to distribute more of the rider's weight along the horse's flanks rather than its back, was widely used by both sides during the war.

Burning of Mr. Mumma's houses and barns at the fight of

LIEUTENANT ROBERT T. COLES
4TH ALABAMA INFANTRY, LAW'S BRIGADE

After surviving a harrowing morning, Lieutenant Coles— recently recovered from a wound received during the Seven Days' Battles—and the remainder of Hood's men now faced two brigades of Greene's division, advancing through the gap created by the flight of McRae's brigade.

In this Alfred Waud sketch, Federal soldiers from Greene's division pull up amid the burning Mumma farm buildings; in the distance an exploding Rebel limber throws up a tower of smoke and flame just in front of the Dunker Church. Ripley's brigade spent the eve of battle bivouacked on the Mumma property. Before advancing to the attack, men from the 3d North Carolina put the house, barn, and several outbuildings to the torch, under orders from D. H. Hill to prevent their use by Yankee sharpshooters.

We had now been engaged, as afterwards learned, almost three hours fighting desperately without any intermission, most of the men had exhausted their ammunition, and all had exhausted themselves in their efforts to drive the enemy from his position. Before accomplishing this, however, the Union General Green, with two fresh brigades made "a terrible and overwhelming attack on our front," which, together with the fire on our right flank, and rear, caused us to fall back. . . . Having no support to take our places in front, and the enemy so heavily reinforced, we feared he would closely follow us up, failed to do so, giving ample time to re-form and replenish our ammunition boxes. General Hood kept his staff and couriers busy going over the field directing the scattered men of the Division to assemble in rear of Dunker Church. Just as we reached the Church, Lieutenant King of F Company, a man born and reared on the Tennessee River in Morgan County, who dropped his plow to enlist in the 4th Alabama, and was promoted from the ranks for sheer merit by the aristocrats of his Company, had here, when some of us stopped for a few minutes, the whole top of his head blown off by a shell. As jovial Captain Karsner, Lieutenant Dan Turner and I were slowly wending our way in that direction, a shell of the enemy from over on the right of the line bursting near us, a fragment struck Karsner's too prominent nose. The shock was so great it knocked him a severe fall, at full length upon his back. We ran to him, thinking he was killed. On examination, as he still remained where he fell, though bleeding profusely, we found

"We had forgotten almost, for the moment, that we were upon a field where more glory was to be achieved, more colors to be captured, more guns taken or silenced, more of the enemy to be placed *hors du combat.*"

the wound very slight. With the blood running down in his eyes and mouth, he presented, lying there, a most ludicrous sight, so much so that it was impossible to avert a smile on our part. He imagined that the missle had gone entirely through his head, so great was the shock; and when he observed that we entertained so little feeling for a "dying" comrade, promptly arose and, still quite dazed, abused us soundly for our lack of sympathy. After being convinced that it was nothing serious he soon regained his usual merry mood. Just then General Hood was seen approaching from the rear. After showing the Division where to re-form, Lieutenant Turner remarked, "Captain, wipe that blood from your face before General Hood reaches us." "No," he said, "I will see if I can make *him* sympathize with me." He then, with his hands, smeared the clotted blood thickly over his face. General Hood exclaimed as he rode up, "My God! Captain, I am sorry to see you so seriously wounded." "Yes, General," he said, "I came very near getting my face shot off." General Hood was as sympathetic as a woman.

PRIVATE JOSEPH L. CORNET
28TH PENNSYLVANIA INFANTRY, TYNDALE'S BRIGADE

The 28th Pennsylvania, nearly 800 strong, looked like a full brigade to McRae's Confederates, who panicked and created the opening for Greene's Federals. Wheeling west into the Cornfield, the 28th and the rest of Tyndale's brigade took Colquitt's men in the flank and pressed on to within 200 yards of the Dunker Church.

We refilled our empty cartridge-boxes, and the boys got to talking of what they had accomplished the little time they had been in the fight. How they had captured several stands of colors, artillery and a number of prisoners, whom we had simply ordered to go to the rear, and how many rebels had been made to bite the dust, etc., when Lieut. Colonel Tyndale said: "Boys don't, yourselves, boast of what you have done, let others speak of it; it is ill manners to talk of it yourselves." At this some one proposed three cheers for Col. Tyndale, which were given with a will. Who would have believed a month before that the 28th would ever cheer that officer? He, the over-strict, yet kind-hearted, but misunderstood Tyndale. No officer ever received a greater compliment from his men than did Tyndale on that day. . . .

. . . We had forgotten almost, for the moment, that we were upon a field where more glory was to be achieved, more colors to be captured, more guns taken or silenced, more of the enemy to be placed *hors du combat,* and more of our men to demonstrate their love of their country by the shedding of their life's blood. At this point Tyndale ordered Co.

Private John P. Murphy of the 5th Ohio, part of Tyndale's brigade, won the Medal of Honor for recovering this flag lost by the 13th Alabama, one of Colquitt's regiments driven out of the Cornfield.

A to deploy as skirmishers. We had hardly moved out when we discovered that a very large body of troops were advancing up the slope towards us. For a little while we were uncertain whether they were friends or foes; but a shot fired by one of their number settled the business. The regiment rose up as one man and poured in another tremendous volley at point blank range. The entire line was now heavily engaged, and the losses on both Union and Confederate sides were very great.

. . . If I mistake not it was here at this position that Bill Moyer, of Co. A, captured a splendid pie-bald horse, supposed to have belonged to a rebel officer. Major Raphail, whose horse had been killed under him, wanted a horse, and accordingly opened negotiations with Moyer for the purchase of the animal. Raphail offered five dollars for him, but Moyer wanted one hundred. What the result of the transaction might have been is uncertain, but it so happened that the lawful owner, a Union officer, came upon the scene about this time, and claimed the fugitive steed, and the horse-trade never took place.

In 1861 Hector Tyndale left his successful importing business to become an officer in the 28th Pennsylvania. At Antietam he commanded a XII Corps brigade with "great gallantry and zeal," according to General Greene. Tyndale suffered two wounds and had three horses shot out from under him. Later, as a brigadier general, he saw action at Chattanooga but resigned in May 1864 due to illness.

Around 9:00 a.m., Captain George V. Moody (above) with two guns of his battery, the Madison (Louisiana) Light Artillery, moved up under heavy musket fire to engage Greene's advancing Federals. One of his officers, Lieutenant John Gorey, was shot in the head as he sighted in the last shot from his gun, but the gallant rearguard action gave the Rebel infantry time to pull back to the West Woods.

Federal II Corps Attack: West Woods and Sunken Road

After the brief lull about 9:00 a.m., the Federals launched a third attack on Lee's troops. John Sedgwick's division of Edwin Sumner's II Corps forded Antietam Creek and marched straight toward the West Woods. Sumner's objective—like Hooker's and Mansfield's before him—was to smash the enemy's left flank and wheel south for Sharpsburg.

Once near the woods, Sedgwick's men were shelled by Rebel artillery and peppered with musket fire from Jubal Early's brigade, Jackson's last reserve, and from the survivors of the early-morning carnage. But the Federals kept on until, suddenly, a torrent of fire blasted Sedgwick's exposed left flank. The barrage came from reinforcements that Lee, sensing a crisis, had detached from Longstreet's corps and sent hurrying north.

First to hit the Federals were Kershaw's, Barksdale's, and Semmes' brigades from Lafayette McLaws' division. These troops were backed by a brigade led by Colonel George T. Anderson. Soon sheets of fire from the Rebels in the West Woods were blasting Sedgwick's men.

Sedgwick and the 65-year-old Sumner, who rode through the lines frantically waving his hat, tried to turn their brigades to meet the attack, but it was too late. In minutes hundreds of men from Gorman's and Dana's brigades had been cut down, while hundreds more were fleeing from the woods and across the Hagerstown pike. By the time Oliver Howard's brigade, bringing up the Union rear, had joined the retreat, Sedgwick had lost almost half of his division—2,255 men killed, wounded, or missing.

Flushed with victory, the Confederates dashed after the Federals, chasing them into the open ground near the pike. Once in the open, however, they were hurled back in turn by devastating fire from I Corps and XII Corps guns positioned to cover the II Corps retreat. McLaws' division lost a third of its men before the lead brigades regained the cover of the woods.

The murderous seesaw fighting continued as George Gordon's brigade from XII Corps, urged on by the now-desperate Sumner, rushed across the Cornfield toward the northern end of the West Woods. But Gordon's men were assailed by Rebels sheltered behind a low ridge in front of the West Woods.

More successful were the XII Corps brigades led by the combative George Greene. Now resupplied with ammunition, they hurled back an assault by Kershaw's brigade, then drove the troops of Manning's brigade 200 yards into the woods behind Dunker Church. No reinforcements arrived to support Greene's near breakthrough, however, and his weary men were eventually forced to retreat by pressure from troops of the brigades of Ransom, McRae, and two regiments under John R. Cooke.

The nearest fresh Federal units were in fact only about a half mile to the southeast —William French's division of Sumner's II Corps, which had followed Sedgwick across Antietam Creek. But French, instead of moving straight ahead, had inexplicably veered south toward the farm of William Roulette —and the center of the Confederate line.

That line was dangerously thin, Longstreet having sent much of his corps north to reinforce Jackson. All that remained were

brigades from D. H. Hill's division, three of them badly torn up in the earlier fighting. Fortunately for the Confederates, the two strongest brigades, led by Robert Rodes and George B. Anderson, were in the center. They occupied a superb defensive position —an old, worn-down country lane called the Sunken Road that made an excellent rifle trench. Before the day was over, it would have a new name: Bloody Lane.

French's three brigades moved smartly ahead, pushing back lines of enemy skirmishers, then climbing a ridge and starting down the other side toward the Sunken Road. Rodes' and Anderson's men, almost invisible in their ready-made trench, held their fire until the Federals were so close, recalled the 6th Alabama's John Gordon, "we might have seen the eagles on their buttons."

Finally the Confederates fired a shattering volley at almost point-blank range, virtually wiping out the first rank of the Union brigade, led by Max Weber and made up mostly of German immigrants. Another volley felled most of the second rank. Weber's survivors stood bravely for a moment, then fell back behind the crest of the ridge. As they retreated, a second brigade commanded by Colonel Dwight Morris was also shot to pieces, as was a third led by Nathan Kimball.

As the slaughter continued, four more Rebel brigades—Pryor's, Posey's, Cumming's, and Wright's—moved past the Piper farm to support D. H. Hill's position in the Sunken Road, and Israel Richardson's Union division arrived to reinforce French.

The first of Richardson's units to attack, the tough Irish Brigade from New York, led by Thomas Meagher, was cut to shreds like those before. But the next, Caldwell's brigade, urged forward by Richardson himself, managed to get around the Confederate right flank. There Colonel Francis Barlow with two New York regiments gained a knoll that looked straight down the Sunken Road. Firing madly, Barlow's men turned the road into a slaughter pen of piled and twisted corpses. Anderson's and Rodes' brigades began to crumble and then—partly because of a confusion in orders—fled for the rear.

The Confederate line now broken, the Federals clambered across the bodies in the Sunken Road, then moved toward the Hagerstown pike. In a desperate attempt to hold, D. H. Hill assembled a ragtag band of survivors and attacked, allowing Longstreet enough time to collect 20 cannon near the Piper farm. Their furious fire halted the Federal advance, and French and Richardson pulled their men back to reorganize. Another thrust by William Franklin's VI Corps, poised less than two miles to the northeast, might have crushed the Confederate center and destroyed Lee's army. But the cautious McClellan refused to order Franklin to attack, dooming the battle to continue its murderous course on another front.

After fording Antietam Creek, Sedgwick's division of Sumner's II Corps headed straight into the West Woods where they were hit hard and driven out with heavy losses. Sumner's other two divisions veered south and ran into a vicious firefight with D. H. Hill's men in the Sunken Road.

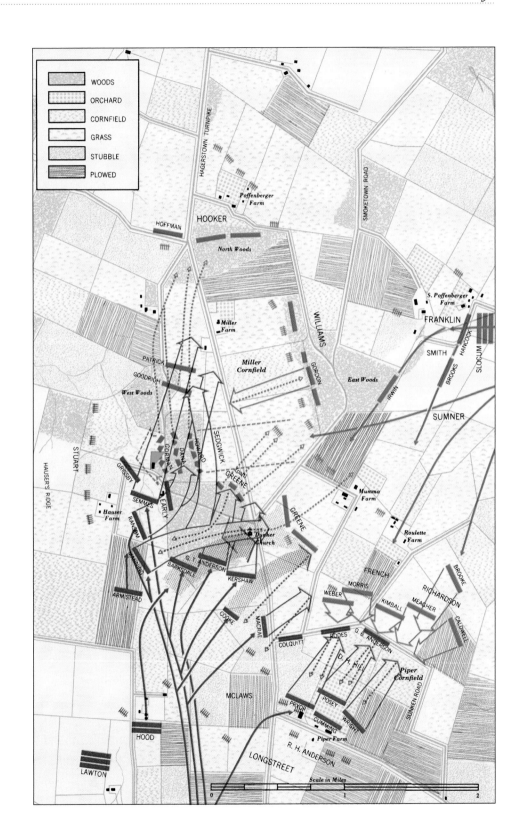

"Our color-bearer fell with a ball through his brain, and one by one all the color-guard went down."

COLONEL JACOB HIGGINS
125TH PENNSYLVANIA INFANTRY, CRAWFORD'S BRIGADE

Determined to acquit themselves well in their first battle, the 125th Pennsylvania under Colonel Higgins advanced right up into the woods around the Dunker Church to support Greene's division. The new regiment had not been there long when it became the first target of Lee's massive counterstroke.

We were then some distance beyond the church, and I detached Co. B and ordered it back to watch the ravine or depression on the other side of the church, and report to me if the enemy attempted to come up to get in our rear. The firing was terrific on both sides. Our color-bearer fell with a ball through his brain, and one by one all the color-guard went down. . . . I saw the Confederates massing for a charge, and then walked back to my own troops.

Gen. Gorman came up and told me that his brigade was some distance back, coming up on my left flank. He then went back to meet his brigade, and at this juncture Capt. Hayett, of Co. B, whom I sent back to the little white church, came down with his company and reported two regiments of the enemy coming up back of the church. Maj. Lawrence had been disabled previous to this engagement, and was not with the regiment, and Lieut-Col. Szink was disabled just as we started in. Adjutant Johnston was the only officer I had to assist me at that time. I ordered a retreat, but could not get a man to move.

They were all blazing away, and I discovered that every officer of the 125th had a musket, firing with the men. I ordered the Adjutant down the line to direct the men to fall back, or they would be all captured, but the brave boy soon fell mortally wounded. By this time that rebel yell, so well known to us afterward, sounded above the din of battle. On they came in solid columns like an avalanche that threatened to sweep all before it, yet the regiment would not move. I yelled at the top of my voice, and very likely said something else, but the men kept firing away into the surging mass in their front until the Confederate column came so close as to shout for us to surrender. Then the 125th broke on a run to the rear.

By this time one of the Confederate regiments that came up back of the church had passed half its length in rear of our regiment marching in column of fours, and the right of our regiment was running toward Rickett's battery, that we had been supporting before we were ordered into the woods. I passed through the Confederate regiment right at its colors. I raised my hand to seize the flag, but something told me I had better not, and I dropped my hand and jostled through the ranks. They spoke not a word. I asked Gen. Imboden, since the war, how that happened, and he told me that they thought we were Confederates charging on that battery. So many of their men wore blue coats, and the rest of their column was right on our heels they took it for granted that we were Confederates. If I had taken their colors it is more than likely we would all have been captured. We went through unmolested, however, and I called to our men to run between the sections of the guns.

Just as we were passing between the guns I saw gunners ram two charges of canister into each gun and fire into the gray column. They cut swaths through the ranks, but did not appear to check them in the least. On they came, and the battery had to limber up and we all went back at a lively gait about two-thirds of the way across the field.

Braving Confederate artillery fire, the three brigades of Sedgwick's division, advancing in a broad front formation, push across open ground toward the West Woods. The artist, James Hope of the 2d Vermont Infantry, condensed some of the action. In reality, the Confederate guns, intended to represent S. D. Lee's batteries, had been driven off before Sedgwick's advance.

SERGEANT WILLIAM H. ANDREWS
1st Georgia Infantry, G. T. Anderson's Brigade

Cheered on by the wounded Confederates they passed along the way, Anderson's Georgians joined up with Kershaw's South Carolina brigade to drive the 125th Pennsylvania and two other Federal regiments out of the woods just north of the Dunker Church. Although Andrews found the carnage appalling, he later wrote, "There are scenes enacted on the field of strife worth a man's life to witness."

General Kershaw's South Carolina Brigade marched within twenty feet of our line and halted a few moments. Again the command "Forward!" was given, and they marched over our line. As they stepped over us General Kershaw asked, "What command?" and when told called for three cheers for the Georgians, which the Palmetto boys gave with a vim. . . . We watched and admired the Palmetto boys as they moved into action without a bobble or a tremor in the line, and as their heads showed over the ridge the Federals opened fire; but the boys moved steadily on until they reached the top of the ridge, when every man fired at the same time. If I had not

been a Georgian, I should have wanted to be one of the Palmetto boys. There is nothing on this green earth half so grand as the sight of soldiers moving into action. A cavalry charge is superb; artillery dashing on the field carries you away; while the deadly infantry moving into the jaws of death causes you to hold your breath in admiration. . . .

The command was given by the right flank, and the boys scaled the fence. I was never able to decide whether I landed on my head or my feet; but I made better time over that fence than I ever did over one before or since. As the boys struck the ground a sheet of flame belched forth, and the sharp report of the rifles seemed to say: "Yankee, you have had your way long enough; we will now have ours." When I looked in front, I saw about sixty yards distant a solid line of blue, and every man working his gun for all it was worth. Directly in front of me I saw the stars and stripes waving to the breeze. How defiant it appeared as it slowly unfolded, then dropped back again around the staff! I thought as I looked that it would be honor enough for one day if I could cause it to strike the ground; and placing my rifle to my shoulder, I took deliberate aim at the color bearer's breast; but as I pressed the trigger my gun snapped. I had to pick the tube, put in powder and cap, and when I looked up the line was a little in advance of me.

Sergeant John W. Franks (left), a member of the 7th South Carolina in Kershaw's brigade, was mortally wounded by artillery fire at Antietam. Before he died the next day, he extracted a promise from John Wilhite—his brother-in-law, who was with him—to take care of his wife, Jane (right), and their two children back home at their plantation, Cedar Hill, in McCormick County, South Carolina. Before retreating with the rest of the army, Wilhite buried Sergeant Franks in an unmarked grave. When Jane Franks died shortly after the battle, Wilhite found the children a new home with an uncle in Georgia.

I saw Lieut. G. B. Lamar, commanding Company F, in front of the line waving his sword and calling on the men to follow him. Thinking my being in the rear might cause the Lieutenant to suspect I was showing some white feathers, under the impulse of the moment I ran through the line to the front. Looking to the left, I saw Capt. R. A. Wayne and one or two other officers holding up the almost lifeless form of Captain Montgomery, who had been shot in the head. I had but a moment to take in the situation, as an order passed along the line to "Charge, boys, and give them the bayonet!" and with the wild Rebel yell ringing in my ears and a wall of bayonets in my rear, I had to move in a hurry.

There is something in a desperate charge, a feeling that cannot be defined or expressed, in the onward rush to victory or defeat. In the wild charge many thoughts passed through my mind, but one question was uppermost: "Should the Federals stand the charge, what would become of me?"

When we were within thirty feet of the Federal line, it wavered, then broke and dashed to the rear. The yell that went up from my throat started from the bottom of my heart. Where the line had stood the earth was covered in blue. I believe I could have walked on them without putting my feet on the ground.

PRIVATE ROLAND E. BOWEN
15th Massachusetts Infantry, Gorman's Brigade

By the time they reached the far side of the West Woods, the men of Gorman's brigade found themselves caught in a horrific cross fire. From the front the brigade took fire from Grigsby's infantry and Pelham's artillery, and from the left it was raked by volleys from Semmes' brigade. Private Bowen's regiment lost 318 men, some of them to the guns of the 59th New York, which mistakenly fired into the backs of the Massachusetts men.

We soon crossed the Antietam, the water being nearly 2 feet deep. After crossing we stoped to ring out our stockings. We then proceeded around the hills so as not to be discovered by the Enemy, and then alternately through wood and field. Soon our approach was discovered by the Enemy and they commenced to Shell us with vengence. The Shell burst thick and fast over and around us, one passed through the ranks of Co. D of our Regmt killing one and wounding three, but we pressed steadily on. Soon we came to a large open field partly planted with corn. This field lies immediately along side the road running from Sharpsburg to Williamsport, and it seemed as if the ground was almost covered with dead and wounded, a large majority of wich were *Confederates*. It appears that Hooker had fought one of the most desperate fights on this field that has been fought since the commencment of the Rebellion. Passing the road, we entered a thin belt of wood. I had hardly steped into the wood when in an instant our left became engaged. The right advance[d] to the front of the wood and into the open field about 20 feet, when I discovered the Rebels a distance of perhaps 30 or 40 rods in strong force. We halted and at it we went. I never had a better chance at them in my life. Well, I guess the bullets flew for about 18 or 20 minits just as fast as we could get them in and out of our guns. I saw a Confederate Officer sitting on a horse up on a knoll. I thought I could fe[t]ch him off that horse, but after trying 3 or 4 times, I give it up thinking I might do better to fire at the crowd. So I don't know wither I hit any body or not. Now the rebs began to fall back. I thought to myself, we have got you now. But almost at the same time I heard a voice from the rear crying out "Fall back." I turned around and said, what does that mean, ain't the rebs falling back themselves. But again the cry "Fall Back." Now some one yelled out, "we are flanked, the rebels are in our rear." I looked and Ah, it was too true. In a moment

"In a moment all was confusion, it was every man for himself. We all run like a flock of sheep."

all was confusion, it was every man for himself. We all run like a flock of sheep. The rebs saw their advantage and with Grape and Canister and Musketry they mowed us down. . . . As soon as we got back a short distance, Ricketts Battery opened with Grape and Canister. This had the good effect of checking the rebs until we got out of the way. We had two Batteries up the road or near the road on the same side we had fought. We fell back on to those and reformed as fast as we could find our men. Some did not appear until the next day.

ANONYMOUS

19TH MASSACHUSETTS INFANTRY, DANA'S BRIGADE

Blasted by Confederate fire from seemingly all sides, Sedgwick's division fell into confusion. "Again and again . . . we formed," wrote an officer of the 19th Massachusetts, "but the fire was too hot." The regiment escaped some of the lethal rain by lying down—except for Colonel Edward W. Hinks, who earned the admiration of his men by remaining on his horse, a display that left him badly wounded.

The fight in the West Woods was the last one for Private Samuel A. Johnson of the 72d Pennsylvania Fire Zouaves, part of Howard's brigade. The 22-year-old bookkeeper was severely wounded in the left arm and discharged in December.

The Division was still in close column by Brigade lines, which made it impossible to manoeuvre, and the moment the lines crossed the old turnpike, afterward called "Dead Lane," and entered the woods, they were met by a storm of fire from small arms and canister from the enemy's artillery. The first volley nearly swept the First Brigade off the earth. The other two Brigades, of course, could use no fire themselves, and at the northern edge of the woods the Nineteenth halted on the top of a ledge. In front, and slightly below were the Forty-Second New York and the First Minnesota, hotly engaged with the rebels, while the Nineteenth, suffering severely from the galling fire of short range, could not reply because of the position of the lines and the conformity of the ground. They were, therefore, ordered to lie down, while the minie balls rained upon them, seemingly as thick as hail stones, and the buzz of canister shot was continual. It was awful to lay there with no chance to reply, but Col. Hinks sat on his horse near the centre of the regiment, amid the heaviest fire of which he seemed to be the special object, watching the movements of the enemy, and, as his men remarked, exhibiting no consciousness of danger. With folded arms and a smile upon his lips, he remained thus at a distance of less than a hundred and fifty yards from the line of the enemy which was pouring its incessant fire upon the position. The first brigade was almost annihilated. One single shot of an Enfield or Springfield rifle could hit a man in the front rank of the first brigade and go through to the rear rank of the last brigade. Soon the front line began to fall back, climbing up the rocky steep to the position of the Nineteenth. Some of the men on the left were firing toward its rear and left.

The rebels covered by a ledge of rock repulsing the troops on the right — in the woods beyond the Dunker ch. antietam

Gen. Sumner's attack

Using what the artist terms a "rock ledge" near the Dunker Church for cover, Confederates in the West Woods fire into the flank of Sedgwick's crowded ranks.

The others yelled to them "What are you doing? Don't you know any better than to fire into our third line?" One of them replied: "You had better look back and see if they are the third line." Where was the third line? No one knew! The wood was clear of any enemy in the immediate rear, but to the left was the rebel line extending back beyond the road and marching down, rolling up the brigades and firing into them.

Gen. Sumner was talking with Col. Kimball, commanding the Fifteenth Massachusetts regiment, when Maj. Philbrick of that regiment shouted: "See the rebels!" Gen. Sumner looked in the direction in which Maj. Philbrick pointed and exclaimed "My God, we must get out of this!"

Howard's brigade was then facing toward the west. He was at once directed to face it to the southwest, but there was not time before the blow fell. French's division had not yet arrived near enough, so that the left of Sumner's Corps was not properly closed on the adjoining force, and the enemy instantly threw troops into the gap, almost surrounding it and bringing an enfilading fire from front and flank and rear to add to the fierceness of the fight. The Division was helpless and a third of its number were cut down in a few minutes.

SERGEANT CHARLES C. CUMMINGS

17TH MISSISSIPPI INFANTRY, BARKSDALE'S BRIGADE

McLaws' division and G. T. Anderson's brigade made short work of the Yankees in the woods around the church. But when some of the Confederates, Barksdale's men among them, pushed on into the open ground beyond, they ran into a hail of canister from a six-gun Federal battery. Sergeant Cummings marveled at his ability to dodge artillery fire unscathed—aided by the use of an enemy soldier as a human shield—but he would later lose his right arm at Gettysburg.

My part of the command charged without halting a moment as soon as we arrived on the field after an all day's and all night's march to get there from the Ferry. . . . We ran up the slope at a double-quick and at the crest of the hill, which we gained a little in advance of the blue boys, we met and routed them by a single fire. We got in the first work, and blue jackets lay thick as leaves in Vallambrosa after that discharge. The old flag fell also, but was quickly snatched up by a plucky boy in blue. It fell again and again was snatched up by another. A third time the flag went down and then we were pressing them so that it seemed our flag, till a Yankee ran back and slung it over his shoulder and ran past the Dunkard Church, trailing its staff out in the open, beyond where they had posted a battery. Six of my company followed after the fleeing flag, seeking to capture it out in the open, and ran into the jaws of this battery before we knew we were "in it." Hamp Woods and Lieut. James rest there yet; Bill McRaven, Jerry Webb and I were spared, as you will see. . . .

. . . As we emerged past the Dunkard Church, which stood in the woodland, and spread ourselves out in the open, for the first time we discovered on the brow of the hill a battery, vomiting grape and canister at us. This did the work for those who fell. When the third man fell we were still running blindly toward the battery, and for a second or so we made sure we would take it, for the gunners had either dodged down or had skedaddled over the knoll it stood on. At any rate no one was in sight, and we thought as we could'nt catch a flag, we would take a battery. But presently the gunner seemed to rise out of the earth and that little battery fairly howled blood and death and double-breasted thunder at us. The grape shot, shrapnel, and what not, pattered around us so that if it had been rain we would all have gotten wet. This caused a blue-coated youth, about fifteen years old, lying behind a stump in

The rare stereoscopic ambrotype at left shows Lieutenant Columbus W. Motes, a photographer from Athens, Georgia, who served with the Troup (Georgia) Artillery in McLaws' division. Motes was wounded in the left hip and right shoulder when the battery took heavy infantry fire supporting the charge of Ransom's brigade. Motes recovered and returned to duty, surviving the war to resume his photographic career in Atlanta.

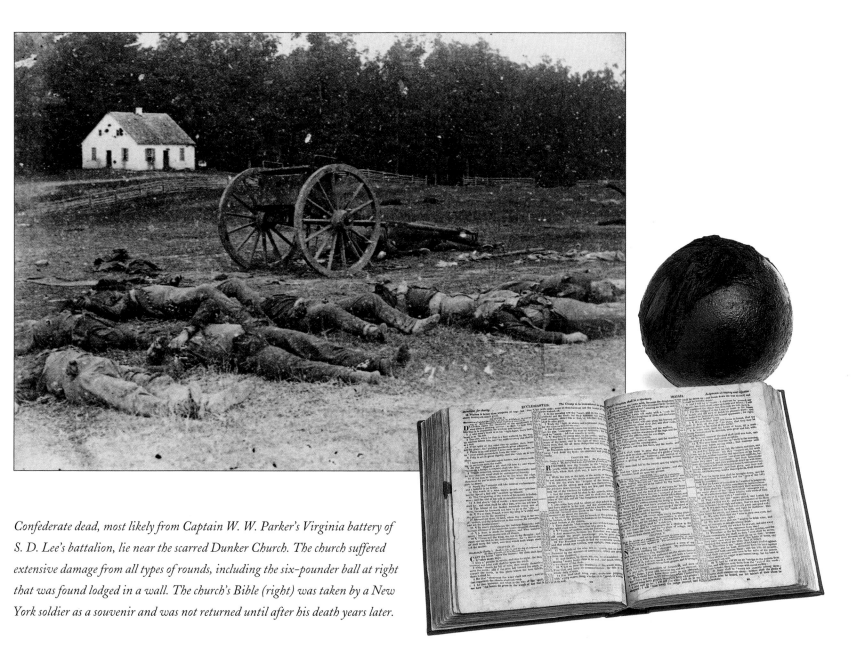

Confederate dead, most likely from Captain W. W. Parker's Virginia battery of S. D. Lee's battalion, lie near the scarred Dunker Church. The church suffered extensive damage from all types of rounds, including the six-pounder ball at right that was found lodged in a wall. The church's Bible (right) was taken by a New York soldier as a souvenir and was not returned until after his death years later.

the field, to wince and move as if to dodge the things slung at us. McRaven saw he was alive and started to run him through with his bayonet, saying he "would get one before they got us all.". . .

. . . So I said: "Bill, give him to me and let me handle him; he's my meat!" I sprang to the boy, in an instant jerked him to his feet with my left hand, doubly strengthened by fear of death from the battery, while the gunner was ramming home another charge, and held him between

me and the battery and retreated, exclaiming to McRaven and Jerry to get behind us and run for the rock fence at the edge of the woods in front of the Dunkard Church. The boy exclaimed: "Don't kill me! I belong to a Maryland regiment; my father is in the Southern Army!" I had my bayonet drawn on him to hold him in line between me and the battery. The gunner stood amazed, afraid to shoot for fear of killing the boy in blue. In this way we reached the rock fence. I was trying to do a difficult act in holding the boy between me and the battery and at the same time climb over the rock fence. He wiggled out of my grasp just in time to let the gunner give a pull with his lanyard. A howl of shot encompassed me. One ricochetted about twenty feet in front of me and bounded up against a roll around my body, consisting of the soldier's bed, an overcoat and blanket. This knocked me over the fence without consulting the order of my going, and my Yankee escaped never to be seen again—in the woods beyond the church. McRaven had also gotten away, which only left Jerry Webb near me, ensconced behind the fence. I felt stunned as if I were shot through, but it was only a bruise, no bones broken, which I soon discovered, after working my legs about the hip joint, preparatory to rising. I had Jerry to peep over the fence to see what the Yankees were doing, and he reported them slowly advancing—"But, sargint," said he, "they seem like they've about enough from the slow way the skirmishers are creeping up on us." I remember reading a Texas story, when a boy back in Mississippi, about an old hunter who was run in a cave by some Indians—"Prairie Flower" was the novel—and how he had the "tender-foot" to run out first and draw the fire and thus give him time to escape. This I tried on Jerry, and the good soul got up and dusted, dodging behind trees, and I followed suit after the fire had been pretty well exhausted at him. They did nothing more than bark the trees for Jerry and me, and I'll bet I can go there to-day and put my hand on those very trees, at the very spot in front of that old white church.

CORPORAL JOHN T. PARHAM
32D VIRGINIA INFANTRY, SEMMES' BRIGADE

Supported by Stuart's artillery, which kept pace with the hard-charging Confederate infantry, Semmes' brigade smashed into Gorman's Federals and drove them back to the North Woods. As Parham later recalled, the 32d Virginia "did its full duty on that terrible, bloody day," in routing Sedgwick from the West Woods.

After a hard march we reached the ford (Boteler's, just below Shepherdstown) at daybreak and crossed the Potomac, and marched up the river opposite Shepherdstown, halted, and two men from each company detailed to fill our canteens. At that time General Jackson rode up and directed General McLaws to strike McClellan about Dunkards' Church and drive him back. . . .

We went on at quick time until halted and ordered to unsling knapsacks and all baggage (except "war-bags," haversacks and canteens); and then on to the field at a double-quick through fields, woods, creeks, fences and most everything. . . . As we emerged from the piece of woods,

As he lay mortally wounded after Gordon's brigade futilely tried to help stem the Rebel onslaught, Lieutenant Colonel Wilder Dwight (far left) of the 2d Massachusetts pulled out a letter he had started earlier and added a few lines. "Dearest Mother," he scribbled, "I am wounded so as to be helpless. Good bye, if so it must be." Pictured with him is his brother William, who accompanied the body home for burial.

"I said to him it was a very dangerous place, so near the colors. He said, 'Yes, everywhere is dangerous here.'"

Colonel Montague gave command, "By company into line!" as we were marching by the flank; but the regiment came into line at one movement and started across that terrible, bloody field. Looking to my right, I witnessed one of the most magnificent sights that I ever saw, or ever expect to see again. It was Barksdale's men driving the enemy up into and through a piece of woods in their front. Their fire was so steady and severe that it looked like a whirlwind was passing through the leaves on the ground and woods. I remarked to Captain Coke, on my left, "to look; was not that the grandest sight he ever saw." He said, "Yes, John, it is grand; but look in our front, my boy, and see what we have to face."

At that time the field in our front was being literally plowed and torn up by shot, shell and minie balls. Colonel Montague gave command that captains take their positions in the centre and rear of their companies. Captain Coke said that he was going to stay by my side, on the right of his company. I said to him it was a very dangerous place, so near the colors. He said, "Yes, everywhere is dangerous here." In a few moments he was shot above the knee and fell. The ambulance corps took him off the field. . . .

On we went until we reached a rocky knoll about, I should judge, seventy-five or one hundred yards from a stone fence, which the enemy were behind, pouring a shower of minies at us. At that point our loss was terrible. The ranks were so scattered, and the dead and wounded so thick, it seemed as if we could go no further. Our rear rank was ten or more paces in our rear, and we were in danger of being shot by our own men. Our flag was shot through seventeen times, and the staff cut in two. I don't think our color-bearer, Bob Forrest, was hurt. I was slightly wounded in the wrist and foot, and it seemed to me that most everybody near the flag was either killed or wounded. Both of my jacket sleeves were bespotted with blood and brains of my comrades near me.

At about this time General Semmes came to our colors, and saw me still shooting away as fast as I could load, and asked where the enemy was located. I told him behind that fence in front. He said, "Yes, and they will kill the last one of us, and that we must charge them." He gave the command to charge. Bob Forrest went forward several paces in front and waited for the line of battle to come up, and Lieutenant

Henry St. Clair, of Company I, ran up to him and said, "Bob Forrest, why in the h——ll don't you go forward with the flag; if you won't go, give it to me," and started for it. Bob Forrest, as brave a man as ever lived, said to him, "You shan't have it; I will carry this flag as far as any man; bring your line up and we will all go up together." They did come up, and took the fence and drove the enemy up the hill.

LIEUTENANT JOSEPH A. MOORE
28TH PENNSYLVANIA INFANTRY, TYNDALE'S BRIGADE

While Sedgwick's men were being cut to pieces, Greene's division, including Tyndale's troops, repulsed attacks by both Kershaw's and Manning's Confederates and actually pushed forward into the West Woods. The Yankees held their position for some time, unaware of Sedgwick's defeat.

As we advanced towards the Dunkard Church a rebel shell struck our flag bearer under the arms and cut him in two. I barely escaped it, being first by his side. Another of the color guard picked up the flag and had not proceeded twenty steps till he was shot, and a third man grasped the old flag carrying it to the fort but was also shot as we advanced steadily driving the rebels back. The fourth color bearer stood bravely through the terrible hail of shell and musketry until we had moved well down the open field facing the Sharpsburg Pike and opposite the old Church. There is a woods extending along the Pike from the church towards Hagerstown—here the

After serving for barely a month, Private John Young Shitle (above) of the 48th North Carolina, Manning's brigade, was mortally wounded on September 17 and died three days later in captivity. He may have been hit during Manning's costly assaults on Greene's division, but family tradition holds that he was struck while reading a letter informing him of the death of his young daughter, Esther.

rebels made a desperate stand. Our whole division was much exposed on the open field. The men were ordered to lay down and the enemy unable to see us made a charge on our lines. Waiting until they had reached within fifty yards of us, our line sprang up and fired low and shot up their column most terribly. After they had fled, that is, such as were not disabled, we could plainly mark the line of their advance when they received our fire, by their dead and wounded laying in our front. After a half-hour's delay another attempt was made on our flank, but they were again driven back with great slaughter. Here the fourth color bearer had the calf of his leg shot away and he handed me the flag. I unfurled it and it was given by Major Pardee to my second sargeant, Robert E. Thompson who carried it successfully throughout the remainder of the battle. The enemy having been unsuccessful in dislodging us from their front and having been terribly punished, it now became our turn to advance, and charged on into the woods and held it. We passed close by the old church. The position in these woods was a bad one as neither on our right or left were we supported by any other troops but having advanced too far, were now in danger of being flanked and probably captured. . . . It was now about 1:30 P.M. My Company had taken into action sixty rounds of cartridge and was twice replenished with forty rounds afterwards, and still the ammunition was exhausted. One hundred and forty rounds of cartridge had been shot away by each man. . . . The orders had been given by Gen. Green, commanding the Division to fall back out of the woods to our former position; about three hundred yards to the rear, but Col. Tyndale held the 28th P.V. in the woods, while the rest of the Division retired. It was not long, however, before the rebels made their appearance on both our flanks, and in front, and opened fire on us. We fell back as rapidly as we could and narrowly escaped capture, and much slaughter. I was one of the last reaching the road, Hagerstown Pike, where the enemy had thrown rails from a fence torn down to build a defense against our approach. As I stepped on this rail pile over which I was retreating, my foot turned on a rail and I fell flat, as if shot. I heard my boys make the remark that Lt. Moore was killed. But unhurt I jumped up and followed after though twenty rods behind all the rest. As I ran up the ascending open field the rebel balls zipped thick and fast about me and struck the ground as rapidly as hail. Every step I expected to fall from the storm of bullets whistling thick around me. But I made the crest of the hill where to my surprise, I saw my brother Frank Moore, 1st Sergeant of Knapp's Battery—hammering at something about one of the guns of the Battery. The only one there, and it was unlimbered from the caison. No other of the Battery men were in sight. I hailed him "Frank, get out of this with all your might—don't you see the rebels coming yonder!" pointing down at the same time to the woods where they were coming in swarms. Frank immediately looked around ran for his gun, quickly aimed a charge of canister at them and then limbered up and drove away. Saving his piece of artillery. I did not wait to linger to see his course but bent rapidly after my regiment.

CAPTAIN NORWOOD P. HALLOWELL

20TH MASSACHUSETTS INFANTRY, DANA'S BRIGADE

With his left upper arm bone shattered by a bullet during the collapse of Sedgwick's division, Captain Hallowell made his way to the Nicodemus house, where many of the Federal wounded sought shelter. The Confederates swept past the house but soon returned when they were repulsed by a makeshift Federal defensive line in the North Woods.

Before long I gained the little farmhouse marked on the maps as the Nicodemus House. The yard was full of wounded men, and the floor of the parlor, where I lay down, was well covered with them. Among others, Captain O. W. Holmes, Jr., walked in, the back of his neck clipped by a bullet. The baggage train had not been up for many a day, so that I had replenished my wardrobe by appropriations of chance clothing from various sources. It so happened that I wore on that day the light blue trousers and dark blue blouse of a private soldier. When the rebels, a little later, were busy in the yard, paroling some and taking others to the rear, paying marked attention, of course, to officers, I was glad to have taken the precaution to remove my shoulder-straps and to conceal them with my sword under a blanket.

The first Confederate to make his appearance put his head through the window and said: "Yankees?" "Yes." "Wounded?" "Yes." "Would you like some water?" A wounded man always wants some water. He off with his canteen, threw it into the room, and then resumed his place in the skirmish line and his work of shooting retreating Yankees. In about fifteen minutes that good-hearted fellow came back to the window all out of breath, saying: "Hurry up there! Hand me my canteen! I am on the double-quick myself now!" Some one twirled the canteen to him, and away he went.

An Irishman in the yard, whose side had been scooped out by a shell, was asked by a rebel whether he could walk. He replied humorously: "Would I be here if I could? I'll just leave it to yourself." And then he died. For a while the farmhouse appeared to be midway between the opposing forces. Shells broke the window panes, and ploughed up the wounded in the yard, but not a shot went through the house.

Sixteen-year-old Walter M. Clark was the newly appointed adjutant of the 35th North Carolina of Ransom's brigade when he took part in the fight in the West Woods. So absorbed was the young lieutenant in the sights and sounds of the battle—his first—that it did not occur to him to dismount from his horse; a veteran of the regiment pulled him from the saddle just as a bullet grazed his hand.

CLARA BARTON
UNION NURSE

When war broke out, Barton left her job at the U.S. Patent Office to head her own relief agency, which in 1881 would become the American Red Cross. Having followed the Union army to Antietam, Barton was a great help to the surgeons on the field and an invaluable comfort to the wounded Union soldiers. When one surgeon laid eyes on her, he exclaimed, "God has indeed remembered us."

We were in a slight hollow and all shell which did not break among our guns, in front, came directly among or over us—bursting above our heads or burying themselves in the hills beyond.

A man lying upon the ground asked for drink—I stooped to give it, and having raised him with my right hand, was holding the cup to his lips with my left, when I felt a sudden twich of the loose sleeve of my dress the poor fellow sprang from my hands and fell back quivering, in the agonies of death—A ball had passed between my body—and the right arm which supported him—cutting through the sleeve, and passing through his chest from shoulder to shoulder.

There was no more to be done for him and I left him to his rest—I have never mended that hole in my sleeve—

I wonder if a soldier ever does mend a bullet hole in his coat?

The patient endurance of those men—was most astonishing as many as could be were carried into the barn, as a slight protection against random shot—just outside the door lay a man wounded in the face—the ball having entered the lower maxillary on the left side, and lodged among the bones of the right cheek—his imploring look drew me to him—when placing his fingers upon the sharp protrubrance, he said Lady will you tell me what this is that burns so—I replied that it must be the ball which had been too far spent to cut its way entirely through—

It is terribly painful he said won't you take it out? I said I would go to the tables for a surgeon "No! No!" he said, catching my dress—"they cannot come to me, I must wait my turn for this is a little wound." You can get the ball, there is a knife in my pocket—please take the ball out for me.

This was a new call—I had never severed the nerves and fibers of human flesh—and I said I could not hurt him so much—he looked up, with as nearly a smile as such a mangled face could assume saying—"You cannot hurt me dear lady—I can endure any pain that your hands can create—please do it,—t'will relieve me so much."

I could not withstand his entreaty—and opening the best blade of my pocket knife—prepared for the operation—Just at his head lay a stalwart orderly sergeant from Illinios—with a face beaming with intelligence and kindness—and who had a bullet directly through the fleshy part of both thighs—he had been watching the scene with great interest and when he saw me commence to raise the poor fellow's head, and no one to support it, with a desperate effort he succeeded in raising himself to a sitting posture—exclaiming as he did so, "I will help do that"—and shoving himself along upon the ground he took the wounded head in his hands and held it while I extracted the ball and washed and bandaged the face.

I do not think a surgeon would have pronounced it a scientific operation, but that it was successful I dared to hope from the gratitude of the patient.

I assisted the sergeant to lie down again—brave and cheerful as he had risen, and passed on to others.

Returning in half an hour I found him weeping—the great tears rolling silently down his manly cheeks—I thought his effort had been too great for his strength—and expressed my fears—"Oh! No! No! Madam," he replied—"It is not for myself I am very well—but—pointing to another just brought in, he said, "This is my comrade and he tells me that our regiment is all cut to pieces—that my captain was the last officer left—and he is dead."

Oh! God—what a costly war—This man could laugh at pain face death without a tremor, and yet weep like a child over the loss of his comrades and his captain.

FRANK LESLIE'S ILLUSTRATED NEWSPAPER.

73

Oct. 25, 1862.]

WOMEN AND CHILDREN OF SHARPSBURG TAKING REFUGE IN THE CELLAR OF THE KRETZER MANSION IN THAT TOWN, DURING THE BATTLE OF ANTIETAM—BURSTING OF A SHELL IN THE WINDOW OF THE CELLAR.
SKETCHED BY OUR SPECIAL ARTIST, MR. F. H. SCHELL.

In this engraving from Leslie's Illustrated, Sharpsburg residents seeking refuge in the cellar of the Kretzer home press together as a shell explodes in a window. As the fighting on the battlefield shifted southward through the day, the number of errant rounds landing in the town increased to a virtual barrage.

"From sheer exhaustion, both sides, like battered and bleeding athletes, seemed willing to rest."

The well-worn farm lane known as the Sunken Road, shown above in a post-battle photograph, served as a natural trench for D. H. Hill's men during their vicious contest with two divisions of the Federal II Corps. The sketch (right), keyed by the artist Edwin Forbes, gives a panoramic view of the battlefield from the high ground east of Antietam Creek. Rendered around midmorning, the sketch shows Sumner's men (#8) advancing on the Confederate position in the Sunken Road (#9). Also depicted are the Philip Pry house (#1), the Dunker Church (#5), the West Woods (#6), and as indicated by #3, "the town of Sharpsburg behind the hill."

COLONEL
JOHN B. GORDON
6TH ALABAMA INFANTRY,
RODES' BRIGADE

*After proving their mettle during
the Seven Days' Battles and at
South Mountain, Gordon and the
rest of Rodes' Alabama brigade
would face perhaps their greatest
test in the Sunken Road. Few
of the brigade's officers, including
Gordon, would pass through the
day unscathed.*

Up to this hour not a shot had been fired in my front. There was an ominous lull on the left. From sheer exhaustion, both sides, like battered and bleeding athletes, seemed willing to rest. General Lee took advantage of the respite and rode along his lines on the right and centre. He was accompanied by Division Commander General D. H. Hill. With that wonderful power which he possessed of divining the plans and purposes of his antagonist, General Lee had decided that the Union commander's next heavy blow would fall upon our centre, and those of us who held that important position were notified of this conclusion. We were cautioned to be prepared for a determined assault and urged to hold that centre at any sacrifice, as a break at that point would endanger his entire army. My troops held the most advanced position on this part of the field, and there was no supporting line behind us. It was evident, therefore, that my small force was to receive the first impact of the expected charge and to be subjected to

the deadliest fire. To comfort General Lee and General Hill, and especially to make, if possible, my men still more resolute of purpose, I called aloud to these officers as they rode away: "These men are going to stay here, General, till the sun goes down or victory is won." Alas! many of the brave fellows are there now.

General Lee had scarcely reached his left before the predicted assault came. The day was clear and beautiful, with scarcely a cloud in the sky. The men in blue filed down the opposite slope, crossed the little stream (Antietam), and formed in my front, an assaulting column four lines deep. The front line came to a "charge bayonets," the other lines to a "right shoulder shift." The brave Union commander, superbly mounted, placed himself in front, while his band in rear cheered them with martial music. It was a thrilling spectacle. The entire force, I concluded, was composed of fresh troops from Washington or some camp of instruction. So far as I could see, every soldier wore white gaiters around his ankles. The banners above them had apparently never been discolored by the smoke and dust of battle. Their gleaming bayonets flashed like burnished silver in the sunlight. With the precision of step and perfect alignment of a holiday parade, this magnificent array moved to the charge, every step keeping time to the tap of the deep-sounding drum. As we stood looking upon that brilliant pageant, I thought, if I did not say, "What a pity to spoil with bullets such a scene of martial beauty!" But there was nothing else to do. Mars is not an aesthetic god; and he was directing every part of this game in which giants were the contestants. . . .

. . . My first impulse was to open fire upon the compact mass as soon as it came within reach of my rifles, and to pour into its front an incessant hail-storm of bullets during its entire advance across the broad, open plain; but after a moment's reflection that plan was also discarded. . . . The only remaining plan was one which I had never tried but in the efficacy of which I had the utmost faith. It was to hold my fire until the advancing Federals were almost upon my lines, and then turn loose a sheet of flame and lead into their faces. I did not believe that any troops on earth, with empty guns in their hands, could withstand so sudden a shock and withering a fire. The programme was fixed in my own mind, all horses were sent to the rear, and my men were at once directed to lie down upon the grass and clover. They were quickly made to understand, through my aides and line officers, that the Federals were coming upon them with unloaded guns; that not a shot would be fired at them, and that not one of our rifles was to be discharged until my voice should be heard from the centre commanding "Fire!". . .

There was no artillery at this point upon either side, and not a rifle was discharged. The stillness was literally oppressive, as in close order, with the commander still riding in front, this column of Union infantry moved majestically in the charge. In a few minutes they were within easy range of our rifles, and some of my impatient men asked permission to fire. "Not yet," I replied. "Wait for the order." Soon they were so close that we might have seen the eagles on their buttons; but my brave and eager boys still waited for the order. Now the front rank was within a few rods of where I stood. It would not do to wait another second, and with all my lung power I shouted "Fire!"

My rifles flamed and roared in the Federals' faces like a blinding blaze of lightning accompanied by the quick and deadly thunderbolt. The effect was appalling. The entire front line, with few exceptions, went down in the consuming blast. The gallant commander and his horse fell in a heap near where I stood—the horse dead, the rider unhurt. Before his rear lines could recover from the terrific shock, my exultant men were on their feet, devouring them with successive volleys.

PRIVATE J. POLK RACINE
5TH MARYLAND (U.S.) INFANTRY, WEBER'S BRIGADE

The three regiments of Weber's brigade—the 5th Maryland, 1st Delaware, and 4th New York—were the first to attack Rodes' and G. B. Anderson's men in the Sunken Road. With bayonets fixed, they advanced to within 80 yards of the road before a Rebel volley cut them down "like grain before a reaper," according to one of Anderson's men. In about five minutes, Weber's brigade lost more than 450 men.

When we came to that beautiful corn field, boys, that was when the trouble began; and just as we crossed that wormfence, which divided the corn and clover fields, oh, but the bullets did fly! I didn't see them, but saw the effects. Men were falling all around us. Our bugler was standing near me, when a cannon-ball struck him in the head and cut it from his shoulders. I think I got some of the blood and brains in my face; I always imagined so. I saw poor Amor Dunbar, standing looking at some horses and cattle that were pasturing in that clover field. It was the last I ever saw of him. He must have been killed there, for no one has ever heard from him since. Just in the middle of the clover field, I saw a mare and colt, two or three cattle, and some sheep, pasturing. They were between two fires—that is, getting our bullets and the enemy's. I saw the old mare stagger and fall, then all but the little colt fell at the first fire. After that we could not see, for the smoke from the burnt powder was so dense that we could see only at close range. But in 15 minutes after the fighting commenced, that little colt ran down our line, apparently unhurt. The most remarkable part of it was, that the next day we found the little thing half a mile down the line. It was full of bullets.

A West Point graduate and Regular Army officer, Confederate general George B. Anderson earned a reputation as a bold yet amiable commander during the fighting around Richmond in May and June 1862. While urging on his men from just behind the Sunken Road, he was hit in the ankle. Anderson returned home to convalesce, but the wound turned septic. Despite the amputation of his leg, he died on October 16, just a day before the birth of his daughter.

LIEUTENANT CHARLES B. TANNER

1st Delaware Infantry, Weber's Brigade

Lieutenant Tanner was wounded three times in a desperate but successful attempt to retrieve the 1st Delaware's regimental colors, dropped when the color guard was mowed down in front of the Sunken Road. Tanner's hard-hit regiment was also fired on by greenhorns in Morris' brigade coming up from the rear.

Our colonel dashed in front with the ringing order: "Charge!" and charge we did into that leaden hail. Within less than five minutes 286 men out of 635, and eight of ten company commanders, lay wounded or dead on that bloody slope. The colonel's horse had been struck by four bullets; the lieutenant-colonel was wounded and his horse killed, and our dearly loved colors were lying within twenty yards of the frowning lines of muskets, surrounded by the lifeless bodies of nine heroes, who died while trying to plant them in that road of death.

Those of us who were yet living got back to the edge of the cornfield, and opened such a fire, that, though the enemy charged five times to gain possession of the flag, they were driven back each time with terrible slaughter. . . .

Charge after charge was made, and the gallant Fifth Maryland, forming on our left, aided in the defense. The fire from our lines directed to the center of that dense mass of Confederates, was appalling. Over thirteen hundred noble dead were covered with earth in that sunken road by the burying party on the following day.

When the Maryland boys joined us, Captain Rickets, of Company C, our regiment, called for volunteers to save the colors, and more than thirty brave fellows responded. It seemed as if they had but just started, when at least twenty, including the gallant leader, were killed and those who would have rushed forward, were forced back by the withering fire.

Maddened, and more desperate than ever, I called for the men to make another effort, and before we marched fifty yards only a scattering few remained able to get back to the friendly corn, in which we sought refuge from the tempest of death. . . .

While covering that short distance, it seemed as if a million bees were singing in the air. The shouts and yells from either side sounded like menaces and threats. But I had reached the goal, had caught up the staff which was already splintered by shot, and the colors pierced with many a hole, and stained here and there with the lifeblood of our comrades, when a bullet shattered my arm. Luckily my legs were still serviceable, and, seizing the precious bunting with my left hand, I made the best eighty-yard time on record, receiving two more wounds.

The colors were landed safely among the men of our regiment just as a large body of Confederate infantry poured in on our flank, compelling us to face in a different direction. We had the flags, however, and the remainder of the First Delaware held them against all comers.

The battered national colors of the 1st Delaware (above) had been presented to the regiment "by the ladies of Wilmington" in 1861. Unusual in that it had only 31 stars—most flags had at least 34—the flag was apparently carried through the rest of the war. The flag's rescuer at Antietam, Lieutenant Tanner, resigned in September 1863 because of lingering trouble with his wounds, but he later signed up with a Pennsylvania unit. For his actions at Antietam Tanner would eventually receive the Medal of Honor.

COLONEL JOHN B. GORDON
6TH ALABAMA INFANTRY, RODES' BRIGADE

Already famous for his ability to evade Federal bullets, Colonel Gordon saw his legend grow as he miraculously survived five wounds at the Sunken Road. Following his return in March 1863 he saw further distinguished service as a general, and after the war served Georgia as a U.S. senator and as governor.

My extraordinary escapes from wounds in all the previous battles had made a deep impression upon my comrades as well as upon my own mind. So many had fallen at my side, so often had balls and shells pierced and torn my clothing, grazing my body without drawing a drop of blood, that a sort of blind faith possessed my men that I was not to be killed in battle. This belief was evidenced by their constantly repeated expressions: "They can't hurt him." "He's as safe one place as another." "He's got a charmed life."

If I had allowed these expressions of my men to have any effect upon my mind the impression was quickly dissipated when the Sharpsburg storm came and the whizzing Miniés, one after another, began to pierce my body.

The first volley from the Union lines in my front sent a ball through the brain of the chivalric Colonel Tew, of North Carolina, to whom I was talking, and another ball through the calf of my right leg. On the right and the left my men were falling under the death-dealing crossfire like trees in a hurricane. . . . Both sides stood in the open at short range and without the semblance of breastworks, and the firing was doing a deadly work. Higher up in the same leg I was again shot; but still no bone was broken. I was able to walk along the line and give encouragement to my resolute riflemen, who were firing with the coolness and steadiness of peace soldiers in target practice. When later in the day the third ball pierced my left arm, tearing asunder the tendons and mangling the flesh, they caught sight of the blood running down my fingers, and these devoted and big-hearted men, while still loading their guns, pleaded with me to leave them and go to the rear, pledging me that they would stay there and fight to the last. I could not consent to leave them in such a crisis. . . .

A fourth ball ripped through my shoulder, leaving its base and a wad of clothing in its track. I could still stand and walk, although the shocks and loss of blood had left but little of my normal strength. . . . I thought I saw some wavering in my line, near the extreme right, and Private

"The first volley from the Union lines in my front sent a ball through the brain of the chivalric Colonel Tew, of North Carolina, to whom I was talking."

Only minutes after he replaced the wounded General Anderson as brigade commander, Colonel Charles C. Tew (above) of the 2d North Carolina was cut down by enemy fire. At right, lying strewn across the Sunken Road are the dead of the 2d North Carolina; the body leaning against the bank at lower right is probably that of Tew.

Vickers, of Alabama, volunteered to carry any orders I might wish to send. I directed him to go quickly and remind the men of the pledge to General Lee, and to say to them that I was still on the field and intended to stay there. He bounded away like an Olympic racer; but he had gone less than fifty yards when he fell, instantly killed by a ball through his head. I then attempted to go myself, although I was bloody and faint, and my legs did not bear me steadily. I had gone but a short distance when I was shot down by a fifth ball, which struck me squarely in the face, and passed out, barely missing the jugular vein. I fell forward and lay unconscious with my face in my cap; and it would seem that I might have been smothered by the blood running into my cap from this last wound but for the act of some Yankee, who, as if to save my life, had at a previous hour during the battle, shot a hole through the cap, which let the blood out.

SERGEANT THOMAS F. GALWEY
8TH OHIO INFANTRY, KIMBALL'S BRIGADE

As members of the only veteran regiments in the division, Galwey and some others in Kimball's brigade were quick to pass off the Confederate repulse of Weber's and Morris' less-experienced commands to a lack of nerve. But when Kimball's men came within range, they too were slaughtered and driven back, leaving French's division with little else to do but take cover and return the fire.

Forward we go over fences and through an apple orchard. Now we are close to the enemy. They rise up in the sunken lane and pour a deadly fire into us. Our men drop in every few files. The ground on which we are charging has no depression, no shelter of any kind. There is nothing to do but to advance or break into a rout. We know there is no support behind us on this side of the creek. So we go forward on the run, heads downward as if under a pelting rain.

About fifty yards on this side of the enemy's improvised trench in the sunken road is a slight elevation. Here we halt. The ground is covered with a soft turf speckled with white clover. . . . This ridge is a cornfield, and just back of it we can see the tops of the trees of an orchard. Line after line of the enemy's troops are advancing along the ridge, through the corn. They come up opposite us and sink out of sight in the sunken lane. It is a mystery that so many men could crowd into so small a space.

In the meantime the work of death and destruction goes on. Two Irishmen are carrying the colors of our regiment today. Sergeant Conlon has the battle flag and Corporal Ready the National Colors. By some miracle these two men, whose bravery is conspicuous, escape all injury. But our men are falling by the hundreds. Our brave Orderly Sergeant, Fairchild, sticks doggedly to his position, his face streaming blood. Jack Sheppard, my old mess-mate, jovial companion, and favorite with everyone, drops. He is shot in a dozen places. He never even groaned! Poor boy! This morning he boastingly said that the bullet was not yet struck that was to kill him! . . .

The fight goes on with unabated fury. The air is alive with the concussion of all sorts of explosions. We are kneeling in the soft grass and I notice for a long time that almost every blade of grass is moving. For some time I supposed that this is caused by the merry crickets; and it is not until I have made a remark to that effect to one of our boys near me and notice him laugh, that I know it is the bullets that are falling thickly around us! It is wonderful how a man can live through such close

danger. I have made up my mind that I shall not, cannot, escape. . . .

Our men are falling fast. General Kimball passes, muttering, "God save my poor boys." Well ought he to pray God in such a moment.

The din is frightful. Alas, no words can depict the horrors of a great battle as they appear to men unaccustomed to them. We had seen a great deal of service before now; but our fighting had been mostly of the desultory, skirmishing sort. What we see now looks to us like systematic killing.

Lieutenant Delaney is shot in the bowels, so some one says. Lieutenant Lantry, poor fellow, is annihilated instantly, near me. The top of his head is taken off by a shell. Our company is narrowing more and more. There is but a small group of us left. Fairchild is bleeding; Campion falls, mortally wounded; Jim Gallagher's head is badly grazed and he rolls, coiled up in a lump, down into a ditch. We thought he was killed, but his brother Charley comes up to us with a bound and a yell, and tells us that Jim's wound is not serious. He has just helped him off.

The Confederate battery at the Dunkard Meeting House is dealing destruction amongst us. They enfilade us with their fire and it seems as though nothing could live through it. The enemy continues to reinforce his line in the sunken lane. Our ammunition is running low. The order is passed along the line for us to charge. There are no bugles to sound it, but we look at one another and, fixing our bayonets, we raise a cheer and go forward.

CAPTAIN EDWIN A. OSBORNE
4TH NORTH CAROLINA INFANTRY, G. B. ANDERSON'S BRIGADE

The road and piled fence, while providing some cover, was hardly a perfect earthwork, and casualties among the Confederates steadily mounted. Reinforcements from Richard H. Anderson's division were brought forward, but their deployment was poorly handled and little but confusion resulted. Osborne, here writing in the third person, took his second wound of the war. He was later captured after being left behind at Shepherdstown.

About nine o'clock the enemy's line of battle appeared, moving in magnificent style, with mounted officers in full uniform, swords gleaming, banners, plumes and sashes waving, and bayonets glistening in the sun. On they came with steady tramp and confident mien. They did not see our single line of hungry shelter from some murderous assault, or securing a more commanding position. Soon Captain Marsh was mortally wounded and borne from the field. The command of the regiment then devolved upon Captain Osborne, who in turn was wounded and borne from the field. One by one the other company officers fell, either killed or wounded, until Second Lieutenant Weaver, of Company H, was in command of the handful of men who were left, and then he was killed bearing the colors of the regiment in his hand. The regiment was left without a commissioned officer; but the men needed none, except for general purposes. There were not more than one hundred and fifty men for duty, every one of whom seemed to realize his own value, and to act with that cool and determined courage which showed that he understood the emergency, and was determined to do his best. All day long the battle raged with almost unabated fury and with varying results, sometimes one side gaining the advantage and then the other.

Second Lieutenant Franklin Weaver of the 4th North Carolina, shown at left (above) with two unidentified comrades, was mortally wounded in the Sunken Road. The North Carolina-made sword (below)—found on the battlefield—has "CSA" worked into the guard and was popular with officers from that state.

jaded and dusty men, who were lying down, until within good musket shot, when we rose and delivered our fire with terrible effect. Instantly the air was filled with the cries of wounded and dying and the shouts of brave officers, trying to hold and encourage their men, who recoiled at the awful and stunning shock so unexpectedly received. Soon they rallied and advanced again; this time more cautiously than before. Our men held their fire until they were within good range again, and again they rose to their feet and mowed them down, so that they were compelled to retire a second time; but they rallied and came again, and the battle now became general all along the line. The roar of musketry was incessant and the booming of cannon almost without intermission. Occasionally the shouts of men could be heard above the awful din, indicating a charge or some advantage gained by one side or the other. Horses without riders were rushing across the field, occasionally a section of artillery could be seen flying from one point to another, seeking

SERGEANT CHARLES A. FULLER
61ST NEW YORK INFANTRY, CALDWELL'S BRIGADE

Sergeant Fuller gave full credit for driving the Rebels from the Sunken Road to Colonel Francis Barlow of the 61st New York, who took over for Brigadier John Caldwell when the general was reported to be hiding behind a haystack in the rear. Promoted to lieutenant in January 1863, Fuller was wounded at Gettysburg and discharged.

As we got a view of the situation it was seen that the rebels were in a sunken road, having sides about four feet in height; this formed for them a natural barricade. Barlow, with the eye of a military genius (which he was) at once solved the problem. Instead of halting his men where Meagher had, he rushed forward half the distance to the rebel line, halted and at once opened fire. We were so near to the enemy, that, when they showed their heads to fire, they were liable to be

knocked over. It did not take them long to discover this, and for the most part, they hugged the hither bank of this sunken road. Barlow discovered that by moving his men to the left and a little forward he could rake the position of the Confederates. This he did, and our firing was resumed with vigor. The result was terrible to the enemy. They could do us little harm, and we were shooting them like sheep in a pen. If a bullet missed the mark at the first it was liable to strike the further bank, and angle back, and take them secondarily, so to speak. In a few minutes white rags were hoisted along the rebel line. The officers ordered "cease firing," but the men were slow of hearing, and it was necessary for the officers to get in front of the men and throw up their guns.

Finally the firing ceased, then Barlow ordered the men forward. They advanced on a run, and when they came to the bank of the sunken road, they jumped the rebels to the rear. Those able to move were glad to get out of this pit of destruction. Over three hundred were taken, who were able to march to the rear.

The dead and wounded were a horrible sight to behold. This sunken road, named by some writers "The Bloody Lane," was a good many rods long, and, for most of the way, there were enough dead and badly wounded to touch one another as they lay side by side. As we found them in some cases, they were two and three deep. Perhaps a wounded man at the bottom, and a corpse or two piled over him. We at once took hold and straightened out matters the best we could, and made our foes as comfortable as the means at hand afforded—that is, we laid them so that they were only one deep, and we gave them drink from our canteens.

Sometime during the battle, Private George B. Worden of the 64th New York lost his identification tag (right). Worden, who was wounded in the head, had a far more elaborate tag than the typical one—a piece of torn paper with a hastily scribbled name pinned to the uniform.

LIEUTENANT WILLIAM W. CHAMBERLAINE
6TH VIRGINIA INFANTRY, PARHAM'S BRIGADE

Caught in the chaos after the collapse in the Sunken Road, Chamberlaine joined up with the scratch artillery force thrown together by a desperate Longstreet. Perhaps prompted by his experience at Antietam, Chamberlaine later transferred to the artillery.

"A Federal soldier turned around and fired deliberately at me, and his ball struck the ground near my feet."

There was a confused crowd at that place, opposite to the entrance to Piper's Lane, but the efforts of the officers succeeded in forming a line along the eastern side of the Turnpike; different commands were mixed. I did not recognize there any of the 6th Virginia. Looking down the Turnpike I saw a gun standing on one side. There was no soldier with it and but one horse hitched to the limber and wounded besides. I requested the assistance of four Infantry soldiers near me, and we drew the gun to the entrance of Piper's Lane and loaded it. The enemy's skirmishers were crossing the lane near Piper's dwelling. Just at that moment Major Fairfax, of General Longstreet's staff, stopped there and dismounted. I asked him if we should fire. He said yes and I handed the lanyard to him. He pulled it and the shell went bounding down the lane by Piper's house. He mounted and rode away. Then some voices were heard saying, "Over here is the place for that gun" and several more Infantry soldiers came and the gun was drawn to the top of the next rise in the Turnpike about fifty yards. From that point could be seen the Dunker Church, and in the field in front of it were lines of the Federals advancing towards the Church. Quite a number participated in getting the gun in position and aiming it at the advancing lines. . . . It was none too soon, for the enemy soon appeared advancing towards our position. A Regiment or small Brigade of Confederates had been advanced from the Turnpike and stationed about one hundred feet east of the same under a slight rise in the ground and some outcropping rock, and their battle flag was waved; that movement, and the appearance of the flag encouraged the rallied men; before that some appeared to be demoralized. Between the orchard and the sunken road was a corn field, the stalks being from four to six feet in height. The enemy's line appeared advancing through the corn about three hundred yards from the Turnpike. The gun was then in just the right position to oppose their line; three shots were fired and struck them where their colors were visible. Their line halted and fell back and was hidden by the corn. In a few moments they appeared again. Three more shots were fired with the same precision; again the line disappeared. Then it advanced the third time, and again it received three more shots equally as true. As the line retired the third time, a Federal soldier turned around and fired deliberately at me, and his ball struck the ground near my feet.

The frock coat at left belonged to Captain Cary F. Grimes of the Portsmouth (Virginia) Light Artillery, who commanded R. H. Anderson's divisional batteries at Antietam. Shortly after Grimes had brought up his guns to pound the Federals advancing across the Piper farm, he was knocked from his horse by a bullet in his thigh. While being carried to the rear he was struck again and killed.

LIEUTENANT WILLIAM M. OWEN
WASHINGTON (LOUISIANA) ARTILLERY

With the Rebel infantry shot up and scattered, it was cannon fire—in particular that of the Washington Artillery battery of Captain M. B. Miller—that played a vital role in staving off the II Corps breakthrough. As the men of Miller's gun crews fell one by one, General Longstreet, wearing a bedroom slipper on a sorely blistered foot, ordered his staff to fill in. "We were already badly whipped," wrote Longstreet, "and were only holding our ground by sheer force of desperation."

The enemy crossed the old road, which we had occupied in the morning, and took position in a cornfield and orchard in advance of it. They had now got within a few hundred yards of the hill which commanded Sharpsburg and our rear. Affairs looked very critical. Longstreet, who had ridden rapidly to the centre, saw at once the condition of affairs, and sent for a battery. The Third company Washington Artillery, Capt. Miller, was ordered to him. As Miller went into position a well-directed shot of the enemy's battery exploded one of his caissons; he immediately unlimbered and opened upon the enemy, who was advancing in force. . . .

As the situation grew more desperate for the Confederates, Surgeon William S. Parran of Lawton's divisional artillery pitched in to help man Miller's battery. Though his efforts helped reestablish the Rebel defense, he was killed by enemy fire.

Miller suffered considerably under the fire of the Federals, losing two of his gunners, and several cannoneers were wounded. . . .

. . . Miller played upon their ranks with cannister. Lieut. Hero was wounded, and Lieut. McElroy having been sent to watch the enemy's movements on the right, Capt. Miller found himself the only officer with his battery. With only men enough left to work a section, he opened upon the enemy with two guns with fine effect, and placed the remaining section under Sergt. Ellis, directing him to take it completely under cover. He then continued the action until his ammunition was nearly exhausted, when Sergt. Ellis brought up the remaining caissons. . . .

When Miller became short-handed, by reason of his loss of cannoneers, the staff officers of Gen. Longstreet, Majors Sorrel, Fairfax, and Thomas Walton, dismounted from their horses and helped work

the guns. Sorrel and Walton were wounded, and the horse of Fairfax was killed. Gen. Longstreet directed the fire of the guns in person, and by example animated the soldiers near him. One line of the enemy's infantry came so near us, that we could see their colonel on horseback waving his men on, and then even the stripes on the corporal's arms. How it made our blood dance and nerves quiver as we saw their colors floating steadily forward, and how heroically and madly we toiled at our guns! Our men worked that day desperately, almost despairingly, because it looked for a time as if we could not stop the blue wave from coming forward, although we were tearing it to pieces with canister and shell. Longstreet was on horseback at our side, sitting side-saddle fashion, and occasionally making some practical remark about the situation. He talked earnestly and gesticulated to encourage us, as the men of the

Later in the day, after the fighting had largely died down, Colonel William Irwin, commanding a VI Corps brigade, ordered the 7th Maine to clear out Rebel sharpshooters on the Piper farm. Shown here in another painting by James Hope, the regiment marches over the corpse-filled Sunken Road into the Piper cornfield, where a deadly cross fire cut down nearly 100 Maine men.

detachments began to fall around our guns, and told us he would have given us a lift if he had not that day crippled his hand. But, crippled or not, we noticed that he had strength enough left to carry his flask to his mouth, as probably everybody else did on that terribly hot day, who had any supplies at command to bring to a carry.

Federal IX Corps Attack: Burnside Bridge

Still feeding his army into the battle piecemeal, McClellan about 10:00 a.m. belatedly ordered Major General Ambrose Burnside's IX Corps to cross Antietam Creek and attack the Confederate right flank. Burnside, thinking he faced a large enemy force, moved cautiously as well. But finally he ordered Brigadier General George Crook's brigade to march toward the handsome stone span crossing the creek below Sharpsburg—known ever after as the Burnside Bridge—and also dispatched Brigadier General Isaac Rodman's division to ford the creek a couple of miles downstream.

The Confederate right was, in fact, held by only five brigades of Brigadier General David R. Jones' division, four of them deployed on ridges south and east of Sharpsburg. Guarding the bridge and its vicinity were three regiments of Georgians and a company of South Carolinians—perhaps 550 men in all—led by Brigadier General Robert A. Toombs.

The Georgians, however, occupied ideal terrain—a steep wooded bluff 100 feet high that loomed over the bridge and the road leading to it on the creek's east bank. The slope was crossed by a stone wall and strewn with boulders that provided Toombs' men with near-perfect rifle pits from which to pick off the enemy attackers.

The initial Federal assaults were fiascos. The men of the 11th Connecticut, deployed as skirmishers for Crook, tried first to gain a foothold on the 125-foot-long bridge. The regiment was quickly thrown back by Rebel fire, losing 139 men—a third of the unit. Then Crook, who had unaccountably failed to scout the terrain, led his brigade of three Ohio regiments blundering into a wood. The troops ended up a quarter mile north of the bridge. Next came James Nagle's brigade from Brigadier General Samuel Sturgis' division. Nagle's attack fell apart when two of his regiments, marching along the road paralleling the creek, were shot to pieces by Toombs' riflemen.

Finally, well past noon, Burnside ordered still another attack by Sturgis' other brigades led by Brigadier General Edward Ferrero. Nearing the bridge, the men of the 51st New York and 51st Pennsylvania ran into such withering fire that they ducked for what cover they could find. At last a handful of Pennsylvanians dashed onto the narrow span—and in a rush the men of both regiments followed.

Firing a few final volleys, Toombs' Georgians ran for the rear—as they had been ordered to do. They were almost out of ammunition and Toombs also knew that Rodman's Federal division, crossing at Snavely's Ford downstream, would soon fall on his flank and rear. Skedaddling fast, the Georgians retreated to positions on another rise a half-mile back. They had done their job, stalling the Federals for three hours.

The bridge secured, the rest of Sturgis' battered division rushed across and soon linked up on the left with Rodman's division and on the right with General Crook's troops, who had discovered a ford 250 yards above the bridge. One strong, swift push, it seemed, would sweep away the Confederate right and possibly destroy Lee's entire army.

But trouble soon developed as General Sturgis, complaining that his troops were low on ammunition and too weary to go on, pulled his division back. As a replacement, Brigadier General Orlando B. Willcox's brigades headed for the front. But with Willcox in reserve a mile east of the creek, more time was lost as his men struggled across the traffic-clogged bridge.

At long last, about 3:00 p.m., the Federals lurched forward, 8,000 men backed by 22 cannon for close support on a front three-quarters of a mile wide. As they came on, one Confederate officer wrote, "the earth seemed to tremble beneath their tread."

Willcox's brigades on the Union right advanced astride the road leading to Sharpsburg. Although harassed by Confederate skirmishers hidden behind haystacks and fences, and hit by blasts from batteries Lee had gathered during the Federal delay, the Federals pushed Joseph Walker's South Carolina brigade back to the outskirts of the town. On the Federal left, Rodman's division, with Colonel Harrison Fairchild's brigade in the lead, charged over a series of ridges and, despite heavy losses from more Confederate batteries, drove back James Kemper's and Thomas Drayton's brigades after a vicious exchange of volleys.

But as the Federals neared Sharpsburg and tried to cut Lee's line of retreat, they were attacked suddenly on the left flank by brigades from the veteran division of Major General A. P. Hill that had just arrived from Harpers Ferry. Hill, alerted by Lee at 6:30 that morning, had marched his men northward at a furious pace, covering 17 miles in less than eight hours. Almost without pausing he threw his 3,000 men into the battle.

Brigadier General Maxcy Gregg's brigade attacked first, hitting Colonel Edward Harland's troops on the Federal far left and throwing back two green Federal regiments with heavy losses. Soon two more of Hill's brigades attacked, punching another hole in the Union line.

With the Federal left broken in a matter of minutes, Brigadier General Jacob Cox—commanding for Burnside on the battlefield—ordered a general withdrawal to the west bank of Antietam Creek. By 5:30 the battle had ended, McClellan refusing to commit reserves that, Longstreet later said, could have "taken Lee's army and everything in it."

The next day, September 18, McClellan failed to attack again or even press his foe, although he could have called on two more fresh divisions just arrived from the rear. Lee for his part called for a truce to bury the dead, then gathered his battered army and retreated to safety across the Potomac at the nearest ford. What might have been a crushing Union triumph—and was certainly the bloodiest one-day clash in American history, with total casualties of 22,717—ended inconclusively in a draw. But Lee's great invasion of the North had been stopped.

Although ordered to attack across the Lower Bridge in midmorning, it was 1:00 p.m. before Burnside's IX Corps was able to drive off the Rebel defenders and get across the span. Resuming the advance, the Federals drove D. R. Jones' Rebel division back toward Sharpsburg. Just as Union elements approached the outskirts of the town, they were struck hard in the flank by A. P. Hill's division, which had just arrived from Harpers Ferry—in time to turn back the last Federal advance.

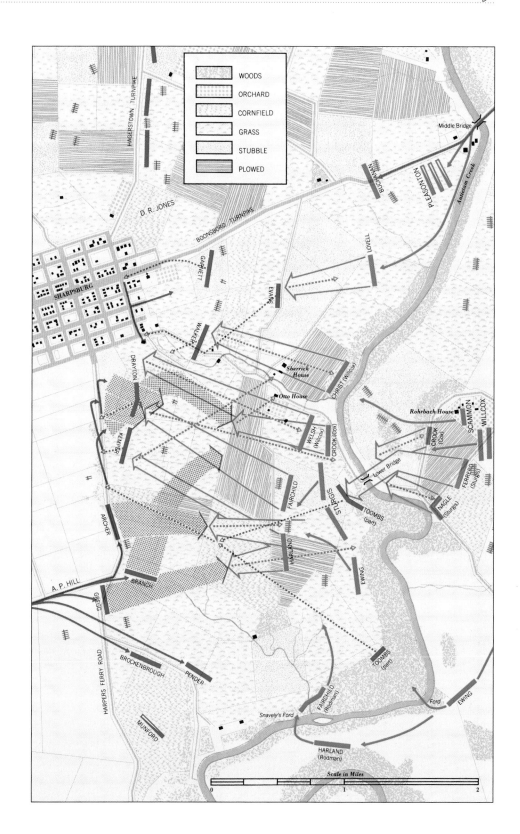

SURGEON THEODORE DIMON

2D MARYLAND (U.S.) INFANTRY, NAGLE'S BRIGADE

Transferred to the 2d Maryland from the 19th New York in June 1862, Dr. Dimon saw service at Second Manassas, Chantilly, and South Mountain before Antietam, and after his appointment was up he served as a volunteer at Gettysburg. Dimon was present when Lieutenant Colonel J. Eugene Duryée, the 2d Maryland's commander, returned with orders from General Sturgis to assault the lower span—Burnside Bridge—across Antietam Creek.

While we were waiting here, having nothing to do but to think of the shells and bullets that were becoming more and more unpleasantly numerous all the while, I found myself getting nervous. After standing it as long as I could, I ordered the Assistant Surgeon to place himself and the men behind the biggest trees he could find and keep everything safe till he received a written order from me—that I was going down to the men to see what was going on. . . .

. . . I turned the point of the hill and came upon the 2nd Maryland lying in a gulch which, after coming up from the Antietam, made a turn to the right, where it afforded a cover for the Regiment. Further to the right, under cover of another hill and in front of us, was Sturgis' staff; Nagle and the rest of the Brigade were in the cornfields to the left.

Soon a staff officer came for Duryea to go up to the General. He went, and after a short confab, turned to come back. As he did so, I noticed that he buttoned up his blouse. This was a sign that work was now at hand. As Duryea came back, he ordered: "Unsling knapsacks." While the men were getting in order, I asked him what was up. He replied that Sturgis had asked him if he wanted to win a star and that he had said yes.

"Well," Sturgis says, "there is a bridge around the other side of this hill, and the Lieutenant Colonel of the 6th New [Hampshire] thinks his regiment too small to head the assault on it, so I offer it to you."

"All right, General," says Duryea, "I'll make a try for that star anyhow."

So he took the head of the Regiment and filed it down the gulch to the river bottom. I followed along.

As we got to level ground on the border of the stream, the bridge was in sight to the right some two or three hundred yards off. The Regiment flanked off across some ploughed ground towards the bridge, the Colonel at the head, pulling down fences. On the opposite side of the stream, some 100 yards or so off, the bank rose perpendicular some 20 or 30 feet, and had been dug out on that side at the bridge end for the road which came from the right of it. The crest of the opposite bank was fringed with bushes and some willow and other trees also grew there. These bushes concealed from sight the enemy, who were laying there waiting till their fire would tell the best.

I was taking observations for a place for the wounded and noticed a barn built of round poles and covered with thatch just to the left of me, and a pool of good-looking water just in front. I unhitched my tin cup and stooped to take a drink of the water. Just at this instant, the enemy poured in their volley. It had seemed comparatively still before that,

Considered one of the most promising members of the West Point class of May 1861, 25-year-old Colonel Henry W. Kingsbury (left) was hit four times and mortally wounded while leading the 11th Connecticut in the doomed first charge at Burnside Bridge. The regiment carried the bullet-torn flag at right in the attack and in every fight up to the war's end.

In the third attempt to take Burnside Bridge, the 51st New York and the 51st Pennsylvania cross the span at last, under fire from Toombs' Georgians along the far bluff. In a change of strategy, the two 51sts charged straight down the hill in front of the bridge rather than approach by the road along the creek. Though stymied at first by Rebel volleys, the Federals ultimately outlasted the Confederates' dwindling ammunition supply.

but now it seemed as if all the noises in the world had broken out at once. The batteries were pretty close down on both sides and they all opened. I noticed some splendid practice of our batteries, their shells bursting just at the willows and limbs of them dropping into the stream, cut off by their fragments. . . .

The Regiment still moving by flank, and at this time all alone, was stopped to throw down the fence on the other side of the field. Duryea had just thrown down the last rail and, as he looked back, he saw the Regiment shrinking and elbowing out under this tremendous fire and just ready to break. The ploughed furrows were thickly dotted with fallen men when down the line came his peculiar-keyed voice which could be, and was, heard through all that infernal noise. "What the hell you doing there? Straighten that line there, forward." The line straightened, like straightening your arm, and on it went for the bridge.

I was now busy getting the wounded to the barn, but learned after-

wards that he could not get to the bridge and have any men left. So, about 30 or 40 yards from it, he halted and faced his men and they commenced returning the enemy's fire. . . .

. . . The action, so far as we were concerned, began about 11 A.M., for I was looking at my watch just before I went down and it was then just 11. About two, as we had finished dressing all in the barn and provided for them as well as we could, I went out to look around. The firing had held up in our vicinity and gone over the other side of the river.

On going towards the bridge, I saw bad signs for the 2nd. There were dead men all along the row and up at the head lay the Adjutant and numbers of others. Just behind was a farm road and in this I found what was left of it resting. . . . My friend, Captain Wilson, was killed, a cannon shot striking him in the forehead and carrying away all the top of his head. There were 400 in line that morning, and 150 had been killed and wounded.

LIEUTENANT THEODORE T. FOGLE
2D GEORGIA INFANTRY, TOOMBS' BRIGADE

The heights overlooking the bridge were manned by a few hundred soldiers from the 2d and 20th Georgia. Outnumbered 20 to 1, the Georgians nevertheless "fought on until their gun barrels were too hot for the naked hands." Lieutenant Fogle, killed at the Wilderness in May 1864, watched as his colonel, William R. Holmes, made a fatal last rush at the Yankees after Toombs ordered a retreat.

At a bridge on the Antietam Creek our Regiment & the 20th Ga., in all amounting to not over 300 muskets held them in check for *four hours & a half* & then we fell back only because our ammunition was exhausted, but we suffered badly, eight cannon just five hundred yards off were pouring grape shot, shell and cannister into us & our artillery could not silence them. We held our post until Major Harris (Cousin William) ordered us to fall back. Our Col. (Col. Holmes of Burke County Ga) was killed about half an hour before. He was as brave a man as I ever saw. He was perfectly cool & calm & did not seem to know what the word danger meant, he had won the confidence of the regiment at the battle of Manassas, poor man he was pierced by three balls after he received his death wound. We could not bring his remains off the field. Three men tried it & two of them were shot down. I wanted to go with them but I knew it was not right to expose myself in that way. Col. Holmes was dead & it was not right for us to risk our lives simply to get his body off the field. Maj. Harris is a brave man but I dont think is quite cool enough. He was struck on the arm but the ball did not enter, only gave him a pretty bad bruise. We went into the fight with only 89 muskets & had eight officers & 35 men killed & wounded. So many of the men were shot down that the officers filled their places & loaded & fired their guns. I fired only once & that was at a bunch of six or seven Yankees not more than 60 yards off. The musket was a smooth bore & loaded with a ball & three buckshot. I won't say whether I hit my mark or not. Mother, I'll give you the benefit of the doubt.

Sergeant Thomas D. Reed (right) carried the bridge with the rest of his regiment, the 51st Pennsylvania. Their reward was the regimental whiskey ration, denied earlier for disciplinary reasons.

LIEUTENANT JOHN W. HUDSON
35TH MASSACHUSETTS INFANTRY, FERRERO'S BRIGADE

In his letter to a friend, Hudson protested glorified "eyewitness" accounts of that day, noting among other things that the attacking Union troops crept, rather than stormed, over the hard-won bridge. At the time, the 26-year-old officer was serving as an aide on Ferrero's staff, giving him an insider's view.

Not hesitating to obey an order which they knew to be the will of McClellan and the direct command of Burnside, through Sturgis & Ferrero, the regimental officers moved without hesitation, and the men at once followed example. Those in the advance saw they had nothing to rush upon and overwhelm, and naturally desired, in self-defense and for the purpose of doing what service

they could, to load and fire as often as any single enemy was to be seen—for nothing like an uncovered rank of rebels was discernible, or indeed, existed. Those of our troops not in the advance crossed somewhat upon those in front—and the whole column while on the bridge appeared like an irregular mob moving nervously, but at a snail's pace, toward the enemy. The unincumbered motions of a tired soldier are distressingly feeble in appearance. So there was much want of all bounding energy in all these movements. But there was no turning back, while there was, to the view of one upon the spot, a patient endeavor to do the most harm to the enemy by the employment of all skill which drill & service had taught these veterans. The column kept up its snail pace, passed the bridge, took the road to the right till it was clear of the bridge, and then, being out of ammunition or nearly so,

took position on the sloping bank of the creek, probably to escape the enfilading fire down the road, if one should come.

The rebels were posted behind trees & natural projections of the rocky, wood covered slope, along the brow of the slope, behind little curious shelters made of rails, in the forms of small lunettes & provided with loopholes (the rails couldn't be laid close you know), and in a few cases up in the trees—all acting like riflemen. They had wounded many upon the knolls, left the effect of their fire along the low land near the road, and galled the assailants of the bridge a good deal, almost without begin seen. Probably 200 might have been the sum of the whole infantry force there—no use for more. It was impossible for them to plant a cannon so as to fire lengthwise of the bridge—physically impossible—& nobody feared it.

A Union soldier poses against the stone wall beside Burnside Bridge (background), next to grave markers of soldiers who were killed trying to cross the span.

" 'General, are you going to send us in again?'
'Yes, my son,' he replied, with a smile,
'you all must do what you can to help drive these people back.' "

PRIVATE ROBERT E. LEE JR.
ROCKBRIDGE (VIRGINIA) ARTILLERY, J. R. JONES' DIVISION

The youngest of the commanding general's three sons, all of whom served in the Confederate army, Private Lee had seen his battery badly mauled during the morning battles at Antietam. Sometime during the early afternoon, he encountered his father busily organizing forces for a counterattack to relieve the pressure on D. H. Hill's sorely depleted command.

As one of the Army of Northern Virginia I occasionally saw the Commander-in-Chief, or passed the headquarters close enough to recognize him and members of his staff; but a private soldier in Jackson's corps did not have much time during that campaign for visiting, and until the battle of Sharpsburg I had no opportunity of speaking to him. On that occasion our battery had been severely handled, losing many men and horses. Having three guns disabled, we were ordered to withdraw and, while moving back, we passed General Lee and several of his staff grouped on a little knoll near the road. Having no definite orders where to go, our captain, seeing the commanding General, halted us and rode over to get some instructions. Some others and myself went along to see and hear. General Lee was dismounted with some of his staff around him, a courier holding his horse. Captain Poague, commanding our battery, the Rockbridge Artillery, saluted, reported our condition, and asked for instructions. The General listened patiently, looked at us, his eyes passing over me without any sign of recognition, and then ordered Captain Poague to take the most serviceable horses and men, man the uninjured gun, send the disabled part of his command back to refit, and report to the front for duty. As Poague turned to go, I went up to speak to my father. When he found out who I was he congratulated me on being well and unhurt. I then said, "General, are you going to send us in again?" "Yes, my son," he replied, with a smile, "you all must do what you can to help drive these people back."

General David R. Jones graduated with the famous West Point class of 1846, which included, among others, McClellan and Stonewall Jackson. Considered competent and reliable, if lacking flare, Jones was left to defend Lee's entire right flank with fewer than 3,000 men. The stress may have been too much for Jones, already a victim of heart disease. The urbane South Carolinian, known affectionately as Neighbor, suffered a heart attack soon after the battle and died four months later.

PRIVATE FRANK M. MIXSON
1ST SOUTH CAROLINA VOLUNTEERS, J. WALKER'S BRIGADE

Posted in the approaches to Sharpsburg, Joseph Walker's South Carolina brigade was about the only Confederate force that stood between the town and Willcox's advancing Yankees. Walker brought his men forward to block Colonel Benjamin C. Christ's brigade, but the Rebels were soon driven back on Sharpsburg.

Our batteries were on the hill above us and were responding all they could. . . . we were ordered up the hill to protect our batteries; the enemy were charging them. We went up the hill at a double quick. Our regiment was on the left of the brigade and we were going left in front, which put us to the front. I was trotting by the side of

Maj. Livingston amid a furor of bursting shells. About half way up the hill Maj. Livingston called to me, saying, "Lead on, Frank, I am wounded." I called to Capt. Knotts, who was the senior captain present, and told him to take command of the regiment. We got in position on the hill in rear of a plank fence and were told not to fire a shot till ordered to do so. While lying behind the fence the Yankees were making their charge and coming down the opposite hill in as pretty a line as on dress parade. In front of us, and about midway, there was a stone fence in another apple orchard. The Yankees were making for this fence, and, as I said before, were moving on it at a double quick and a regular dress parade line. The old captain commanding our batteries had shot himself out of balls, and, all his horses being killed, he ordered his men to cut off the trace chains. With these he loaded his pieces and fired. It seemed that as the chains reached the ranks they spread themselves out full length and cut their way broadside through. The old captain jumped up, yelled, and ordered another load, with about the same result. This was done several times, and finally the column began to waver and weaken. At this point a Yankee colonel rode to the front with drawn sword and rallied his men, who were about to give way. Just then I said to Kite Folk, from Bamberg, a boy like myself, but a year or two older, "Let us shoot him." I picked up a gun lying near me and Kite and I put our guns through the fence and fired together. The colonel fell and was carried from the field. The enemy fell back, but very soon came again.

PRIVATE WILLIAM BREARLEY
17TH MICHIGAN INFANTRY, CHRIST'S BRIGADE

Many men inexperienced in combat, including Private Brearley, were baptized in the blood of Antietam. The 16-year-old Brearley had signed on in August 1862 with the new 17th Michigan Infantry, a regiment that had seen its first action just days earlier. Brearley's letter to his father shows how quickly a young soldier's romantic ideas of war changed amid the storm of gunfire.

It was rather Strange music to hear balls scream within an inch of my head. I had a bullet strike me on the top of the head just as I was going to fire and a piece of Shell struck my foot—a ball hit my finger and another hit my thumb I concluded they ment me. the rebels played the mischief with us by raising a U.S. flag. We were ordered not to fire and as soon as we went forward they opened an awful fire from their batteries on us we were ordered to fall back about

After recovering from typhoid, Private Albert N. Stone posed for this photograph before returning to the 4th South Carolina Battalion of J. Walker's brigade. Stone was wounded at Antietam but survived the rest of the war unscathed.

1/2 miles, I staid behind when our regiment retreated and a line of Skirmishers came up—I joined them and had a chance of firing about 10 times more—. . . Our Generals say they (the rebels) had as strong a position as could *possibly* be and we had to pick into them through an old chopping all grown up with bushes so thick that we couldent hardly get through—but we were so excited that the "old scratch" himself couldent have stopt us. We rushed onto them evry man for himself—

Charged with making soldiers out of the men of the two-week-old 17th Michigan, Colonel William H. Withington broke in his green troops at Fox's Gap, three days before colliding with Walker outside Sharpsburg. The two battles cost the regiment more than 200 men. Fearless under fire, Withington had rescued his commanding officer at First Manassas and earned a Medal of Honor.

all loading & firing as fast as he could see a rebel to Shoot at—at last the rebels began to get over the wall to the rear and run for the woods. the firing increased tenfold then it sounded like the rolls of thunder—and all the time evry man shouting as loud as he could—I got rather more excited than I wish to again. I dident *think* of getting hit but it was almost a miricle that I wasent the rebels that we took prisoners said that they never before encountered a regiment that fought so like "Devils" (so they termed it) as we did—every one praised our regiment—one man in our company was Shot through the head no more than 4 feet from me he was killed instantly. . . . I saw some of horidest sights I ever saw—one man had both eyes shot out—and they were wounded in all the different ways you could think of—the most I could do was to give them water—they were all very thirsty—. . . . Our Colonel (Withington) was formerly a captain of the Mich 1st—he is just as cool as can be, he walked around amongst us at the battle the bullets flying all around him—he kept Shouting to us to fire low and give it to them.

PRIVATE ALEXANDER HUNTER
17TH VIRGINIA INFANTRY, KEMPER'S BRIGADE

To Willcox's left was Fairchild's New York brigade led by the 9th New York Zouaves, advancing, as one Confederate put it, as dense "as Pharaoh's locusts." Waiting for them were the Rebels of D. R. Jones' last two brigades, numbering between them, as Private Hunter was well aware, fewer than 600 men.

In about half an hour it came. Then the artillery was silent, and the infantrymen, who had lain there face downward, exposed to the iron hail, now arose, placed their cartridge boxes in position, rested their muskets on the lower rail, and with clenched teeth, fast beating hearts and hurried breath, braced themselves for the shock. The fence was not built on the top of the hill, but some fifty feet from the crest; consequently we could not see the attacking force until they were within pistol shot of us. We could hear the rat-a-plan of their drums, the stern commands of their officers, the muffled sound of marching feet.

Colonel Corse gave but one order—"Don't fire, men, until I give the word." As we lay there with our eyes ranging along the musket barrels, our fingers on the triggers, we saw the gilt eagles of the flagpoles emerge above the top of the hill, followed by the flags drooping on the staffs, then the tops of the blue caps appeared, and next a line of the

This shell jacket belonged to 20-year-old Lieutenant Frank C. Littleton of the 17th Virginia. Captured during the Seven Days' Battles, Littleton was exchanged and returned to duty just six weeks before Antietam. He was mortally wounded on the afternoon of September 17 and died eight days later across the Potomac River at Shepherdstown.

fiercest eyes man ever looked upon. The shouts of their officers were heard, urging their men forward. Less brave, less seasoned troops would have faltered before the array of deadly tubes leveled at them, and at the recumbent line, silent, motionless and terrible, but if there was any giving away we did not see it. They fired at us before we pulled trigger and came on with vibrant shouts. Not until they were well up in view did Colonel Corse break the silence, and his voice was a shriek as he ordered:

"Fire!"

All the guns went off at once, and the whole brigade fire seemed to follow our volley, and the enemy's line, sadly thinned, broke and went over the hill. Every man in our line began to load his musket with frenzied haste. Only three or four of the Seventeenth were shot, the fire of the enemy being too high.

We had barely loaded and capped the muskets when the blue line came with a rush and we fired now without orders. Before we could load a third time the two lines of battle of the Federals, now commingled as one solid bank of men, poured a volley into us that settled the matter. It killed or wounded every officer and man in the regiment except five, of whom I was fortunate enough to be one.

Just as the bluecoats were climbing the fence I threw down my musket and raised my hand in token of surrender. Two or three stopped to carry me back to the rear. The rest kept on, urged by their officers, in the direction of the village of Sharpsburg.

For his stand on the outskirts of Sharpsburg, Colonel Montgomery D. Corse (left) earned both the praise of General Lee and a promotion to brigadier. Wounded in the foot during the fight, Corse fell into the hands of the 9th New York, but he was liberated soon after, during A. P. Hill's counterattack. That evening, however, Corse's 17th Virginia could count only a handful of men.

"We had barely loaded and capped the muskets when the blue line came with a rush and we fired now without orders."

LIEUTENANT MATTHEW J. GRAHAM
9TH NEW YORK INFANTRY, FAIRCHILD'S BRIGADE

The outnumbered Confederate force defending the approaches to the town exacted a heavy price among the Zouaves of the 9th New York. Two-thirds of Lieutenant Graham's fellow soldiers in the regiment were killed or wounded—eight from one shell. Some of Fairchild's men made it into the streets of Sharpsburg, only to be recalled by their officers, who were intent on regrouping their forces.

The practice of the rebel artillerymen was something wonderful in its accuracy; they dropped shot and shell right into our line repeatedly. They kept the air fairly filled with missiles of almost every variety, from shrapnel to railroad iron. The shrapnel or canister was very much in evidence. I saw one of our men in hospital afterward who had nine gunshot wounds in his right arm. I watched solid shot—round shot—strike with what sounded like an innocent thud in front of the guns, and, bounding over battery and park, fly through the tree tops, cutting some of them off so suddenly that it seemed to me they lingered for an instant undecided which way to fall. These round shot did not appear to be in a hurry. They came along slowly and deliberately, apparently, and there appeared no harm in them until they hit something.

I was lying on my back, supported on my elbows, watching the shells explode overhead, and speculating as to how long I could hold up my finger before it would be shot off, for the very air seemed full of bullets, when the order to get up was given. I turned over quickly to look at Colonel Kimball, who had given the order, thinking he had become suddenly insane; never dreaming that he intended to advance in that fire, and firmly believing that the regiment would not last one minute after the men had got fairly on their feet. Sure enough, there was Kimball, looking all right. He repeated the order: "Get up the Ninth!" and, I thought, looked directly at me. We got up and went forward, passing at once into a cornfield. The fence over which my men were swarming was at that moment knocked down by a shell. From the corn we crossed over a meadow, then over a strip of plowed land, and

E. A. Kimball

Lt. Col. comding 9th N.Y. Vol

Commanding the 9th New York Infantry was Lieutenant Colonel Edgar A. Kimball, a tough-skinned former newspaper editor. After his regiment had been savaged by Confederate artillery during the first minutes of the Federal advance, Kimball encouraged his soldiers by shouting, "Bully Ninth! Bully Ninth! Boys, I'm proud of you! Every one of you!"

then another piece of grass. We halted twice, I think, to rest and dress the line, although dressing was not necessary, as every man was in his place. The loss was frightful. I could see the regiment—the line— shortening perceptibly as we advanced. We could hear the crash of the missiles through the ranks, and strange as it may seem, that sound brought like a flash to my mind a saying of Lanne's when describing the Battle of Austerlitz: "I could hear the bones crash in my division like glass in a hailstorm."

The charge ended, so far as I was concerned, in what appeared to be a grand finale. We had been advancing over what I remember as rolling, but at the same time rising ground; we had reached what looked like the summit of this particular ridge, when we were met by what I remember as a crashing volley of musketry. We all went down together, although I was hit not with a bullet, but with a grapeshot. The fronts of the companies had by that time become so narrow that I found myself right at the colors. The companies did not average, I think, above twelve or fifteen men each, at that stage. When I recovered myself after I fell—that is, got into position to see about me, and after the men had passed over me, some stumbling over and others stepping on me, which occupied but a moment, nearly everybody was down on the ground. The whole color guard lay prone, the colors on the ground. One or two of the men staggered to their feet and reached for the colors, but were shot down at once. Then there was what seemed a spontaneous rush for them by a dozen or more men from several companies, who were shot down in succession as each one raised his flag. One of these whom I noticed was Lieutenant Myers, who was hit just as he picked up one of them. The flags were up and down, up and down, several times in a minute. Lebaier at last seized one of them, and swinging it around his head was profane for the first and only time, I think, shouting to his company, "Up, damn you, and forward!" I could see only toward the right of the line as I lay. I saw four commissioned officers in front of the line. Kimball, Horner, Lebaier and McKechnie, all shouting forward as the men sprang to their feet. McKechnie was on the stone wall with his fez on the point of his sword waving his men on.

Shown at left are the jacket and fez belonging to Sergeant Latham A. Fish of the 9th New York Infantry, known also as Hawkins' Zouaves. The bullet-pierced canteen was found near the panoramic scene shown below, depicting the already hard hit New Yorkers exchanging fire with the remnants of the Rebel battle line on the outskirts of Sharpsburg.

LIEUTENANT JOHN A. RAMSAY

ROWAN (NORTH CAROLINA) ARTILLERY, HOOD'S DIVISION

Writing in the third person, Ramsay recounts the critical moment on the Confederate right when he served as the eyes of General Robert E. Lee. Shortly before, Ramsay's guns had opened up on the Federals, "soon breaking their line and throwing them into confusion."

About 3 o'clock P.M. the right section's ten-pounder Parrotts, commanded by Lieutenant Ramsay, had obtained a supply of ammunition and started to the front. Near Sharpsburg we met a large number of straggling soldiers going to the rear, and farther on officers were trying to rally the men and form them into line and nearly abreast of Sharpsburg we met General Lee. General Lee seeing Lieutenant Ramsay's telescope, said to him: "What troops are those?" pointing to the position occupied by Captain Reilly's Battery on the day before. Lieutenant Ramsay drew his telescope from the case and handed it to General Lee. He held up his wounded hand (fingers in bandages) and said: "Can't use it. What troops are those?" Lieutenant Ramsay dismounted and adjusting the glass, replied: "They are flying the United States flag." General Lee pointed at another body of troops, nearly at right angles from the others, and said: "What troops are those?" Lieutenant Ramsay replied: "They are flying the Virginia and Confederate flags." General Lee said: "It is A. P. Hill, from Harper's Ferry," and ordered Lieutenant Ramsay to place his guns on a little knoll on the right of the road and fire on those people (pointing in the first-named direction). Lieutenant Ramsay then said: "General Lee, as soon as we fire we will draw the enemy's fire." General Lee replied: "Never mind me." Both of the gunners of the right section, James M. Pitman and Ignaz Schoesser were experts, and the first shell exploded in the middle of the line, the next a little to the right of the first, and by the time each gun had thrown five shells the enemy had disappeared. General Lee, with a pleasant smile, said: "Well done! Elevate your guns and continue the fire until these troops (pointing towards them) come near your line of fire, then change your position to the ridge on the right of the line and fire on the troops beyond the creek." General Lee then rode off, and the section kept up a steady, effective fire until General A. P. Hill's troops came near the line of fire.

CORPORAL BERRY G. BENSON

1ST SOUTH CAROLINA INFANTRY, GREGG'S BRIGADE

Coming up at the double-quick from the Potomac River crossing, Gregg's brigade smashed into Harland's Federal troops, who were moving through the Otto family's cornfield to reinforce Fairchild. At one point the Federals briefly held their fire, when they mistook the blue state colors being waved above the corn by the Carolinians for a Union banner.

We were ordered to the field, whither we went in rapid march, crossing the Potomac at Boteler's Ford, the water being hip deep. All wet and draggled we hurried on to the field of battle, and took position upon the Confed. right. Advancing through a cornfield, there suddenly rose before us a line of the enemy, whom we drove in disorder at the first fire.

Running rapidly forward through the corn, we stopped at the top of

With his hands still bandaged from the fall at Manassas, General Lee had to decline the offer of Lieutenant Ramsay's telescope, shown at left.

the hill and poured a galling fire into the fleeing foe. Many of them stopped in a little hollow in the corn at the foot of the hill, afraid to attempt the passage of the open slope beyond. Into them grouped here in a crouching disorderly line, we poured volley after volley, doubtless with terrible execution. I say volleys, and here was the only time in battle that I now remember firing to be done by command. Maj. Alston many times gave the command, "Right wing—ready—aim—fire—Load! Left wing—ready—aim—fire!—Load!" with splendid effect, for the line obeyed as a drill.

Besides those lying in the ravine, part of the enemy's line had taken refuge behind a stone fence or ridge of rocks which did not appear to protect them fully, for by ones and twos and threes they were continually breaking from it and fleeing across the open slope beyond. These with those who fled the ravine fairly dotted the green slope. And now amongst them, spurring down the hillside, came galloping an officer, mounted upon a black horse, waving his sword and endeavoring to rally the scattered line. Our eyes all turned to him, a fair mark, and half a thousand rifles were aimed, and a storm of bullets sped on their mission. Both horse and rider fell. . . .

Suddenly and unexpectedly, whilst we were thus having things our own way, came a volley from our flank which drove us back precipitately, and we had hardly chance to deliver a shot ere we were being hotly pursued. I found myself dropping behind; for my pantaloons (which I had found at Manassas Junction) proved to be of weak stuff and had already begun to rip at the bottom of the left leg. And now being wet by fording the river, they were heavier, so that running caused them to split further and further, so that now every time I threw the left leg forward, the breeches leg flew forward and wrapped around my right leg. Bullets whistled around me thick, for I must have been a conspicuous target. A bullet struck me on the right side of the head, leaving a black mark on my gray felt hat. Feeling it strike, I stopped, seized the cloth in my hands and tore the leg off a foot above the knee, and "skedaddled."

Our line did not run far, but jumped into a gully and fronted, awaiting in this natural breastwork the advance of the enemy. But they did not come, nor were we ordered forward. Sitting down there, one of the men asked me if that was a bullet hole in my drawers. Looking down I saw two holes near the bottom of the leg, and unrolling it (for they had been made for a good deal longer man than me) I found in all six holes, one bullet having doubtless passed through three folds of the cloth. And so I came out of the battle of Sharpsburg or Antietam half trouserless.

"At length, we sought some stacks, and a barn, resolved not to ride farther; but there, on the straw and in the buildings, were the dead."

SERGEANT GEORGE W. BEALE
9TH VIRGINIA CAVALRY, F. LEE'S BRIGADE

At day's end, the Confederates, having faced frightful odds, had bravely staved off ferocious assaults, while McClellan's men could boast that they had turned back Lee's bold foray into the North. But Beale's account attests to the human toll, as survivors were left to deal with the ghastly results of the 12-hour battle.

When the night's approach put an end to the fighting on this field, we were allowed to seek some camp near by for food and rest. Wherever we rode for this purpose, however, the ground seemed to be occupied with dead or wounded men. At length, we sought some stacks, and a barn, resolved not to ride farther; but there, on the straw and in the buildings, were the dead. I sought an empty wagon in the barnyard and fastened my horse to a wheel. Next morning, under the wagon, lay a young soldier, fair and noble in his death, with his clothes partly unfastened and his clinched fingers near the ghastly wound in his abdomen from which he had died. The last scene on which my eye rested that night before it closed, in such close comradeship with the dead, was that of a small group with a flickering lantern beside a fence near by, who were digging a grave and rudely raising the earth over some fellow-soldier who had fallen.

Return to Virginia

Dawn of September 18 revealed a scene of unparalleled carnage. More than 22,000 Union and Confederate soldiers had been killed, wounded, or captured. Nearly 4,000 corpses were strewn over the rolling countryside surrounding the shell-torn town of Sharpsburg. The battle along Antietam Creek would stand as the bloodiest single day in American history, and it was a sight no survivor would ever forget.

"I have heard of the dead lying in heaps," Union artillery officer Emory Upton wrote his sister, "but never saw it till this battle. Whole ranks fell together." Stonewall Jackson's aide, Henry Kyd Douglas, recalled: "It was a dreadful scene, a veritable field of blood. My horse trembled under me in terror, looking down at the ground, sniffing falteringly as a horse will over or by the side of

Federal soldiers, part of a burial detail, stand among Confederate dead on the Miller farm in this Alexander Gardner photograph. Owing to the September heat, most of the dead were quickly buried in mass graves, only to be disinterred later and moved to family plots or other cemeteries.

human flesh; afraid to stand still, hesitating to go on, his animal instinct shuddering at this cruel human misery."

Both armies were exhausted, and except for a few brief skirmishes and an occasional exchange of artillery fire the day passed without significant fighting. Content with having checked Lee's invasion, McClellan trumpeted the grim stalemate as a great victory, writing his wife, Nellie, "Those in whose judgement I rely tell me that I fought the battle splendidly & that it was a masterpiece of art." With 14 Rebel guns and nearly 40 flags as trophies, the Federal commander informed General in Chief Halleck that "victory was complete." But in reality the victory was far from total.

Despite his army's staggering losses, two of McClellan's corps—the V and VI—had been only partially engaged. Given the Federals' numerical advantage, a renewed offensive on September 18 might well have succeeded in destroying all or part of Lee's forces. But Little Mac was content to rest on his laurels. "Everybody looks pleased," noted McClellan's staff officer David Hunter Strother, "but I feel as if an indecisive victory was in our circumstances equivalent to a defeat."

Confederate officers likewise recognized

that McClellan had missed a golden opportunity. "Not twice in a life time does such a chance come to any general," noted Lieutenant Colonel E. Porter Alexander. "The Confederate army was worn & fought to a perfect frazzle."

Although Lee held his ground on the 18th, he realized that to remain north of the Potomac was to court disaster. That night the Army of Northern Virginia pulled back and headed toward a new base of operations at Winchester, Virginia. "We do not boast a victory," admitted Lee's adjutant, Walter Taylor. Some of Lee's officers expressed deep regret at the outcome and questioned the wisdom of Lee's having given battle at Sharpsburg in the first place. But all had nothing but praise for their soldiers, many of whom had paid the ultimate sacrifice for the Confederacy. "The fight of the 17th has taught us the value of our men," Taylor wrote, "who can even when weary with constant marching & fighting & when on short rations, contend with and resist three times their own number."

McClellan's tentative efforts to pursue Lee's column met with near disaster for the Federals on September 20, when troops of the V Corps forded the Potomac south of Shepherdstown. The Confederates counterattacked. While most of the Federals managed to make their escape, the 118th Pennsylvania regiment was cut off and driven over a precipitous bluff, whereupon, as Marylander Jonathan T. Scharf recalled, "our men shot them like dogs in the river." Before risking another crossing, McClellan decided to rest and resupply his war-weary soldiers, many of whom had been lacking proper clothing, footwear, and accouterments since the end of the Peninsula campaign three months earlier. "I have *hundreds* of men in my command without shoes," General George Meade wrote his wife. "Our artillery horses and train animals have been literally starving." But Lee's ragged and depleted units were in even worse shape; and by failing to press on, McClellan fell into increasing disfavor with President Lincoln and his senior advisers.

But if the great bloodletting at Antietam failed to achieve the decisive victory Lincoln desired, Lee's retreat was at least perceived as a strategic success for the Union. And the president was determined to take moral and political advantage of Lee's withdrawal. On September 22 Lincoln gathered his cabinet and announced his intention to issue the Emancipation Proclamation he had drawn up two months earlier, decreeing freedom for the Confederacy's 3.5 million slaves. The proclamation was decried in the South and hotly debated in the North. Some abolitionists felt the president had not gone far enough. "I can't see what *practical* good it can do now," wrote Massachusetts officer Robert G. Shaw. "Wherever our army has been, there remain no slaves, and the Proclamation will not free them where we don't go." But Lincoln well knew that by linking the Northern war effort to the abolition of slavery, he was effectively denying the Confederacy any hope of foreign recognition. Because of Antietam and the Emancipation Proclamation, the Confederacy would have to continue fighting alone.

In early October Lincoln visited the Army of the Potomac, ostensibly to learn the details of the recent battle, but in reality to try to get McClellan moving again. The general demurred, as he did again 10 days later in response to the president's written appeal. "Are you not over-cautious when you assume that you can not do what the enemy is constantly doing?" Lincoln asked. "If we never try, we shall never succeed." It was October 26 before McClellan finally got under way, crossing the Potomac and moving southward toward the town of Warrenton, Virginia. But Lincoln had had enough of his cautious army commander. At 11:30 on the night of November 6, McClellan received orders to relinquish command of the Army of the Potomac to Major General Ambrose E. Burnside.

Urging his subordinates to give unqualified loyalty to his successor, McClellan bade an emotional farewell on November 10 to the soldiers who had never ceased to admire and trust the Young Napoleon. Ohioan Thomas Galwey described the "half-shout and half-sob" that swept through the ranks as the general rode past in a last review of the troops, some of whom yelled out: "Send him back! Send him back!" Galwey thought, "A very mutinous feeling is apparent everywhere."

But McClellan departed, and the grumbling gave way to grim determination. "The Army are not satisfied with the change," Brigadier General Winfield Scott Hancock wrote his wife, Almira, "and consider the treatment of McClellan most ungracious and inopportune. Yet I do not sympathize with the movement going on to resist the order. 'It is useless,' I tell the gentlemen around me. 'We are serving no one man; we are serving our country.' "

BATTLE OF ANTIETAM CASUALTIES

FEDERAL

Killed	2,108
Wounded	9,540
Missing	753
Total	12,401

CONFEDERATE

Killed	1,546
Wounded	7,752
Missing	1,018
Total	10,316

MARYLAND CAMPAIGN CASUALTIES

FEDERAL

Total	27,000

CONFEDERATE

Total	14,000

"A few months before I could not have taken a mouthful of food and swallowed it in the presence of a corpse."

CORPORAL WILLIAM B. WESTERVELT

27TH NEW YORK INFANTRY, BARTLETT'S BRIGADE

Federals and Confederates alike found no rest on the day after the battle, having to deal with casualties on both sides numbering more than 22,000. Among the burial parties dispatched to dig graves for the already decomposing bodies was veteran Westervelt, whose tour of duty had hardened him to the toll of battle.

Thursday, Sept. 18th.—Just before daylight we were called in line, as that is considered the favorable time to surprise a camp, and we did not intend to be caught napping. Here we stood, leaning on our guns, while in the rear of us were the artillerymen with guns shotted and lanyard in hand ready to attach to the prime, and send death and destruction into the ranks of an advancing foe. All remained quiet, however, and soon after sunrise we were ordered to stack arms and break ranks. Soon [a] score of small fires were kindled with cornstalks and small twigs, and the coffee cup—that inseparable companion of the soldier—was steaming, and meat frying, and we soon sat down to our morning meal right among the dead that, already in the hot September sun, began to give forth a very unpleasant odor. This only shows to what extent we could adapt ourselves to our surroundings. A few months before I could not have taken a mouthful of food and swallowed it in the presence of a corpse. Now, although they showed unmistakable signs of decomposition, we did not mind it, even though they lay so thick we were obliged to lift some of them out of our way to make room for our lines of battle. . . .

Stretcher carriers now came up, and while they carried off scores of

In this drawing by Alfred Waud, a Federal and a Confederate officer shake hands under a white flag near the Dunker Church during a truce on the day after the battle. Both sides needed the time to collect their dead and wounded. During the respite, North Carolinian Calvin Leach recorded in his diary, "It seemed very curious to see the men on both sides come together and talk to each other when the day before were fireing at each other."

wounded we turned in with pick and shovel, in the capacity of grave diggers, and like most everything else done by the army, our grave digging was on a wholesale scale. We first dug a grave six feet wide and about sixty feet long. In this grave, or rather trench, were placed side by side, forty of a South Carolina regiment. A few rods from this was another that contained thirty more. This disposed of all that lay close to our lines, and as we had but few tools for digging, it took most of the day to complete our wholesale interments. . . .

Friday, September 19th.—At daylight we were again under arms, when our picket line reported no signs of the enemy in our front. At sunrise they were ordered to advance, when it was discovered they had made good use of their time during the cessation of hostilities, and were safe with their supply trains, and artillery south of the river, leaving most of their wounded, however, in our care. About noon we got orders to move, and as we crossed the battle field the stench from the unburied dead almost took our breath away. We soon crossed the Sharpsburg Pike, where the dead lay in every conceivable position; one with his rammer half drawn from his gun, as he had finished loading his piece, having his gun in one hand and the rammer in the other, with a small, round hole through his forehead, his countenance being but slightly disfigured, but more expressive of surprise than pain. Others noticed his look as well as myself, and as Bogart expressed it, "he was astonished at how quick we killed him." Another was killed in the act of biting off the end of a cartridge, and lay with his hand still at his mouth. One of them had been killed just as he was climbing a fence, and in his death grip had caught the top rail where, in his half standing position he looked like one in the act of leaping over, and our men had fired repeatedly at him, thinking him still alive and trying to escape. I counted sixteen bullet holes in the lower part of his back that had been made after he was dead.

A makeshift grave marker fashioned from a wood plank bears the name, rank, and regiment of 21-year-old Lieutenant Arthur W. Speight, one of seven officers of the 3d North Carolina Infantry killed in action at Antietam.

BRIGADIER GENERAL ALPHEUS S. WILLIAMS
Division Commander, Army of the Potomac

When Major General Joseph Mansfield was mortally wounded early during the second Federal assault of the day, Alpheus Williams ably took command of the XII Corps, steadying his largely inexperienced troops through some of the heaviest fighting. Later, in the lull following the battle, Williams was riding over the area where his soldiers had fought and happened upon a scene of eerie beauty in the midst of the devastating ruin.

I took the delay to ride over the field of battle. The Rebel dead, even in the woods last occupied by them, was very great. In one place, in front of the position of my corps, apparently a whole regiment had been cut down in line. They lay in two ranks, as straightly aligned as on a dress parade. There must have been a brigade, as part of the line on the left had been buried. I counted what appeared to be a single regiment and found 149 dead in the line and

about 70 in front and rear, making over 200 dead in one Rebel regiment. In riding over the field I think I must have seen at least 3,000.
In one place for nearly a mile they lay as thick as autumn leaves along
a narrow lane cut below the natural surface, into which they seemed
to have tumbled. Eighty had been buried in one pit, and yet no impression had apparently been made on the unburied host. The cornfield
beyond was dotted all over with those killed in retreat.

The wounded Rebels had been carried away in great numbers and
yet every farmyard and haystack seemed a large hospital. The number
of dead horses was high. They lay, like the men, in all attitudes. One
beautiful milk-white animal had died in so graceful a position that I
wished for its photograph. Its legs were doubled under and its arched
neck gracefully turned to one side, as if looking back to the ball-hole in
its side. Until you got to it, it was hard to believe the horse was dead.

SERGEANT ROBERT W. SHAND
2D SOUTH CAROLINA INFANTRY, KERSHAW'S BRIGADE

The hard fighting of September 17 gave way to a quiet morning on the Antietam battlefield, affording both Union and Rebel troops the opportunity to eat breakfast, tend their wounded, and bury their dead. For Shand, a Columbia native who had joined the colors in April 1861, it was a chance to replace the pair of shoes he had been marching in since the day he enlisted.

In August there had been shipped to me from home a box in which was a pair of shoes, but we had been on the move since, and it was long after Sharpsburg that the box reached me. And the shoes that I had on were worn away, nor could I get any from the quartermaster. At this time the uppers of my old pair were practically gone and I kept the broken soles to my feet by an arrangement of strings around my feet and ankles. In this condition I fought thro' the Battle of Sharpsburg, or Antietam as it is called by our friends, the enemy.

Early Thursday morning, I went out among the Yankee dead to get a pair of shoes. I picked out my size and was in the act of removing them from his feet, when he opened his eyes and said: "Can't you wait until I am dead?" I replied that I really thought he was dead, and that, even then I would not have disturbed him but for the fact that I was barefooted. I gave him water, and passed on: it was all I could do. I got my shoes from another, first making sure that he was dead. In our company was a Swede, a tailor from Columbia, named Kaletrom: We called him Kaslosh. He was small and his feet were small. He too went out on a shoe hunt. On his return he was asked if he had found his shoes. He said he had found only one pair that would fit, but the fellow was not quite dead yet. He went again later in the day, and again returned without the shoes. When asked what was the matter, he replied: "The damned rascal ain't dead yet."

Graceful even in death, this horse met its end in a field near the East Woods (background). Its lifelike pose prompted one soldier to note that it "was the only pleasing picture on this battlefield." Its rider, believed to be Colonel Henry B. Strong of the 6th Louisiana Infantry, was also killed in the battle.

CAPTAIN GEORGE F. NOYES
STAFF, BRIGADIER GENERAL ABNER DOUBLEDAY

Persuaded to leave his thriving law practice when war broke out, Noyes saw uneventful duty guarding Washington and Fredericksburg, and serving as judge-advocate at a court-martial, until the summer of 1862. Despite having seen action at Second Manassas, he was unprepared for the carnage and destruction he witnessed in the aftermath of the fighting at Antietam.

My route carried me over the late battle-field, and I spent much of the afternoon, part of the time in company with a friend, in visiting some of the most severely-contested points, to be awe-struck, sickened, almost benumbed by its sights of horror. Within this space of more than a mile square, this spot, once beautiful with handsome residences and well cultivated farms, isolated, hedged in with verdure, sacred to quiet, calm, content, the hottest fury of man's hottest wrath had expended itself, burning residences and well-filled barns, plowing fields of ripened grain with artillery, scattering every where through cornfield, wood, and valley the most awful illustrations of war. Not a building about us which was not deserted by its occupants, and rent and torn by shot and shell; not a field which had not witnessed the fierce and bloody encounter of armed and desperate men.

Let us first turn off to the left of the Hagerstown turnpike; but we must ride very slowly and carefully, for lying all through this cornfield are the victims of the hardest contest of our division. Can it be that these are the bodies of our late antagonists? Their faces are so absolutely black that I said to myself at first, this must have been a negro regiment. Their eyes are protruding from the sockets; their heads, hands, and limbs are swollen to twice their natural size. Ah! there is little left to awaken our sympathy, for all those vestiges of our common humanity which touch the sympathetic chord are now quite blotted out. These defaced and broken caskets, emptied of all that made them manlike, human, are repulsive merely. Naught remains but to lay them away quietly, where what is now repulsive shall be resolved into its original elements, shall be for a time . . . and shall reappear in new forms of life hereafter.

PRIVATE ROLAND E. BOWEN

15TH MASSACHUSETTS INFANTRY, GORMAN'S BRIGADE

Eager for a fight when he enlisted in July 1861, Bowen found himself writing to Elam Ainsworth, father of his boyhood friend, Henry, who had been killed in the blistering action in the West Woods. A year of active duty had taken its toll. In another letter to a friend, Bowen wrote, "You want to know why not enlist. . . . Enlist if you want to. Come in the 15th so I can Bury you."

Well, now I began to look around to see who was killed. At this time I did not even know the loss of our own Co., only that I knew that Capt. Simonds was killed. He was not hurt untill after the retreat. The rebs continued to shell us and one struck capt. S. in the breast killing him almost instantly. Well, I went down to Co. H and inquired after Henry, but all any one knew about him was

that when we had the order to *fall back* he was not hurt but started back with the rest. But as I told you it was every man for himself. So no one knew anything about Henry. I told them that I guessed he had only got lost from the Regmt. and would come in before long, but night came on and he did not make his appearance.

I expected the battle would be renewed on Thursday the 18th, but it was not. Thursday night came, but Henry came not. Now the question arose, is he Killed, is he Wounded or is he Lost. Ah, it can't be the latter for he would have come back before now. My only hope was that he might be wounded. I could not believe he was Dead. Yet in order to believe that, I must know it. Friday morning came and with it the news that the rebels had gone over the river into Va. Some of the boys at once started to find and bury the dead. I did not go. Now the mystery is revealed. Here in the wood under the cliffs of a ledge his remains are found. Unlike the rest of the Dead, he looks very natural. Its quite evident he has not been dead so long as the rest. Furthermore there is straw laid under him as if put there by the rebels that he might die as comfortable as posible. Blood is seen upon his clothes as if the ball struck him in the back just above the [ ] and passed through his right side. No particular examination was made to see where the ball struck him. They only judged from the blood on his clothes. Some think he had only been dead a few hours when found. I am of a different opinion. I don't think he lived over 24 hours after being wounded, for this reason. His pockets had been rifled and his shoes taken off. Now had he lived until after dark Thursday night, these things would not have been taken as that was the night the rebels left. I don't believe they would take any thing from a wounded man, especially his shoes, so I think he must of died on Thursday, Sept 18th, 1862.

Now when I heard he was dead, which was 10 or 11 oc on Friday the 19th, I went righ[t] over to the battle field to find his body so that I could bury it in a separate grave. I looked over a number of hundreds of bodies but I could not find Henry any where. So I went down to the front of the wood, and here I found a burying party from the 15th under a Lieu[tenant] from Co. H. I asked him if he had got the body of Henry Ainsworth. Yes said he and have just covered the corpes over. Said I, I am sorry. I wished to see it and bury it separately. But I was too late, he was buried. Perhaps you don't know how we bury the dead. Let me tell you about this particular *trench* and that will suffice for the whole. The trench in wich Henry is buried is situated near a log cabin just out side the garden fence. I believe its on the West side. The trench was 25 feet long, 6 feet wide and about 3 feet deep. The corpes were buried

Four days after they fell in battle, two anonymous Confederates, their units unknown, lie bloated and decomposing in the warm September sun, in a field believed to be on the heights just west of Antietam Creek. Unable to bury more than a small number of its 1,546 dead before retreating across the Potomac, Lee's army left interment of its fallen comrades to the Federals, who attended to the burial of their own men before that of their enemies.

Civilians watch as troops of the 130th Pennsylvania dig trenches for mass graves near the Sunken Road and the Roulette farm lane, in this gouache by special artist Frank Schell. News of the slaughter spread quickly, and the battlefield was soon besieged by families hoping to find their wounded or claim their dead.

by Co., that is the members of each Co. are put together. Co. H was buried first in the uper end of the trench next the woods. They are laid in two tiers, one top of the other. The bottom tier was laid in, then straw laid over the head and feet, then the top tier laid on them and covered with dirt about 18 inches deep. Henry is the 3rd corpes from the upper end on the top tier next to the woods. Mr. Ainsworth, this is not the way we bury folks at home. I am sorry, but I was too late to have it different. Then there is a board put up at each end of the trench with the simple inscription, "15th Mass. buried here." There is 39 men in the trench with Henry. There is others of our Regmt buried near by. Some of our men had their clothes taken off by the rebels. Henry did not have anything taken but shoes and what was in his pockets.

A Union soldier looks down on the grave of Lieutenant John A. Clark of the 7th Michigan. A simple inscribed headboard marks the grave; beside it lies the crumpled body of a young Confederate. Clark (left), a veteran of the Peninsula campaign, was killed during Sedgwick's advance into the West Woods.

Civilians help lift a wounded soldier into a Federal wagon as other volunteers assist a field surgeon performing an amputation, in this sketch by Alfred Waud. The more than 17,000 wounded at Antietam so overwhelmed local facilities that a woman from a nearby town wrote, "They filled every building and overflowed into the country round,—wherever four walls and a roof were found together—every inch of space, and yet the cry was for room."

PRIVATE GEORGE A. ALLEN
76TH NEW YORK INFANTRY, HOFMANN'S BRIGADE

Having survived the deadly artillery battle in the early hours on the 17th, Private Allen, assisting a wounded comrade off the battlefield, was detailed for duty as a hospital steward by a surgeon in charge. Until his discharge in April 1863 for a heart problem, Allen would devote his days to caring for the Antietam wounded at the Reformed Church hospital in Keedysville, Maryland.

The principle hospital was established in the brick church near the upper end of the town. Boards were laid on top of the seats, then straw and blankets, and most of the worse cases of wounded were taken to this, the headquarters. Comrades with wounds of all conceivable shapes were brought in and placed side by side as thick as they could lay, and the bloody work of amputation commenced. The Surgeons, myself and a corps of nurses with sleeves rolled up, worked with tender care and anxiety to relieve the pain and save the lives of all we could. A pit was dug just under the window at the back of the church and as soon as a limb was amputated I would take it to the window and drop it outside into the pit. The arms, legs, feet and hands that were dropped into that hole would amount to several hundred pounds. On one occasion I had to fish out a hand for its former owner, as he insisted that it was all cramped up and hurt him. . . .

Most of the wounded got it into their heads that no one but myself could dress their wounds, change their bandages, etc., so I had to do the most of it, and was kept busy for several weeks, night and day. For three weeks I never realized that I had not slept at all. I was in several battles and on many hard marches, but nothing ever wore me as that did. At night I would drop down upon the sofa in the pulpit, but no sooner had I closed my eyes than some one of the many amputees would call me to change a bandage or something. When a patient gets it in his head that you can handle his stump more carefully than any one else, you're elected.

COLONEL JOHN B. GORDON
6TH ALABAMA INFANTRY, RODES' BRIGADE

Recuperating from severe wounds, Gordon considered himself fortunate to have at his side his devoted wife, Fanny, who accompanied her husband throughout his campaigns. But her constant presence so annoyed General Early that he was once heard to wish that the Federals would capture her.

"Summoning all my strength, I said: 'Here's your handsome husband; been to an Irish wedding.'"

Mrs. Gordon was soon with me. When it was known that the battle was on, she had at once started toward the front. The doctors were doubtful about the propriety of admitting her to my room; but I told them to let her come. I was more apprehensive of the effect of the meeting upon her nerves than upon mine. My face was black and shapeless—so swollen that one eye was entirely hidden and the other nearly so. My right leg and left arm and shoulder were bandaged and propped with pillows. I knew she would be greatly shocked. As she reached the door and looked, I saw at once that I must reassure her. Summoning all my strength, I said: "Here's your handsome husband; been to an Irish wedding." Her answer was a suppressed scream, whether of anguish or relief at finding me able to speak, I do not know. Thenceforward, for the period in which my life hung in the balance, she sat at my bedside, trying to supply concentrated nourishment to sustain me against the constant drainage. With my jaw immovably set, this was exceedingly difficult and discouraging. My own confidence in ultimate recovery, however, was never shaken until erysipelas, that deadly foe of the wounded, attacked my left arm. The doctors told Mrs. Gordon to paint my arm above the wound three or four times a day with iodine. She obeyed the doctors by painting it, I think, three or four hundred times a day. Under God's providence, I owe my life to her incessant watchfulness night and day, and to her tender nursing through weary weeks and anxious months.

Allowing himself to be taken prisoner, Dr. John M. Gaines, a surgeon with the 8th Virginia Infantry, remained in Boonsboro to care for the hundreds of Confederate wounded unable to return to Virginia. There he became friends with Dr. O. J. Smith, a Boonsboro physician and Confederate sympathizer whose daughter, Helen Jeanette, Gaines would marry after the war.

could get all the attention required, though at present I canot see how it can be done, not Knowing how long I have to remain at this Hospital.

I wish You would come instantly to see me, but bring none of the Ladies with You.

You will take the Cars to Frederik City and from there every body can tell You, the direction McClellans Army took. You can also see in the News Papers, what Place the Battle was fought on. Do not give up, until You find me.

Inquire for the wounded of General Howards Brigade/late Burns/ commanded by Col: De Witt Baxter.

Your affectionate
friend
Edward Fulton
Comp. N. 72nd Reg. P.V.
Philadelphia Fire Zouaves.

PRIVATE EDWARD A. FULTON

72D PENNSYLVANIA INFANTRY, HOWARD'S BRIGADE

Private Fulton received a leg wound during the fighting in the West Woods. His thighbone, fractured by a bullet, failed to mend properly, and he was discharged from duty in spring 1863. While recuperating, Fulton was anxious for home.

*S*tonewall Barn Hospital
near Sharpsburgh Maryland
Septbr 21/62
Dear Sis!

A friend of mine is writing this, to let You Know, that I was very badly wounded at the last Battle, but I hope not so bad, as at first supposed.

In the early part of the action a ball stroke me in the thigh and afterward another one stroke me in the left thigh, passing clear through the left thigh, and entering the right one, breaking the bone. It was at first thought, that I would loose my life, but I think I shall only loose my right leg. A piece of a shell also stroke me in the left foot, while I was laying wounded on the field. I was also stroke by a ball, on the mouth. I wish You would devise some means of getting me home, where I

Second Presbyterian Church Hospital, Frederick City, Maryland

Women of Frederick, Maryland, minister to wounded soldiers at the Second Presbyterian Church hospital in this sketch by 19-year-old Charles F. Johnson, a private in the 9th New York. With his regiment heavily engaged in the IX Corps attack, Johnson took a bullet in the hip. He was forced to spend several weeks in the hospital but rejoined his unit the following spring.

PRIVATE ROBERT G. CARTER

22D MASSACHUSETTS INFANTRY, BARNES' BRIGADE

Federal units dogging the Confederate rear guard were overwhelmed by A. P. Hill's men as they tried to form battle lines on the Rebel side of the Potomac at Shepherdstown. Hill bragged that "the Potomac was blue with the floating bodies of our foe." Carter, only 16 when he was mustered in a month earlier, witnessed the fate of the hapless 118th Pennsylvania, the so-called Corn Exchange regiment.

Early on the morning of the 20th we were ordered to make a reconnaissance in force across the Potomac, at Blackford's ford. This had been used by Lee, both in coming into and retreating from Maryland. It was, where we forded it, some distance below the dam, quite shallow, a little over the knees, with a somewhat pebbly bottom, but not many large rocks. We were to ascertain the whereabouts of Lee's rear guard. We had no trouble in finding it. Innocent of the diversion which was in store for us, we splashed and paddled our way along. Some of the men had taken off both shoes and stockings; others, perhaps the majority, had kept them on; these were the wise ones, for we had use for them on our return.

The cavalry were met returning. The splashing of their horses sent the water flying into the faces of some of our grumblers who, out of spite, shouted out, "Are there any dead cavalrymen ahead? What guerillas do you belong to?" etc., etc.; to which the answer came back promptly, "Yes, you bummers, we do the fighting and leave the dead cavalrymen for the 'dough boys' to pick up. Go to the rear, you 'worm crushers!' "

The chaffing continued until the river was crossed. We were then hurriedly, and with sharp commands, formed into line of battle, ordered to "load at will," and by the flank were directed to move by a narrow cart path up a rather sheltered ravine, on one side of which was a protecting bank, and on the other a rather abrupt bluff that formed the bank of the Potomac.

We again hastily formed line of battle. A crack, a crash, followed by another and another in quick succession directly over our heads, came from our batteries on the Maryland shore, and was the first intimation we had that a rebel line of battle was rapidly moving down upon us.

"Fix bayonets!" came the command, followed by "Lie down!" and although from our sheltered position we could not then see the enemy's line, a moment later the roll of musketry from the right of our brigade told us that the engagement had begun. . . .

As the firing surged along the line toward us, and the men commenced firing at the grey line now beginning to show up over the bank, we were ordered to withdraw. As we fell back, the 118th Pennsylvania, which had received the full force of the blow thus far, did not follow us, and being overwhelmed by superior numbers, were driven from their position on the extreme right to the crest of the bluff, where many were killed, wounded or captured, and driven pell-mell over its precipitous slopes.

Our passage back to the Maryland shore was a hard one, higher up and nearer the dam; the river was full of snares and pitfalls and up to our necks in many places, besides being very rocky.

As we emerged from the stream and passed through Berdan's Sharpshooters, in the dry bed of the Canal, we halted for a moment to gain our breath. While resting here, a little officer of the 118th Pennsylvania came in behind us. He was dripping with water. In his *enthusiastic energy* to move across and get to the rear, he had not stopped to see how many of the regiment had followed. Waving his sword, he shouted in a high and squeaky voice—"Follow me, all that are left of the gallant

Refusing to withdraw without orders received through the proper chain of command, Colonel Charles M. Prevost, commander of the 118th Pennsylvania Infantry, was largely responsible for the rout of his untried troops.

FRANK LESLIE'S ILLUSTRATED NEWSPAPER.

69

Oct. 25, 1862.]

CAMPAIGN IN MARYLAND—BATTLE AT DAM NO 4, POTOMAC RIVER, BETWEEN LUTTERFIELD'S BRIGADE AND A LARGE REBEL FORCE.—From a Sketch by our Special Artist, Mr. F. H. Schell.

'Corn Exchange!' " He turned as he did so, and there behind stood one half drowned little corporal, smaller than himself, beside a very tall private. Both the officer and corporal pieced together could hardly have equalled his size. We broke out into uncontrollable laughter at the absurdity of the group. It seems that the order for the brigade to withdraw across the river had not reached this regiment on the right for some still unexplained reason, or they attempted to retire when too late, but, either on account of the chaffing they received, or the sensitiveness which they naturally felt at this, their first battle, from that time on there was a lack of *cordiality* between the rest of the brigade and our brethren from the Keystone State, who stoutly asserted that we ran away and left them to their fate, and whenever on picket, scrambling for water at a small spring, gathering rails, or "reaching" for straw, there were numerous collisions, although no bloodshed, between the

Federal artillerymen on the Maryland shore of the Potomac fire their guns over the green troops of the 118th Pennsylvania to cover their retreat across the river near Boteler's Ford just below Shepherdstown.

two commands. A conversation on picket occurred shortly after between one of our sharp-witted Irishmen and a member of the "Corn Exchange" regiment. The latter was upholding their cause and its gallant conduct in staying, while our fellow was very strongly arguing that "any regiment after being ordered to retreat, that did not do so, deserved all they got," etc. The other angrily rejoined, "If you had behaved as well as the *'gallant* Corn Exchange,' the Johnnies would have been whipped." "Oh begorra! 'Corn Exchange!' 'Corn Exchange!' " said Pat, "there is no such regiment as that now. It is the *'Cob* Exchange,' for didn't the 'rebs' shell all the corn off yez the other day?"

PRIVATE ANDREW J. PROFFITT

18TH NORTH CAROLINA, BRANCH'S BRIGADE

A native of Wilkes County, Proffitt, a schoolteacher, was one of four brothers who served in the Confederate army. Together with his brother Alfred Newton ("A. N." in the account below), Proffitt enlisted on August 22, 1862, but his regiment was held in reserve at Antietam. In a letter to his parents, Andrew described his first encounter with the Yankees at the Battle of Shepherdstown.

We turned on them and had a bloody engagement. We formed in line of battle about one mile from them and made a general charge. exposed the hole way to the heavist bombing said to be by old soldiers that they ever saw but we routed them and drove them back across the river about 9 or 10 oclock. I suppose we lost a great many but the yankees lay on the field in heaps and piles. we got all their arms knap sacks and all they had with [them and] many prisoners. as they crossed the river we give them fits. A. N. and I shot as long as we could see a blue coat exposed to the fire of 8 batteries. the bombs burst round our heads with terrific fury and showers of grape and canister fell mingled with limbs of trees thick around us but the God of heaven protected us from their power which I hope he will ever do. we wer so much exhosted from the fatigues of the charge that we threw a way all our clothes & blankets only what we have on but that is all right we will get more. A. N. was slightly struck on the arm with a piec of shell or something. he droped his gun. I asked him if he was hurt he said not he grabed his and fought like a heroe while the sweat droped fast from his brow.

Not having been issued weapons until September 15, the Wilkes County recruits in the 18th North Carolina, among them Private Alfred N. Proffitt (left), first fired their Springfield rifle muskets five days later, at Federals retreating across the Potomac River at Boteler's Ford. Alfred Proffitt's wound, suffered in the exchange, was so slight that it went unreported in the company's records.

DR. OLIVER WENDELL HOLMES SR.

Holmes, a Boston physician and author, imagined the worst the night he got word that his son had been shot through the neck on the Antietam battlefield. The next morning the distraught father began a journey to Maryland by train and horse-drawn wagon. He spent days in a fruitless and frustrating search for his boy. Finally, on a train bound for Philadelphia, father and son were reunited.

It was getting late in the evening when we began our rounds. The principal collections of the wounded were in the churches. Boards were laid over the tops of the pews, on these some straw was spread, and on this the wounded lay, with little or no covering other than such scanty clothes as they had on. . . . I could not help thinking the patients must be cold; but they were used to camp-life, and did not complain. . . . I saw one poor fellow who had been shot through the breast; his breathing was labored, and he was tossing, anxious and restless. The men were debating about the opiate he was to take, and I was thankful that I happened there at the right moment to see that he was well narcotized for the night. Was it possible that my Captain could be lying on the straw in one of these places? Certainly *possible,* but not probable; but as the lantern was held over each bed, it was with a kind of thrill that I looked upon the features it illuminated. Many times, as I went from hospital to hospital in my wanderings, I started as some faint resemblance—the shade of a young man's hair, the outline of his half-turned face—recalled the presence I was in search of. The face would turn towards me and the momentary illusion would pass away, but still the fancy clung to me. There was no figure huddled up on its rude couch, none stretched at the road-side, none toiling languidly along the dusty pike, none passing in car or in ambulance, that I did not scrutinize, as if it might be that for which I was making my pilgrimage to the battle-field. . . .

The time approached for the train to arrive from Hagerstown, and we went to the station. . . .

To-day there was the delay spoken of, but nothing worse. The expected train came in so quietly that I was almost startled to see it on the track. Let us walk calmly through the cars, and look around us.

In the first car, on the fourth seat to the right, I saw my Captain; there saw I him, even my first-born, whom I had sought through many cities.

"How are you, Boy?"

"How are you, Dad?"

"The hidden cisterns of the soul may be filling fast with sweet tears, while the windows through which it looks are undimmed by a drop or a film of moisture."

Such are the proprieties of life, as they are observed among us Anglo-Saxons of the nineteenth century, decently disguising those natural impulses that made Joseph, the Prime-Minister of Egypt, weep aloud so that the Egyptians and the house of Pharaoh heard,—nay, which had once overcome his shaggy old uncle Esau so entirely that he fell on his brother's neck and cried like a baby in the presence of all the women. But the hidden cisterns of the soul may be filling fast with sweet tears, while the windows through which it looks are undimmed by a drop or a film of moisture.

Weeks after being wounded at Antietam, Oliver Wendell Holmes Jr., future associate justice of the Supreme Court, returned to duty at Falmouth, Virginia, only to be hospitalized for dysentery and later wounded at Fredericksburg.

SUSAN BRANCH

Although reports of the unprecedented bloodletting at Antietam quickly reached the Confederate states, reliable information on casualties was not readily available. For Susan Branch, daughter of Brigadier General Lawrence O'Bryan Branch, the anguish of waiting for news of her father would turn to despair when she received word of his death. General Branch was hit in the head by a sharpshooter's bullet while following the action through his field glasses.

Raleigh, Sept. 23rd 1862.
My Very dear dear Aunt
Oh how sad is the news which was yesterday transmitted to us through the telegraph. It seems very hard for us to realize, nevertheless it is true. I will try and give you the circumstances as well as it is in my power. On last Sunday evening just as we were going to Church, a dispatch was brought us, saying that it was reported in Richmond that Pa was killed. Oh such a shock it was. We had not even heard that he was in the battle. All day Sunday we endured the suspense, not knowing whether it was a mere idle rumor coming from a straggler from the battle field, or whether it was a sad reality as it has proven to be. Sunday night at about 10 o'clock we had another dispatch, saying that Pa was safe, for the gentleman that telegraphed had seen an aid of Genl. A. P. Hills, who said that Pa was unhurt. We continued to receive these contradictory dispatches, one from the President, and another through Commodore Chaney, until late Yesterday evening when we had a dispatch from Major Englehardt, who is one of Pa's staff officers, saying that Pa was shot by a rifle ball through the head, Wednesday evening

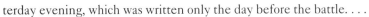
just about sundown, and died instantly in Mr. Englehardt's arms. He said that he would be at Stanto to-day with his body, and would probably reach here Thursday. Oh Aunt Sue, it is terrible, terrible to bear. What is home with out him, or what will it ever be? Ma says do come to see her, for it will be the greatest comfort in the world to us all to see you. It was Pa's wish that you should come, and do come if you possibly can, but if you cant dont distress yourself about it. Ma says you know she has already loved you but now it is increased ten fold. Do come to see us. . . . Ma has a letter here that she received from Pa yes-

terday evening, which was written only the day before the battle. . . .

The thought is almost unbearable that he should be so cut off from a dependent family. I hope we will all be reunited once more in that land of rest, where there is neither trouble nor sorrow. Ma says she will write to you in a day or two, just as soon as she is able to do any thing, but do come and see us if you can, for it will be the greatest comfort in the world to us all. Do write to us if you can not come. Believe me my ever dearest aunt, your most devoted niece.

Sue Branch.

In the absence of news from the front, Varina Davis, the Confederate first lady, offered Mrs. Lawrence Branch hope in the note below that her husband might be safe. General Branch (right) was the ninth Confederate of his rank to fall that day.

ANNA HOLSTEIN
VOLUNTEER NURSE

When her husband, William, a volunteer nurse, returned home with stories of the suffering he saw on the battlefield of Antietam, Anna Holstein abandoned her work with the Soldiers' Aid Society for the more challenging task of nursing the wounded. Holstein and her husband left their home in Upper Merion, Pennsylvania, and headed for Sharpsburg, Maryland, to begin what would amount to three years of service in field hospitals of the Army of the Potomac. Recalling those years, Holstein wrote of an encounter with a widow at Antietam.

Among the many who came to visit the Battlefield was a young wife whose frantic grief I can never forget. She came hurriedly as soon as she knew her husband was in the battle, only to find him dead and buried two days before her arrival. Unwilling to believe the facts that strangers told her—how in the early morning they had laid him beside his comrades in the orchard, she still insisted upon seeing him. Accompanying some friends to the spot she could not wait the slow process of removing the body but in her agonizing grief, clutched the earth by handfuls where it lay upon the quiet sleeper's form. And when at length the slight covering was removed and the blanket thrown from off the face, she needed but one glance to assure her it was all too true. Then passive and quiet beneath the stern reality of this crushing sorrow, she came back to the room in our house. The preparations for taking the body to Philadelphia were at once made for her and with his remains she left for her desolate home.

183

"Instead of a decided brilliant victory and the end of the war, we have a doubtful victory and the enemy left to recruit at will and prolong the contest indefinitely."

SURGEON DANIEL M. HOLT

121ST NEW YORK INFANTRY, BARTLETT'S BRIGADE

Receiving his U.S. Army commission in August of 1862, Holt, a successful country doctor from Newport, New York, was at the age of 42 the oldest staff member of his regiment. The physician was shocked by the ruin and carnage in the wake of Antietam, and in the account below he lambastes his commander for failing to pursue and crush the weakened Rebel army.

At last, the Confederates under a flag of truce, asking the privilege to bury their dead, vacated their position and crossed the Potomac into Virginia where they now are. We ought to have utterly routed and destroyed their army had the effort been made, for they were completely discouraged and ready to accept any terms of capitulation or surrender had it been pressed upon them, but no! McClellan thought too much of them and let them off as they liked, into the precincts of their own state, thus giving them length of days and vitality of action which we had in our hands to withhold. It is sickening to see such parleying with rebels when we have the power to do differently. It looks almost like treason upon the part of our officers to let the bars down and tell them to get away as quickly as possible. I believe and shall ever believe, that General McClellan could have made his own terms with Lee at Antietam, but for some reason unexplained, the reverse was the case and instead of a decided brilliant victory and the end of the war, we have a doubtful victory and the enemy left to recruit at will and prolong the contest indefinitely.

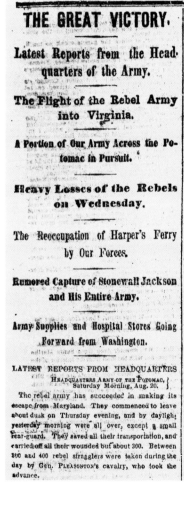

Within a few days of the battle at Antietam, stories of the bloody contest appeared in both Northern and Southern newspapers. Despite headlines trumpeting a Union victory in the New York Times (above, left) and claims of a Confederate advantage by the Charleston Daily Courier (above, right), the battle ended in a tactical stalemate, with staggering losses on both sides.

CAPTAIN SHEPHARD G. PRYOR
12TH GEORGIA INFANTRY, J. A. WALKER'S BRIGADE

In the wake of the bloodshed at Antietam, a shaken and subdued Rebel army retreated across the Potomac into Virginia. Writing to his wife in Americus, Georgia, Pryor, who survived the Maryland campaign unscathed, keenly felt the Confederate losses.

LIEUTENANT GEORGE W. WHITMAN
51ST NEW YORK INFANTRY, FERRERO'S BRIGADE

The September 22 Emancipation Proclamation set off reverberations among the rank and file of the Union army. Soldiers who were abolitionists embraced the measure with enthusiasm. Others, such as Walt Whitman's brother George, harbored doubts about the proclamation's effectiveness.

Dear the heavyest fight of the war was fought in Md near & at Sharpsburg Wednesday the 17th all of our forces was engaged during the day fought all day the 12th Ga went into the fight with 110 men had 63 killed and wounded more than half our number great many other reg suffered similar to ours then again there was some that lost but fiew there was 14 of our rg killed dead on the field others since died from their wounds the war is becomeing more desperate dayly I think which makes me have some hopes that it will end this winter the prospects ahead though looks dark and gloomy our army has been verry successfull all this summer I fear this Md trip has injured us more than done good wee lost more than wee gained in it I think the lost of the enemy killed was twice as many as our from what I could see on the field after the fight it was a draw fight. . . . I have yet strong hopes of getting home to live in peace once more Oh what a world of trouble is this now not a house but what mourns the loss of some dear relative or friend it will take years to blot out this generation will have to pass away first I have written about all that I can this time I wrote you yesterday that Probe was killed in the fight of wednesday you may get this first I mourn his loss as though he was my own dear brother he was a true soldier Oh his little family what will they do but there are thousands in a worse condition than his Il stop here My love to all.

Everything now is quiet and it is quite a releif to be out of the sound of canon after hearing it almost daily, and sometimes nightly, for two or three weeks. I think the late rebel movement into Maryland has been a very unfortunate one for them, as they did not meet with anything like the encouragement from the Marylanders that they expected, and I believe that after the battle of Bull Run they firmly expected to invade Pennsylvania if not capture Washington and Baltimore, and now to be badly beaten twice, and driven back with such terrible loss, must be very discouraging and had it not been for bad management, cowardice, or treachery at Harpers Fery, I believe we could have bagged the most of their army. . . .

I expect there will shortly be some promotions made in the regt and I think I stand a good chance to be made a 1st Lieut. I think, after Cap gets back if everything remains quiet I shall try for a furlough to come home for a few days and see you all. I have stuck pretty close to business since I have been sogering, and the regt never went on a march or into a fight without my being on hand. (I see by the papers that Uncle Abe has issued a proclamation declaring the slaves free in all the States that are in rebellion on the first of next Jan. I dont know what effect it is going to have on the war, but one thing is certain, he has got to lick the south before he can free the niggers,) and unless he drives ahead and convinces the south, before the first of January, that we are bound to lick them, and it would be better for them to behave themselvs and keep their slaves, than to get licked and lose them, I dont think the proclamation will do much good.

Executive Mansion,

Washington, Sep. 26. , 1862.

Major John J. Key.

    Sir

        I am informed
that in answer to the question
"Why was not the rebel army
bagged immediately after the battle near Sharpsburg" propounded
to you by Major Levi C. Turner,
Judge Advocate &c. You answered
"That is not the game" "The object is that neither army shall
get much advantage of the other; that both shall be kept in
the field till they are exhausted, when we will make a compro-
mise, and save slavery".
    I shall be very happy if you
will, within twenty four hours

from the receipt of this, prove to
me by Major Turner, that you
did not, either literally, or in
substance, make the answer stated—

                Yours

                A. Lincoln

At about 11 o'clock A.M. Sep.
27. 1862. Major Key & Major
Turner appear before me.
Major Turner says, "As I remember it, the conversation was, I
asked the question why we did
not bag them after the battle
at Sharpsburg? Major Key's reply
was that was not the game.
that we should tire the rebel-
els out and ourselves, that
that was the only way the

In the absence of a decisive Federal victory at Antietam, rumors circulated that the objective had not been victory but a stalemate that might lead to a negotiated peace. An irate President Lincoln learned that one Major John J. Key, brother of an aide to General McClellan, had expressed such an opinion and wrote him to ask if it was true. When Key owned up, Lincoln dismissed him. Above, in Lincoln's hand, is the letter to Key (or a copy of it), followed by the president's notes on Key's response.

LIEUTENANT JAMES ABRAHAMS
GILMORE'S COMPANY OF WEST VIRGINIA CAVALRY,
SCAMMON'S BRIGADE

For four days in October, President Abraham Lincoln toured the Antietam battlefield, reviewing the troops, surveying the wreckage the battle had wrought, and lending support to the fighting men of the Army of the Potomac. Although he lacked a military bearing, the commander in chief nevertheless made a good impression on the troops, as Lieutenant Abrahams recalled.

ere President Lincoln visited and reviewed the troops. In appearance, Lincoln was not a prepossessing figure, especially on horseback; tall, thin and angular, with arms and legs that seemed out of all proportion to his body, but with a kindly, anxious face, furrowed with care and anxiety. As he passed along the lines his black cloth suit and high plug hat contrasted strangely with the gold and glitter of McClellan and his staff, but he seemed to look right into the soul of each individual soldier and although he uttered not a word, yet he left an abiding impression that he was our fast and sympathizing friend.

Eager to capitalize on the Confederate retreat and the moral impact of the Emancipation Proclamation, Lincoln yearned to pursue the Rebels into Virginia. In a continuing effort to spur McClellan into action, the frustrated president traveled to the battlefield on October 1. Here he is shown conferring privately with his reluctant general on October 4, the last day of his visit. Content with having captured dozens of Confederate flags, one of which is seen in the lower left corner, the Young Napoleon cited numerous excuses for remaining in camp. Lincoln later lamented, "He has got the slows."

CORPORAL AUSTIN C. STEARNS
13TH MASSACHUSETTS INFANTRY, HARTSUFF'S BRIGADE

No amount of prodding from the president could set McClellan in motion. It was nearly six weeks after the battle before he stirred. On October 26 the Army of the Potomac, now reinforced to 110,000 troops, crossed the Potomac on a new pontoon bridge at Berlin, Maryland, and headed south in pursuit of Lee's army. As Stearns would remember, McClellan's delay caused the men to march in miserable conditions. Not two weeks later, it would also lead to the general's dismissal.

At length, after repeated urgeings by the President and when there was no more excuses to offer, after the golden days of Oct. had passed, after the rebel army was thoroughly rested and its ranks filled, then the "Young Napoleon" was ready to move the grand "Army of the Potomac," was ready to inaugurate a campaign from the Potomac if the President would assume all responsibilities. The good man said he was ready, and would assume each and all responsibilities if the army would only move. Consequently, at the close of a cold and wet sabbath day in the gloomy month of Nov., with the winds sighing in the treetops of our camp, orders came to pack up. We could hardly beleive that after idling away so many sunny days that we would be compeled to break camp and brave the storm of a November night. We boys delayed to strike our tents hoping there might be a mistake or the order countermanded. But the order was imperitave and "fall in" was soon given. Quickly striking and rolling up our wet tents and straping on our knapsacks, we bid adieu to our camp where we had passed two months comparitively doing nothing.

We had hardly passed the borders of our camp when darkness set in and, with the roads filled with men and teams, our progress was nessarily slow. It was terriable marching, the mud was deep, and cobble stones were plenty, adding to a pitch dark night. Henry Vining, hitting his foot against a stone, fell full length into the mud, and on regaining his feet again with the assistance of others, he called out to his brother in a most pitiful tone "Albion, I'm all mud"; this served for a by-word during our entire time of service whenever we saw anyone laboring under circumstances that was not at all favorable for them.

COLONEL CHARLES S. WAINWRIGHT
ARTILLERY COMMANDER, I CORPS

On November 7 General McClellan received orders from President Lincoln directing him to relinquish command of the Army of the Potomac. He took the blow stoically, but later in a letter to his wife he expressed regret, writing: "Alas for my poor country! I know in my inmost heart she never had a truer servant." On November 10 the general was shown a moving display of loyalty by his troops, as described by Colonel Wainwright.

McClellan took leave of this corps today; he had previously bid adieu to the others. About noon the whole corps except the pickets and guards was drawn up in rear of the camps of the Second and Third Divisions. Accompanied by General Reynolds and both their staffs, he rode slowly along the lines, the men all saluting as he passed. Such a sight I shall never see again. Not a word was spoken, no noisy demonstration of regret at losing him, but there was hardly a dry eye in the ranks. Very many of the men wept like children, while others could be seen gazing after him in mute grief,

one may almost say despair, as a mourner looks down into the grave of a dearly loved friend. The General himself was quite overwhelmed, as well he might be, to see such affection and devotion testified towards him. Napoleon's farewell at Fontainbleau may have been more impressive—doubtless it was, for the French are great at scenic effect. But I could not have supposed there would be such a display of feeling from Americans. I do not know how the feeling was shown in the Second, Fifth, and Sixth Corps, but it must have been quite as strong as in this, which, except the Third Division, has only been under his command for two months.

After the review, the General passed an hour or two at our headquarters, and bade a personal farewell to all the officers who gathered there, of whom there must have been sixty or more. I remained near him the whole time, determined to see for myself just how he acted, and to hear just what he said. All on being introduced expressed their great regret at parting with him, some using expressions with regard to his removal which they had no right to use, and a few even going so far as to beg him to resist the order, and saying that the army would support him. These last he reproved gently but strongly. To everyone personally he expressed his high opinion of General Burnside, and begged them to transfer to him all the devotion and zeal they had ever shown for himself. Whatever might be their opinion of McClellan as a general, no one who saw and heard him today as I did could help pronouncing him a good and great man: great in soul if not in mind.

Doffing his kepi, General McClellan bids farewell to the Army of the Potomac near Warrenton, Virginia, on November 10, 1862, in this sketch by Alfred Waud. McClellan's successor, General Ambrose E. Burnside, rides beside him. For the last time, cheering soldiers in the tens of thousands turned out, corps by corps, in a final review to honor their beloved leader. "I never before had to exercise so much self-control," McClellan wrote his wife. "The scenes of to-day repay me for all that I have endured."

"Mr. Brady has done something to bring home to us the terrible reality and earnestness of war."

NEW YORK TIMES
REPORTER

Having raced to the Antietam battlefield, photographers Alexander Gardner and James F. Gibson, working between September 18 and 21, made pictures of the dead. Weeks later they exhibited their work at the New York gallery of Mathew Brady, their employer. For the first time the American public were exposed to the sight of war dead—American corpses on an American battlefield, no less —and the Brady exhibition attracted throngs of visitors. As noted by a reporter in his review of the show, the stark, unromanticized images of the Antietam dead had a stunning effect; the conflict had been to many, heretofore, faceless.

The living that throng Broadway care little perhaps for the Dead at Antietam, but we fancy they would jostle less carelessly down the great thoroughfare, saunter less at their ease, were a few dripping bodies, fresh from the field, laid along the pavement. There would be a gathering up of skirts and a careful picking of way: conversation would be less lively, and the general air of pedestrians more subdued. As it is, the dead of the battle-field come up to us very rarely, even in dreams. We see the list in the morning paper at breakfast, but dismiss its recollection with the coffee. There is a confused mass of names, but they are all strangers; we forget the horrible significance that dwells amid the jumble of type. The roll we read is being called over in Eternity, and pale, trembling lips are answering to it. Shadowy fingers point from the page to a field where even imagination is loth to follow. Each of these little names that the printer struck off so lightly last night, whistling over his work, and that we speak with a clip of the tongue, represents a bleeding, mangled corpse. It is a thunderbolt that will crash into some brain—a dull, dead, remorseless weight that will fall upon some heart, straining it to breaking. There is nothing very terrible to us, however, in the list, though our sensations might be different if the newspaper carrier left the names on the battle-field, and the bodies at our doors instead. . . .

Mr. Brady has done something to bring home to us the terrible reality and earnestness of war. If he has not brought bodies and laid them in our door-yards and along the streets, he has done something very like it. At the door of his gallery hangs a little placard, "The Dead of Antietam." . . . You will see hushed, reverend groups standing around these weird copies of carnage, bending down to look in the pale faces of the dead, chained by the strange spell that dwells in dead men's eyes. It seems somewhat singular that the same sun that looked down on the faces of the slain, blistering them, blotting out from the bodies all semblance to humanity, and hastening corruption, should have thus caught their features upon canvas, and given them perpetuity for ever. But so it is.

These poor subjects could not give the sun sittings, and they are taken as they fell, their poor hands clutching the grass around them in spasms of Pain, or reaching out for a help which none gave. . . . It is a bleak, barren plain and above it bends an ashen, sullen sky; there is no friendly shade or shelter from the noonday sun or the midnight dews; coldly and unpityingly the stars will look down on them and darkness will come with night to shut them in. But there is a poetry in the scene that no green fields or smiling landscapes can possess. Here lie men who have not hesitated to seal and stamp their convictions with their blood,—men who have flung themselves into the great gulf of the unknown to teach the world that there are truths dearer than life, wrongs and shames more to be dreaded than death. And if there be on earth one spot where the grass will grow greener than on another when the next Summer comes, where the leaves of Autumn will drop more lightly when they fall like a benediction upon a work completed and a promise fulfilled, it is these soldiers' graves.

There is one side of the picture that the sun did not catch, one phase that has escaped photographic skill. It is the background of widows and orphans, torn from the bosom of their natural protectors by the red remorseless hand of Battle, and thrown upon the fatherhood of God. Homes have been made desolate, and the light of life in thousands of hearts has been quenched forever. All of this desolation imagination must paint—broken hearts cannot be photographed.

These pictures have a terrible distinctness. By the aid of the magnifying-glass, the very features of the slain may be distinguished. We would

Two days after the battle, distended bodies of Confederates from J. R. Jones' division still lie along the west side of the Hagerstown Turnpike on the Miller farm.

scarce choose to be in the gallery, when one of the women bending over them should recognise a husband, a son, or a brother in the still, lifeless lines of bodies, that lie ready for the gaping trenches. For these trenches have a terror for a woman's heart, that goes far to outweigh all the others that hover over the battle-field. How can a mother bear to know that the boy whose slumbers she has cradled, and whose head her bosom pillowed until the rolling drum called him forth—whose poor, pale face, could she but reach it, should find the same pillow again—whose corpse should be strewn with the rarest flowers that Spring brings or Summer leaves—when, but for the privilege of touching the corpse, of kissing once more the lips though white and cold, of smoothing back the hair from the brow and cleansing it of blood stains, she would give all the remaining years of life that Heaven has allotted her—how can this mother bear to know that in a shallow trench, hastily dug, rude hands have thrown him. She would have handled the poor corpse so tenderly, have prized the boon of caring for it so dearly—yes, even the imperative office of hiding the dead from sight has been done by those who thought it trouble, and were only glad when their work ended.

GLOSSARY

abatis—A defensive barrier of fallen trees with branches pointed toward the enemy.

ball and buck—A round of ammunition consisting of a bullet and three buckshot.

battery—The basic unit of artillery, consisting of four to six guns.

Belgians—Belgian-made muskets, usually flintlocks, refitted with rifling, or grooves cut in the barrel, and modified to take a percussion cap.

Berdan's Sharpshooters—The 1st U.S. Sharpshooters Regiment, named after its founder, Hiram Berdan, a well-known marksman.

Bucktails—Nickname for the 13th Pennsylvania Reserves. Recruits were required to bring in a deer's tail as proof of their prowess with a rifle. The men then wore the tails in their hats.

butternut—The color, variously described as yellowish brown, tan, or brownish gray, of the common homespun Confederate uniform for those who could not afford to acquire cloth of the official gray. It became a general Northern term for a Confederate soldier.

caisson—A cart with large chests for carrying artillery ammunition. It is connected to a horse-drawn limber when moved.

canister—A tin can containing lead or iron balls that scatter when fired from a cannon. Used primarily in defense of a position as an antipersonnel weapon.

cap—Technically a percussion cap. A small, metal cover, infused with chemicals and placed on the hollow nipple of a rifle or revolver. When struck by the hammer the chemicals explode, igniting the powder charge in the breech.

change front—To alter the direction a body of troops faces in order to deliver or defend against an attack.

Corn Exchange Regiment—Nickname of the 118th Pennsylvania Volunteer Infantry. Named for the Philadelphia Corn Exchange Market.

double-quick—A trotting pace.

doughboy—A Federal infantryman. The term derives either from the brass uniform buttons resembling a dumpling or "doughboy," or from the white clay or "dough" used to whiten dress uniform belts.

elevating screw—A mechanism located under the breech of an artillery piece and used to raise or lower the angle of fire.

Enfield rifle—The Enfield rifle musket was adopted by the British in 1853, and the North and South imported nearly a million to augment their own production. Firing a .577-caliber projectile similar to the Minié ball, it is fairly accurate at 1,100 yards.

forage—To search for and acquire provisions from nonmilitary sources. To soldiers of the Civil War it often meant, simply, stealing.

grapeshot—Iron balls (usually nine) bound together and fired from a cannon. Resembling a cluster of grapes, the balls break apart and scatter on impact. Although references to grape or grapeshot are numerous in the literature, some experts claim that it was not used on Civil War battlefields.

hardtack—A durable cracker, or biscuit, made of plain flour and water and normally about three inches square and a half-inch thick.

hors de combat—French for "out of combat," meaning dead or disabled.

lanyard—An artillerist's cord with a handle on one end and a clip connector for a friction primer on the other. The friction primer is inserted into the touchhole on an artillery piece. When the gunner jerks the lanyard, friction in the touchhole ignites powder in the breech, firing the weapon.

limber—A two-wheeled, horse-drawn vehicle to which a gun carriage or a caisson is attached.

lunette—A crescent-shaped fortification, usually for artillery.

mess—A group of soldiers who prepare and eat meals together, or to eat such a meal; the place where such a meal is prepared and eaten.

Minié ball—The standard bullet-shaped projectile fired from the rifled muskets of the time. Designed by French Army officers Henri-Gustave Delvigne and Claude-Etienne Minié, the bullet's hollow base expanded, forcing its sides into the grooves, or rifling, of the musket's barrel. This caused the bullet to spiral in flight, giving it greater range and accuracy. Appears as minie, minnie, and minni.

musket—A smoothbore, muzzleloading shoulder arm.

muster—To assemble. To be mustered in is to be enlisted or enrolled in service. To be mustered out is to be discharged from service, usually on expiration of a set time.

Napoleon—A smoothbore, muzzleloading artillery piece developed under the direction of Napoleon III. It fires a 12-pound projectile (and therefore is sometimes called a 12-pounder). The basic light artillery weapon of both sides, Napoleons were originally cast in bronze; when that material became scarce in the South, iron was used.

oblique—At an angle. Units would be ordered to fire or move in a direction other than straight ahead.

open order—A loose formation in which, while rough lines might be maintained, men were more widely spaced than in normal formations.

parole—The pledge of a soldier released after being captured by the enemy that he will not fight again until properly exchanged.

Parrott guns—Muzzleloading, rifled artillery

pieces of various calibers made of cast iron with a unique wrought-iron reinforcing band around the breech. Patented in 1861 by Union officer Robert Parker Parrott, these guns are more accurate at longer range than their smoothbore predecessors.

picket—One or more soldiers on guard to protect the larger unit from surprise attack.

pick the tube—To clear the touchhole or vent of a musket or cannon with a wire pick.

prime—To pour gunpowder into the touchhole or vent of a cannon or musket.

rammer—An artillerist's tool used to force the powder charge and projectile down the barrel of a gun and seat them firmly in the breech. Also, another word for the ramrod of a shoulder arm.

red legs—See *Zouaves.*

redoubt—An enclosed, defensive stronghold, usually temporary.

rifle—Any weapon with spiral grooves cut into the bore, which give spin to the projectile, adding range and accuracy. Usually applied to cannon or shoulder-fired weapons.

rifle pits—Holes or shallow trenches dug in the ground from which soldiers can fire weapons and avoid enemy fire. Foxholes.

right shoulder shift—A position for holding a musket in which the butt of the gun is held in the right hand at just below chest height, the breech area rests on the right shoulder, and the muzzle points skyward. The rough equivalent of the modern *shoulder arms.*

section of artillery—Part of an artillery battery consisting of two guns, the soldiers who man them, and their supporting horses and equipment.

shelter tent—Also called a *tente d'abri,* pup tent, or dog tent, it consists of two shelter halves (each carried by a single soldier) buttoned together and hung over a ridgepole.

shrapnel—An artillery projectile in the form of a hollow sphere filled with metal balls packed around an explosive charge. Developed by British general Henry Shrapnel during the Napoleonic Wars, it is used as an antipersonnel weapon. A fuse ignites the charge at a set distance from the gun, raining the balls down on the enemy. Also called spherical case.

skirmisher—A soldier sent out in advance of the main body of troops to scout out and probe the enemy's position. Also, one who participates in a skirmish, a small fight usually incidental to the main action.

small arms—Any hand-held weapon, usually a firearm.

soger—Noun and verb for *soldier* and *to soldier.*

solid shot—A solid artillery projectile, oblong for rifled pieces and spherical for smoothbores.

Springfield rifle—The standard infantry shoulder arm of both sides; named for the U.S. arsenal at Springfield, Massachusetts, which produced it in 1861, 1863, and 1864 models. The term eventually referred to any similar weapon regardless of where it was made.

stack arms—To set aside weapons, usually three or more in a pyramid, interlocking at the end of the barrel with the butts on the ground.

vent—A small hole in the breech of a weapon through which a spark travels to ignite the powder charge and fire the piece.

worm fence—Also known as a snake fence, in which split rails are stacked alternately and at an angle producing a zigzagging line.

Zouaves—Regiments, both Union and Confederate, that model themselves after the original Zouaves of French Colonial Algeria. Known for spectacular uniforms featuring bright colors—usually reds and blues—baggy trousers, gaiters, short and open jackets, and a turban or fez, they specialize in precision drill and loading and firing muskets from the prone position.

ACKNOWLEDGMENTS

The editors wish to thank the following for their valuable assistance in the preparation of this volume:
Scott Anderson, Antietam National Battlefield, Sharpsburg, Md.; Doug Bast, Boonsboro Museum of History, Boonsboro, Md.; Tom Beckman, Historical Society of Delaware, Wilmington; Eric Blevins, North Carolina Division of Archives and History, Raleigh; Gerry Caughman, State Capitol, Hartford, Conn.; Paul Chiles, Antietam National Battlefield, Sharpsburg, Md.; Gregory A. Coco, Bendersville, Pa.; Sharon Dicks, University of Michigan, Ann Arbor;
Colonel Keith Gibson, Virginia Military Institute Museum, Lexington; Jeff Goldman, Maryland Historical Society, Baltimore; George E. Gorman IV, West Grove, Pa.; Randy W. Hackenburg, U.S. Army Military History Institute, Carlisle Barracks, Pa.; Alice Hanes, Portsmouth Naval Shipyard Museum, Portsmouth, Va.; Scott Hann, Mays Landing, N.J.; Corinne Hudgins, The Museum of the Confederacy, Richmond; Mary Ison and Staff, Reference Library, Prints and Photography Department, Library of Congress, Washington, D.C.; Lawrence T. Jones III, Confederate Calendar Works, Austin, Tex.; Paul Loane, Cherry Hill, N.J.; Steve Massengill, North Carolina Division of Archives and History, Raleigh; Greg Mast, Roxboro, N.C.; Sharon Minix, University of Michigan, Ann Arbor; Nick Noyes, Maine Historical Society, Portland; David Wynn Vaughan, Atlanta; John F. Weaver, McLean, Va.; Ernie Wetterer, Antietam National Battlefield, Sharpsburg, Md.; George S. Whiteley IV, Atlanta; Michael J. Winey, U.S. Army Military History Institute, Carlisle Barracks, Pa.; Tony Zeoli, Brockton City Hall, Brockton, Mass.

PICTURE CREDITS

The sources for the illustrations are listed below. Credits from left to right are separated by semicolons; from top to bottom by dashes.
All calligraphy by Mary Lou O'Brian/Inkwell, Inc. Dust jacket: front, Library of Congress Neg. No. B8171-570; rear, The Dawes Arboretum. 6, 7: Map by Paul Salmon. 8: Library of Congress. 15: Map by Walter W. Roberts, overlay by Time-Life Books. 16: Maryland Historical Society, Baltimore. 17: Frank & Marie-Thérèse Wood Print Collections, Alexandria, Va. 18: Courtesy Arthur Kent; courtesy Dave Zullo, copied by Evan H. Sheppard. 19: Courtesy National Library of Medicine—courtesy Don Troiani Collection, photographed by Larry Sherer. 20: National Archives; from *The Story of a Cannoneer under Stonewall Jackson,* by Edward A. Moore, published by J. P. Bell, Lynchburg, Va., 1910, copied by Larry Sherer. 22: Courtesy Dave Zullo, photographed by Evan H. Sheppard. 23: Bill Turner; Frank & Marie-Thérèse Wood Print Collections, Alexandria, Va. 25: Courtesy Bill Turner, copied by Philip Brandt George—Confederate Memorial Hall, photographed by Larry Sherer. 26: Courtesy Mrs. Benjamin Rosenstock. 27: Courtesy Doug Bast/Boonsboro Museum of History, photographed by Larry Sherer. 28: Library of Congress. 30: Archives Department, University Library, Dundee, Scotland. 31: Courtesy North Carolina Division of Archives and History. 33: Map by Walter W. Roberts. 34: Library of Congress Neg. No. 23725-262-11967; The Civil War Library and Museum, Philadelphia, copied by Blake Magner. 35: Bill Turner—Virginia Military Institute Museum, Lexington, photographed by Larry Sherer (2). 36: Massachusetts Commandery of the Military Order of the Loyal Legion of the United States and the U.S. Army Military History Institute (MASS-MOLLUS/ USAMHI), Carlisle Barracks, Pa., copied by Peter Ralston. 37: U.S. Army Military History Institute (USAMHI), Carlisle Barracks, Pa., copied by A. Pierce Bounds. 39: Michael Kraus, Creston, Ohio. 40: Library of Congress Neg. No. 21368 262-5278; USAMHI, Carlisle Barracks, Pa., copied by A. Pierce Bounds. 41: Special Collections Library, Duke University. 42: Frank & Marie-Thérèse Wood Print Collections, Alexandria, Va. 43: Made from a copy in the North Carolina Collection, University of North Carolina Library at Chapel Hill, of an original owned by Alfred T. Clifford. 44, 45: National Archives. 46: Richard Carlile Collection; USAMHI, Carlisle Barracks, Pa., copied by A. Pierce Bounds. 47: Lightfoot Collection. 48: Division of Military and Naval Affairs, State of New York, photographed by Henry Groskinsky. 49: Courtesy Doug Bast/Boonsboro Museum of History, photographed by Larry Sherer—Antietam National Battlefield, Sharpsburg, Md., photographed by Larry Sherer. 50, 51: Library of Congress; painting by Lach-

lan Field, courtesy Joseph Whitehorne, photographed by Henry Beville. 52: Library of Congress Neg. No. B815-1179. 55: Map by Walter W. Roberts. 56: The Museum of the Confederacy, Richmond, copied by Larry Sherer. 57: Library of Congress Neg. No. B8171-595. 59: Library of Congress Neg. No. B815-576. 61: Map by Walter W. Roberts. 62: MASS-MOLLUS/USAMHI, Carlisle Barracks, Pa., copied by A. Pierce Bounds. 63: From *History of the Doles-Cook Brigade: Army of Northern Virginia,* by Henry W. Thomas, The Franklin Printing and Publishing Co., Atlanta, 1903, copied by Philip Brandt George; Mrs. Lucille G. Parrish, Dry Branch, Ga., courtesy Gregory A. Coco Collection, photographed by Mike Brouse. 64: Courtesy Gregory A. Coco Collection, photographed by Mike Brouse. 65: Courtesy the Commonwealth of Massachusetts and the Bureau of State Office Buildings (2)—courtesy Brockton City Hall, photographed by Jeffrey R. Dykes. 66, 67: Eleanor S. Brockenbrough Library, The Museum of the Confederacy, Richmond, photographed by Katherine Wetzel; Library of Congress Neg. No. B811-577A. 68: The Dawes Arboretum. 69: Courtesy Scott Hann, photographed by Marty Lerario; Library of Congress. 70, 71: MASS-MOLLUS/USAMHI, Carlisle Barracks, Pa., copied by Peter Ralston; Library of Congress Neg. No. B811-560. 72: Confederate Research Center, Hillsboro, Tex.—Eleanor S. Brockenbrough Library, The Museum of the Confederacy, Richmond, photographed by Katherine Wetzel. 73: Archives Division, Texas State Library, Austin; courtesy George E. Gorman IV. 74: From *Deeds of Valor,* Vol. 1, edited by W. F. Beyer and O. F. Keydel, The Perrien-Keydel Company, Detroit, 1903; National Archives Neg. No. 111-B-4091. 76: Antietam National Battlefield, Sharpsburg, Md., photographed by Larry Sherer. 77: Painting by L. E. Faber, West Point Museum, U.S. Military Academy, photographed by Henry Groskinsky. 79: Map by R. R. Donnelley & Sons Co., Cartographic Services, overlay by Time-Life Books. 80, 81: USAMHI, Carlisle Barracks, Pa., copied by A. Pierce Bounds—Library of Congress; National Archives Neg. No. 111-BA-61. 82: Soldiers & Sailors Memorial Hall Museum, Pittsburgh, photographed by John Krachinski; Confederate Calendar Works, Austin, Tex. 83: Courtesy Cape Fear Museum, Wilmington, N.C., 1981.45.15, UDC Collection. 84: From *The Twenty-Seventh Indiana Volunteer Infantry in the War of the Rebellion, 1861-1865, First Division, 12th and 20th Corps,* by A Member of Company C, Monticello, Ind., 1899. 85: Massachusetts Historical Society; courtesy Miss Jean Freeman, photographed by Henry Mintz—Antietam National Battlefield, Sharpsburg, Md., photographed by Larry Sherer. 86, 87: Library of Congress; Alabama Department of

Archives and History, Montgomery. 88: Alabama Department of Archives and History, Montgomery, Neg. No. 86.3953.1. 89: MASS-MOLLUS/USAMHI, Carlisle Barracks, Pa., copied by A. Pierce Bounds; Eric D. Rivenbark. 91: Map by Walter W. Roberts. 92, 93: MASS-MOLLUS/ USAMHI, Carlisle Barracks, Pa., copied by A. Pierce Bounds—painting by James Hope, courtesy Antietam National Battlefield, Sharpsburg, Md., photographed by Larry Sherer. 94, 95: Courtesy Stephen McLeod, photographed by Glen Johnson. 96: Courtesy Scott Hann, photographed by Marty Lerario. 97: Library of Congress. 98: Collection of Steve Folio, photographed by George S. Whiteley IV. 99: MASS-MOLLUS/USAMHI, Carlisle Barracks, Pa., copied by A. Pierce Bounds; Antietam National Battlefield, Sharpsburg, Md., photographed by Larry Sherer (2). 100: Courtesy Scott Hann, photographed by Marty Lerario. 101: MASS-MOLLUS/ USAMHI, Carlisle Barracks, Pa., copied by A. Pierce Bounds. 102: Courtesy Mildred E. Lecroy, photographed by Henry Mintz. 103: MASS-MOLLUS/ USAMHI, Carlisle Barracks, Pa., copied by A. Pierce Bounds; from *The Papers of Walter Clark,* Vol. 1, edited by Aubrey Lee Brooks and Hugh Talmage Lefler, University of North Carolina Press, 1948, copied by Philip Brandt George. 104: National Archives Neg. No. 111-B-1857. 105: Frank & Marie-Thérèse Wood Print Collections, Alexandria, Va. 106, 107: The Huntington Library, San Marino, Calif.; The Valentine Museum, Richmond, Cook Collection, No. 2832—Library of Congress. 109: Collection of North Carolina Museum of History, courtesy Bennett Place, N.C. State Historic Site; from *Deeds of Valor,* Vol. 1, edited by W. F. Beyer and O. F. Keydel Company, The Perrien-Keydel Company, Detroit, 1903. 110: Courtesy Historical Society of Delaware, Wilmington. 111: Courtesy Mr. and Mrs. Edward D. Sloan Jr., Greenville, S.C., photographed by Henry Mintz; Library of Congress Neg. No. B8171-565. 112, 113: Courtesy John F. Weaver, McLean, Va.—courtesy Doug Bast/ Boonsboro Museum of History, photographed by Larry Sherer; courtesy Division of Military and Naval Affairs, State of New York, photographed by Randall Perry. 114: Library of Congress; Antietam National Battlefield, Sharpsburg, Md., photographed by Larry Sherer. 115: From *Memoirs of the Civil War,* by Captain William W. Chamberlaine, Press of Byron S. Adams, Washington, D.C., 1912, copied by Philip Brandt George; Portsmouth Naval Shipyard Museum, photographed by Charles Ledford. 116, 117: Eleanor S. Brockenbrough Library, The Museum of the Confederacy, Richmond, photographed by Katherine Wetzel; painting by James Hope, courtesy Antietam National Battlefield, Sharpsburg, Md., photographed by

BIBLIOGRAPHY

BOOKS

Battles and Leaders of the Civil War: North to Antietam. Ed. by Robert Underwood Johnson and Clarence Clough Buel. New York: Castle Books, 1956.

Beale, G. W. *A Lieutenant of Cavalry in Lee's Army*. Boston: Gorham Press, 1918.

Benson, Susan Williams, ed. *Berry Benson's Civil War Book*. Athens: University of Georgia Press, 1991.

Beyer, W. F., and O. F. Keydel, eds. *Deeds of Valor*. Detroit: Perrien-Keydel, 1903.

Blackford, W. W. *War Years with Jeb Stewart*. New York: Charles Scribner's Sons, 1945.

Blakeman, A. Noel, ed. *Personal Recollections of the War of the Rebellion*. Wilmington, N.C.: Broadfoot, 1992.

Borcke, Heros von. *Memoirs of the Confederate War for Independence*. Philadelphia: J. B. Lippincott, 1867.

Bowen, Roland E. *From Ball's Bluff to Gettysburg . . . and Beyond*. Ed. by Gregory A. Coco. Gettysburg, Pa.: Thomas Publications, 1994.

Brown, Philip F. *Reminiscences of the War, 1861-1865*. Blue Ridge Springs, Va., 1912.

Carter, Robert Goldthwaite. *Four Brothers in Blue*. Austin: University of Texas Press, 1978.

Chamberlaine, William W. *Memoirs of the Civil War*. Washington, D.C.: Press of Byron S. Adams, 1912.

Clark, Walter, ed. *Histories of the Several Regiments and Battalions from North Carolina in the Great War, 1861-'65*. Vol. 1. Wendell, N.C., 1982 (reprint of 1901 edition).

Coffin, Charles Carleton. *Stories of Our Soldiers*. Vol. 2. Boston: Journal Newspaper, 1893.

The Confederate General. Vols. 1 and 3. Ed. by William C. Davis. Harrisburg, Pa.: National Historical Society, 1991.

Dawes, Rufus R. *Service with the Sixth Wisconsin Volunteers*. Marietta, Ga.: E. R. Alderman & Sons, 1890.

Frassanito, William A. *Antietam: The Photographic Legacy of America's Bloodiest Day*. New York: Simon & Schuster, 1978.

Fuller, Charles A. *Personal Recollections of the War of 1861*. Hamilton, N.Y.: Edmonston Publishing, 1990 (reprint of 1906 edition).

Galwey, Thomas F. *The Valiant Hours*. Harrisburg, Pa.: Stackpole, 1961.

Gibbon, John. *Personal Recollections of the Civil War*. Dayton: Morningside Bookshop, 1978 (reprint of 1928 edition).

Gordon, John B. *Reminiscences of the Civil War*. New York: Charles Scribner's Sons, 1904.

Gould, John Mead. *Joseph K. F. Mansfield, Brigadier General of the U.S. Army*. Portland, Maine: Stephen, Berry, Printer, 1895.

Hallowell, N. P. *Selected Letters and Papers of N. P. Hallowell*. Peterborough, N.H.: Richard R. Smith, 1963.

Hartwig, D. Scott. *The Battle of Antietam and the Maryland Campaign of 1862*. Westport, Conn.: Meckler, 1990.

Harwell, Richard B., ed. *The Union Reader*. New York: Longmans, Green, 1958.

Hill, A. F. *Our Boys*. Philadelphia: John E. Potter, 1865.

History of the Thirty-Fifth Regiment Massachusetts Volunteers, 1862-1865. Boston: Mills, Knight, 1884.

Holstein, Anna Morris. *Three Years in Field Hospitals of the Army of the Potomac*. Philadelphia: J. B. Lippincott, 1867.

Holt, Daniel M. *A Surgeon's Civil War*. Ed. by James M. Greiner, Janet L. Coryell, and James R. Smither. Kent, Ohio: Kent State University Press, 1994.

Johnson, Clifton, comp. *Battleground Adventures*. Boston: Houghton Mifflin, 1915.

Lord, Edward O., ed. *History of the Ninth Regiment*. Concord, N.H.: Republican Press Association, 1895.

McDaniel, J. J. *Diary of Battles, Marches and Incidents of the Seventh S.C. Regiment*. N.p., [1862].

Manarin, Louis H. *North Carolina Troops, 1861-1865: A Roster*. 8 vols. Raleigh, N.C.: State Department of Archives and History, 1866.

Mixson, Frank M. *Reminiscences of a Private*. Columbia, S.C.: State Co., 1910.

Monroe, J. Albert. *Battery D, First Rhode Island Light Artillery at the Battle of Antietam, September 17, 1862*. Providence: Providence Press, 1886.

Moore, Edward A. *The Story of a Cannoneer under*

Stonewall Jackson. New York: Neale, 1907.

Nisbet, James Cooper. *Four Years on the Firing Line.* Hackson, Tenn.: McCowat-Mercer Press, 1963.

Noyes, George F. *The Bivouac and the Battlefield.* New York: Harper & Brothers, 1863.

Owen, William Miller. *In Camp and Battle with the Washington Artillery of New Orleans.* Boston: Ticknor, 1885.

Priest, John M. *Antietam: The Soldiers' Battle.* New York: Oxford University Press, 1989.

Racine, J. Polk. *Recollections of a Veteran.* Elkton, Md.: Appeal Printing Office, 1894.

Sears, Stephen W. *Landscape Turned Red.* Boston: Houghton Mifflin, 1983.

Schildt, John W. *Drums along the Antietam.* Parsons, W.Va.: McClain Printing, 1972.

Shaw, Robert Gould. *Blue-Eyed Child of Fortune.* Ed. by Russell Duncan. Athens: University of Georgia Press, 1992.

Shotwell, Randolph Abbott. *The Papers of Randolph Abbott Shotwell.* Vol. 1. Ed. by J. G. de Roulhac Hamilton. Raleigh: North Carolina Historical Commission, 1929.

Stearns, Austin C. *Three Years with Company K.* Ed. by Arthur A. Kent. Rutherford, N.J.: Fairleigh Dickinson University Press, 1976.

Stevens, John W. *Reminiscences of the Civil War.* Hillsboro, Texas: Hillsboro Mirror Print, 1902.

U.S. War Department. *The War of the Rebellion.* Series I, Vol. 19, Part I-Reports. Washington, D.C.: Government Printing Office, 1887.

Wainwright, Charles S. *A Diary of Battle.* Ed. by Allan Nevins. New York: Harcourt, Brace and World, 1962.

Waitt, Ernest Linden, comp. *History of the Nineteenth Regiment Massachusetts Volunteer Infantry, 1861-1865.* Baltimore: Butternut and Blue (reprint of 1906 edition).

Whitman, George Washington. *Civil War Letters of George Washington Whitman.* Ed. by Jerome M. Loving. Durham, N.C.: Duke University Press, 1975.

Wiley, Bell Irvin. *The Life of Billy Yank.* Baton Rouge: Louisiana State University Press, 1981.

Williams, Alpheus S. *From the Cannon's Mouth.* Ed. by Milo M. Quaife. Detroit: Wayne State University Press, 1959.

Worsham, John H. *One of Jackson's Foot Cavalry.* Ed. by James I. Robertson Jr. Jackson, Tenn.: McCowat-Mercer Press, 1964.

PERIODICALS

Andrews, W. H. "Tige Anderson's Brigade at Sharpsburg," *Confederate Veteran,* 1908, Vol. 16.

Bartlett, Joseph J. "Crampton's Pass." *National Tribune,* December 19, 1889.

Bradwell, I. G. "General Lee at Sharpsburg." *Confederate Veteran,* 1921, Vol. 19.

"Brady's Photographs: Pictures of the Dead at Antietam." *New York Times,* October 20, 1862.

Cornet, Joseph L. "The 28th Pennsylvania at Antietam." *Grand Army Scout and Soldiers' Mail,* September 22, 1883.

Cummings, Charles C.:
"Mississippi Boys at Sharpsburg." *Confederate Veteran,* 1897, Vol. 5.
"Storming Maryland Heights." *Confederate Veteran,* 1915, Vol. 23.

Frye, Dennis E. "Stonewall Attacks!—The Siege of Harpers Ferry." *Blue and Gray,* August-September 1987.

Garnett, James M. "The Battle of Antietam." *Southern Historical Society Papers,* 1891, Vol. 31.

Hamby, W. R. "Hood's Texas Brigade at Sharpsburg." *Confederate Veteran,* 1908.

Higgins, Jacob. "At Antietam: The Gallant Services of the 125th Pennsylvania." *National Tribune,* June 3, 1886.

Holmes, Oliver Wendell, Sr. "My Hunt after the Captain." *Atlantic Monthly,* December 1862.

Hudson, John W. "Tired Soldiers Don't Go Very Fast." Ed. by John M. Priest. *Civil War Times Illustrated,* January-February 1992.

Hunter, Alexander:
"The Battle of Antietam or Sharpsburg." *Southern Historical Society Papers,* 1903.
"A High Private's Account of the Battle of Sharpsburg." *Southern Historical Society Papers,* 1882.

Parham, John T. "Thirty-Second at Sharpsburg." *Southern Historical Society Papers,* Vol. 34.

Pittman, Samuel E. "How Lee's Special Order Was Found." *National Tribune,* June 25, 1925.

Robertson, James I., ed. "A Federal Surgeon at Sharpsburg." *Civil War History.* June 1968.

Sears, Stephen W. "Fire on the Mountain." *Blue and Gray,* December-January 1986-1987.

Schell, Frank H. "Sketching under Fire at Antietam." *McClure's,* February 1904.

Williams, Charles R. "Diary and Letters of Rutherford B. Hayes." *Ohio State Archaeological and Historical Society,* 1922-1926.

OTHER SOURCES

Abrahams, James. Memoirs, n.d. Carlisle Barracks, Pa.: U.S. Army Military History Institute, *Civil War Times Illustrated Collection.*

Barton, Clara. "Works and Incidents." Notes, n.d., MS Lecture no. 11. Washington, D.C.: Library of Congress.

Branch, Susan. Letter, September 23, 1862. Branch Family Papers. Raleigh: North Carolina State Archives.

Coles, R. T. "History of the Fourth Regiment, Alabama Volunteer Infantry, C.S.A., Army of Northern Virginia." Unpublished manuscript, n.d. Montgomery: Alabama Department of Archives and History.

Daffan, Katie. "My Father As I Remember Him." [Texas]: Private printing, [1906].

DeRosset, W. L. Letter, June 1, 1886. John M. Gould Papers. Hanover, N.H.: Dartmouth College, Antietam Collection.

Dugan, Ivy W. Letter, October 1, 1862. Dugan Papers. Athens: University of Georgia Press.

Foard, Fred C. Unpublished personal account, n.d. Raleigh: North Carolina State Archives.

Fogle, Theodore. Letters, n.d. Atlanta: Emory University.

Fulton, Edward. Letter, September 21, 1862. Southbury, Conn.: Don Troiani Collection.

Graham, M. J. "Concerning the Battle of Antietam." Unpublished manuscript, 1894. Rush Hawkins Papers. Providence: Brown University.

Leach, Calvin. "Diary of Calvin Leach." Unpublished manuscript, n.d. Chapel Hill: University of North Carolina.

Moore, Joseph A. Unpublished account, n.d. Carlisle Barracks, Pa.: U.S. Army Military History Institute.

Proffitt, Andrew J. Letter, September 22, 1862. Proffitt Family Papers. Chapel Hill: University of North Carolina, Southern Historical Collection.

Pryor, Shephard Green. "Letters 1861-1863 of Captain Shephard Green Pryor of the Muckalee Guards . . ." Bound, unpublished letters. Atlanta: Georgia Department of Archives and History, 1940.

Shand, Robert W. "Incidents in the Life of a Private Soldier in the War Waged by the United States against the Confederate States, 1861-1865." Unpublished manuscript, n.d. Columbia: University of South Carolina, South Caroliniana Library.

Smith, Otis D. "Reminiscences." Unpublished manuscript, n.d. Thach Papers. Chapel Hill: University of North Carolina, Southern Historical Collection.

3d Wisconsin Veterans Association. "Proceedings of the 17th Annual Reunion of the 3d Wis. Vet. Association, Held At Waupun, Wis. Sept. 17-18, 1907."

Warner, Adoniram J. "Save the Flags." Unpublished manuscript, n.d. Carlisle Barracks, Pa.: U.S. Army Military History Institute.

Westervelt, William B. Memoir, n.d. Carlisle Barracks, Pa.: U.S. Army Military History Institute.

Work, Phillip. A. "First Texas Infantry Regiment of the Texas Brigade at the Battles of Boonsboro Gap and Sharpsburg." Unpublished manuscript. Sharpsburg, Md.: Antietam National Battlefield, n.d.

INDEX

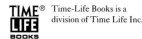 Time-Life Books is a
division of Time Life Inc.

TIME LIFE INC.
PRESIDENT and CEO: George Artandi

TIME-LIFE BOOKS
PRESIDENT: John D. Hall
PUBLISHER/MANAGING EDITOR: Neil Kagan

VOICES OF THE CIVIL WAR

DIRECTOR, NEW PRODUCT DEVELOPMENT:
Curtis Kopf
MARKETING DIRECTOR: Pamela R. Farrell

ANTIETAM

EDITOR: Henry Woodhead
Deputy Editors: Kirk Denkler (principal), Harris J. Andrews,
Philip Brandt George
Picture Editor: Marion Ferguson Briggs
Art Director: Barbara M. Sheppard
Associate Editor/Research and Writing: Gemma Slack
Senior Copyeditors: Donna D. Carey, Mary Beth
Oelkers-Keegan
Picture Coordinator: Paige Henke
Editorial Assistant: Christine Higgins

Initial Series Design: Studio A

Special Contributors: Mark Galan, Brian C. Pohanka, David S.
Thomson, Barry Wolverton (text); Martha Lee Beckington,
Charles F. Cooney, Steve Hill, Robert Lee Hodge, Henry
Mintz, Liz Soderberg, Anne Whittle (research); Jayne
Rohrich Wood (copyedit); Roy Nanovic (index).

Correspondents: Christine Hinze (London), Christina
Lieberman (New York).

Vice President, Director of Finance: Christopher Hearing
Vice President, Book Production: Marjann Caldwell
Director of Operations: Eileen Bradley
Director of Photography and Research: John Conrad Weiser
Director of Editorial Administration: Judith W. Shanks
Production Manager: Marlene Zack
Quality Assurance Manager: James King
Library: Louise D. Forstall

Consultants

Brian C. Pohanka, a Civil War historian and author, spent six
years as a researcher and writer for Time-Life Books' Civil
War series and Echoes of Glory. He is the author of *Distant
Thunder: A Photographic Essay on the American Civil War* and
has written and edited numerous works on American military
history. He has acted as historical consultant for projects
including the feature film *Glory* and television's *Civil War
Journal.* Pohanka participates in Civil War reenactments and
living-history demonstrations with the 5th New York Volunteers, and he is active in Civil War battlefield preservation.

Ted Alexander is Chief Historian at Antietam National Bat-
tlefield. He is the author of three books and more than 100
articles and book reviews for publications such as *Blue and
Gray Magazine, Civil War News,* and the *Washington Times.*
Active in preservation issues, he is the past president of the
Harpers Ferry Civil War Round Table and founder and past
president of the Cumberland Valley Civil War Round Table.
He lectures frequently for Civil War Round Tables and or-
ganizations such as the Smithsonian Institution and Johns
Hopkins University.

Scott Hartwig is a historian at Gettysburg National Military
Park and has worked for the National Park Service since 1979.
He attended the University of Wyoming, where he studied
under E. B. "Pete" Long, author of *The Civil War Day by
Day.* Hartwig's publications include numerous essays and
articles and *The Maryland Campaign of 1862: A Bibliography.*

First printing. Printed in U.S.A.
Published simultaneously in Canada.
School and library distribution by Time-Life Education,
P.O. Box 85026, Richmond, Virginia 23285-5026.

TIME-LIFE is a trademark of Time Warner Inc. U.S.A.

Library of Congress Cataloging-in-Publication Data
Antietam / by the editors of Time-Life Books.
    p. cm.—(Voices of the Civil War)
    Includes bibliographical references and index.
    ISBN 0-7835-4704-8
    1. Antietam, Battle of, Md., 1862.
    2. Maryland Campaign, 1862.
I. Time-Life Books. II. Series.
E474.65.A58 1996
973.7'33—dc20   96-3090
                                                  CIP

For information on and a full description of any of the Time-
Life Books series listed above, please call 1-800-621-7026
or write:

Reader Information
Time-Life Customer Service
P.O. Box C-32068
Richmond, Virginia 23261-2068